Peruvians Dispersed

Peruvians Dispersed

A Global Ethnography of Migration

Karsten Paerregaard

LEXINGTON BOOKS

A division of
ROWMAN & LITTLEFIELD PUBLISHERS, INC.
Lanham • Boulder • New York • Toronto • Plymouth, UK

LEXINGTON BOOKS

A division of Rowman & Littlefield Publishers, Inc.
A wholly owned subsidiary of The Rowman & Littlefield Publishing Group, Inc.
4501 Forbes Boulevard, Suite 200
Lanham, MD 20706

Estover Road
Plymouth PL6 7PY
United Kingdom

British Library Cataloguing in Publication Information Available

Library of Congress Cataloging-in-Publication Data

Paerregaard, Karsten.
  Peruvians dispersed : a global ethnography of migration / Karsten Paerregaard.
    p. cm.
  Includes bibliographical references and index.
  ISBN-13: 978-0-7391-1837-5 (cloth : alk. paper)
  ISBN-10: 0-7391-1837-4 (cloth : alk. paper)
  1. Peruvians—Foreign countries. 2. Peru—Emigration and immigration. I. Title.
  JV7511.P34 2008
  304.80985—dc22   2007044989

Printed in the United States of America

⊗™ The paper used in this publication meets the minimum requirements of American
National Standard for Information Sciences—Permanence of Paper for Printed Library
Materials, ANSI/NISO Z39.48–1992.

This book is dedicated to my parents.

Contents

Acknowledgments

This book is an ethnographic study of Peruvians who have emigrated in search for new lives outside Peru. It is based on a methodology that requires that the researcher follows and lives with Peruvians wherever they go. Considering that Peru's emigrant population today counts more than two million and is dispersed in four continents this has implied a global odyssey that includes visits to such cities as Miami, Los Angeles and Paterson, New Jersey, in the United States, and to Canada, Japan, Spain, Italy, Argentina, Chile and, of course, Peru. During this odyssey I have met a large number of people who in one way or the other have provided me with a new and informative perspective on not only how the migration experience transforms Peruvians' worldview but also how Peruvians change the world. The majority of these people were Peruvians or descendants of Peruvians but I have also met migrants from other nationalities and, not to forget, North Americans, Spaniards, Japanese, Argentineans, and others, who in different ways have contact with Peruvians.

I want to thank all these people for helping me to make this book possible. In particular, my gratitude goes to the following. In Miami I have shared many moments of joy as well as concern with Andrea and Silvia Sierra who always have offered me their warm support. My thanks also go to Tito Dominguez and to Sandy and Brian Page who helped me rent a car and offered me shelter and excellent food and wine. Elena Sabogal and Alma Suarez introduced me to Peruvian life in Miami and offered me stimulating intellectual company. I am also in dept to Nicario Jiménez with whom I have had exciting conversations about his work as *retablista* in both Miami and Lima.

In Los Angeles, I want to thank Oscar Trigoso and Silvia Dominguez for the hospitality and attention that I received during my stay in their house in

Long Beach. I am also grateful to my friend and colleague Michael Kearney who not only let me stay in his house but also took interest in my study and shared his research experience in migration with me. Paul Gelles is another colleague and friend who always has offered me shelter and taken his time to discuss issues of mutual interest. In Bakersfield I am indebted to Victor Flores who introduced me to the life of Peruvian sheepherders in California and their struggle to improve their working conditions. My thanks also goes to Pedro Li, Jorge Luís Placencia, Javier Decarpio, and Rómulo Melgar.

My stay in Paterson, New Jersey, was short but very intense. Manuel Cunza, Lorenzo Puertas, and Felix Araujo provided me with helpful information on Peruvian migration to this city.

In Spain, I am in dept to Chavica, Charo, Esperanza, Miguel, and Amelia Dominguez who not only have helped me contacting Peruvians in Barcelona but also offered me shelter on many occasions and perhaps most important a good laugh. Telmo and Vanesa rented me a room in their crowded flat and have always been very kind to me. I am also thankful to Melvin Samaniego, Ninoska Palomino, Eduardo Evanán, and Alfonso Cárdenas. Finally, I want to thank you my colleagues Angeles Escrivá and Mary Crain for their intellectual support.

In Italy, where I've only spent short periods of time in Milan, my regards go to Rosa, Raúl, and Amanda Mallma—and, of course, their parents and sister in Huancayo.

In Japan, Marco and Rosa María Tamayoshi and their two daughters, Sayuri and Naomi, have taken me in on all my visits to Japan. Their hospitality is overwhelming and they will always be in my mind. I also want to thank my friend Shinya Watanabe for letting me stay in his flat in Mito and for being so kind to me. My thanks also go to Pilar Aniya for introducing me to Peruvians in Japan.

In Argentina, my colleague Brenda Pereyra instructed me in the labyrinths of Argentina's migration policy and offered my good company. I am specially in debt to my late friend and colleague Eduardo Archetti for introducing me to the intellectual circles of Buenos Aires. Casilda Mallma and Gloria Samaniego also offered me help.

In Chile my thanks go to Lorena Nuñez, Carolina Stefoni, and Francisco Malouf, who introduced me to the Peruvian colony in Santiago and offered my good company.

Special thanks go to the consuls at the Peruvian Embassies and Consulates in Miami, Los Angeles, Paterson, Barcelona, Milan, Tokyo, Buenos Aires, and Santiago who took time to talk with me.

My odyssey started and ended in Peru. Here special thanks go to my parents-in-law and sisters- and brothers-in-law who pick me up in the airport and take me in as a yet another member of the family whenever I come to Peru. Some privilege! I am also indebted to my compadre and colleague Teófilo Altamirano with whom I have shared many moments of good company and to Carla Tamagno and her parents in Huancayo who always receive me with open arms. My thanks also go to my colleagues Ulla Dalum Berg and Ayumi Takaneka with whom I have had many stimulating conversations about Peruvian migration. Many others have supported me and although they are not mentioned here they should know that their support has been of great help.

At the Department of Anthropology in Copenhagen I want to thank all my colleagues. In particular, I want to express my gratitude to Karen Fog Olwig, Kirsten Hastrup, Susan Reynolds Whyte, Michael Whyte, and Michael Jackson for their encouraging support and for always believing that this book would materialize one day.

The grant that I received from the Danish Research Council made this research and publication possible.

Finally, special thanks go to my wife, Ana María, and my two daughters, Laura and Sofie and my parents, Peer and Grethe, for always waiting for me during my countless journeys to the end of the world—in the search for Peruvians.

Chapter 6 is based on an article published in *Journal for Ethnic and Migration Studies*, vol. 34 (2008).

Chapter One

Introduction

The Extended Field

I'm interviewing Javier in his mechanical workshop in downtown Los Angeles. "Why did you come to the U.S.?" I ask this sixty-two-year old Peruvian man. He replies, "In 1984 I went to the U.S. Embassy in Lima to apply for a tourist visa. But they turned me down. I got very upset and started to argue with the official. He didn't like that and asked for help to have me thrown out. But before leaving the Consulate I shouted at the official, 'I'm going to your f—— country anyway. When I get there I'll s—— in front of your door.'" Javier smiles at me and says, "A few days later I quitted my job, sold my house and cars, flew to Mexico and crossed the border to the United States illegally." Today Javier has permanent residency in the United States and lives together with his wife in a small flat in Los Angeles where he makes a living repairing cars.

In recent years embassies or consulates, their more modest equivalents, have become the battleground for thousands of Third World citizens applying for tourist, residence, or work permits to travel to the developed world. Wrapped in diplomatic mystery these institutions, which are the representations of foreign states in a nation's territory, appear distant and inaccessible to common people. Moreover, embassies and consulates are often located in modern downtown areas or upper-class neighborhoods like the U.S. Consulate in Lima, which allows their officials and employees to enjoy privileges and lifestyles that are foreign to the majority. Yet once inside embassies or consulates the enticing images of exotic countries shrouded by elegant glamour rapidly fade. Here bureaucratic rigidity and obscure procedures reign, and the visitor is met with an attitude of mistrust and severity, particularly if he or she is a citizen of the country hosting the embassy or consulate. Legally on foreign soil, the "local" is regarded as a "stranger" and his or her requests are submitted to the most critical inspection. Identification papers and personal

1

histories are examined over and over again, and the interrogators are instructed not to engage in personal communication with the visitors. As a foreign subject the petitioner's sole right is that of requesting permission to enter the country. The decision whether to grant or refuse that request is taken in accordance with the country's immigration laws and lies entirely in the hands of the embassy or consulate officials, with no court of appeal. Not surprisingly, Javier felt upset when his application was turned down.

BETWEEN EXCLUSION AND INCLUSION

Population movements have shaped Peru in significant ways since the time of the Incas but it is only in the past twenty years that emigration has gained momentum. Altamirano asserts that in 1980 the number of Peruvians living outside Peru was 500,000, in 1992 one million and in 1996 1.5 million out of a total population of approximately 24 millions (2006: 118). Today the author estimates the same figure to have reached 2.5 million constituting almost 10 percent of the Peruvian population that today has reached 26 million (Altamirano 2006: 118).[1] Compared to other international migrant groups, such as Mexicans, Turks, Chinese, or Indians, this is not, of course, a large population in sheer numbers. Yet Peruvian emigration calls for close attention for other reasons. First, Peruvians from all sectors of Peruvian society are represented in the country's migrant population. Upper- as well as middle- and working-class Peruvians, urban professionals as well as highland peasants, police officers as well as street vendors, women as well as men, old as well as young, and mestizos as well as Indians and other ethnic groups are leaving the country in large numbers. Second, unlike other Latin American or Caribbean migrants who tend to concentrate in one or two countries and cities (Cubans in Miami, Puerto Ricans in New York, Mexicans in Los Angeles but also other U.S. cities, Jamaicans in London, and so on)[2] Peruvians disperse in many places. Of course, in the contemporary world it is not unusual for migrant populations to establish strong international links between two or perhaps three countries. Thus many Asian and African populations have strong migrant ties to several European, Middle Eastern, or North American cities and countries (e.g., the Turks, Algerians, Moroccans, Bangladeshis, Pakistanis, and Filipinos).[3] Similarly, intra-continental links of migration are common in many parts of Africa, Asia, and Europe.[4] However, few migrant populations are as heterogeneous in terms of geographical dispersal and social diversity as the Peruvian, which makes it a unique case study to revise current attempts to theorize international migration that predominantly draw on studies of migrant populations that either are physically concentrated in one or two destinations (as in the case of the concept of transnationality) or represent self-conscious, homogeneous social formations (as in the case of the concept of diaspora).

This book examines the historical changes and economic and political circumstances in Peru that have prompted Javier and millions of other Peruvians to migrate to the United States, Spain, Japan, and Argentina and describes how the country's population movements have evolved in the last fifty years. Analytically, the book uses ethnographic research to explore how Peruvians, on the one hand, adapt to the receiving context in the United States, Spain, Japan, and Argentina and, on the other, experience and interpret, collectively as well as individually, this adaptation. In order to do this, I study migration as a process of inclusion and exclusion shaped by two forms of differentiation. First, an external process of differentiation that is generated by shifting immigration policies and demands for foreign labor in the receiving societies. These structural changes constantly cause division among those Peruvians who are granted status as legal immigrants opposed to those who are classified as undocumented or unauthorized immigrants and those who succeed to achieve social mobility opposed to those who fail to do so. Second, an internal process of differentiation produced by the conflicts and strife that periodically occur within the migrant communities. Such tensions are usually triggered by the relations of not only reciprocity and trust but also exploitation and inequality that Peruvians draw on to create support networks and migrant institutions in the receiving societies. The distinction between an external and an internal process of differentiation allows me to operate on two analytical levels: one that brings to the fore migrants' own experiences and viewpoints and another that locates this presentation within the wider context of power relations and political forces that structure the migration process. The aim of such an inquiry is to investigate not merely how the two forms of differentiation mediate migrants' efforts to establish new lives in North American, Spanish, Japanese, and Argentinean society but also how their adaptation to the receiving societies transforms Peruvians' own ideas of class, nationality, ethnicity and regionality and, ultimately, changes their sense of belonging.

In order to understand the social and political meaning of the two processes of differentiation I make use of Agamben's definition of the concepts of inclusion and exclusion and his suggestion that in the modern world order not all humans meet the requirements to be qualified as political subjects and hereby obtain the right to be granted status as citizens (or legal residents). As an example of such an exception he mentions the refugees who remain included in politics solely through an exclusion (Agamben 2006: 11). Agamben calls such a relation an *inclusive exclusion* (Agamben 2006: 21) and claims that "If refugees . . . represent such a disquieting element in the order of the modern nation-state, this is above all because by breaking the continuity between man and citizen, *nativity* and *nationality*, they put the originary fiction of modern sovereignty in crisis" (Agamben 2006: 131).[5] In other words, because the refugees remind us of the distinction between the natural life and the political life and hereby the difference between birth and nation they are associated with social disorder. In contrast to the relation of inclusive exclusion that places refugees and other aliens on the margin of society and excludes them from becoming formal members of modern society, Agamben asserts that other social groups may be victims of a relation of *exclusive inclusion*. Although he refrains from defining the exact meaning of such a relation Agamben's use of the term suggests that he refers to those sectors of the native population that enjoy formal citizenship but are excluded from practicing it, economically or socially.

In as much as the majority of Peruvian migrants are in high demand on the labor markets in the industrialized world as cheap, unskilled workers but nevertheless are excluded from the legal rights that other members of these countries enjoy they are submitted to a relation of inclusive exclusion similar to the refugee that Agamben describes. And although only a small number of Peruvians living in the United States, Spain, Japan, and Argentina actually are refugees many live in a state of exception because they fail to comply with the requirements to obtain legal status and therefore initiate their new lives as immigrants as undocumented aliens at the mercy of money loaners, people traffickers, and corrupt police and immigration officers and at the risk of being incarcerated and returned to Peru or, what is even worse, violated or killed. Others enter their new countries of settlement as legal aliens on a tourist or student visa, which they overstay when the visa expires. Now unauthorized immigrants, they live on the margins of society constantly hiding to avoid deportation. Yet others travel with forged ID papers or the papers of somebody else. Because such a strategy implies taking up a new life in the name of another person it brings migrants in conflict with not only the law and the immigration authorities but also their own networks and relatives. Paradoxically, however, in some of the countries where Peruvians take residence and find work the governments turn a blind eye to their undocumented or unauthorized presence and offer periodical amnesties to regularize their irregular status. Hence, the relation of inclusive exclusion implies the tacit recognition and official rejection of migrants at one and the same time, which makes the lives of many Peruvians in the United States, Spain, Japan, and Argentina both seemingly stable and utterly fragile.

In fact, many migrants are familiar with marginalization and exclusion from their previous lives in Peru. Historically, Peru's class structure has been sustained by a political system that favors a minority of rich Peruvians at the cost of the majority of poor Peruvians in terms of access to education, health, and other public resources. However, this form of exclusion, which produces what Agamben calls an exclusive inclusion, differs noticeably from the inclusive exclusion that Peruvians suffer in the United States, Spain, Japan, and Argentina. Whereas the latter tolerates immigrants' continuous presence but denies them the same legal rights as the native population the former formally recognizes all Peruvians as citizens but nevertheless prevents the bulk of the population from exercising their legal rights in practical terms. In Peru this form of exclusion is based on a national ideology dividing the population into ethnic and regional groups (Mendoza 2000: 9–18; de la Cadena 2000: 20–34). On the one hand, a mestizo world concentrated in the coastal region that is related to Western culture, associated with Peru's national heritage and regarded as synonymous with progress and, on the other, an indigenous world located in the rural hinterland that is imagined as the reminiscence of a barbarian past and an obstacle to modernization and development (Paerregaard 1997a: 203–33; Turino 1991: 271–81). Although ongoing rural-urban migration processes and a severe economic and political crisis in the past two decades have changed the power balance between the country's social classes and challenged the hegemonic order that upholds its economic difference and social inequality continue to divide Peruvian society and exclude large numbers of Peruvians from enjoying the same rights as the dominating classes. As a result, many regard emigration as the most adequate strategy to change social status and although migrants often find themselves constrained by new ties of exploitation and domination in the receiving societies they tend to view such relations as a resource rather than as an obstacle to find work, obtain legal status, and climb up the social ladder.

To scrutinize ethnographically how Peruvians create networks and design strategies to first escape the exclusive inclusion that prevents them from exercising their legal rights in Peru and later overcome the inclusive exclusion that thwarts them from obtaining social mobility in the receiving societies I map out the ties and linkages that they establish between their places of origin in Peru and new countries of settlement. Such ties and linkages, I suggest, serve to not merely confirm their continuous loyalty to their home communities but also maintain households that are divided across national borders (Alicea 1997; Pribilsky 2004) and overcome the barriers that migrants face in the receiving societies (Portes 2001). Several scholars have suggested that we employ the terms space or field to study exactly how such transnational engagements are organized and practiced (Rouse 1991; Levitt and Glick Schiller 2004; Pries 1999). According to Levitt and Glick Schiller, "The concept of social fields is a powerful tool for conceptualizing the potential array of social relations linking those who move and those stay behind" (Levitt and Glick

Schiller 2004: 1009) and in the case of transnational social fields, these "connect actors through direct and indirect relations across borders" (Levitt and
Glick Schiller 2004: 1009). Similarly, Pries proposes that we explore contemporary processes of international migration as transnational social spaces, by
which he is referring to the new forms of "interlacing coherence networks"
that emerge from these processes (Pries 1999: 26). In his view, such social
spaces are "spacially diffuse or pluri-local, at the same time comprising a social space that is not exclusively transitory" (Pries 1999: 26).

In my view, however, the use of the concepts of field and space evokes a
notion of migration as a movement in an open and flat terrain that people may
cross more or less untroubled by economic and political institutions. Rather
than examining Peruvian migration as a social field or space that exists independently of external power structures I suggest that we view Peruvians'
transnational activities as a movement in social networks and institutional
practices that simultaneously include and exclude migrants in their efforts to
obtain legal status, find work, and create new lives (Mahler 1995; Menjívar
2000). Because many Peruvians travel illegally and therefore are forced to
rely on the economic support of relatives and friends in the receiving countries the networks they use to emigrate are often tormented by tensions between those who provide support for others and those who benefit from such
support. By the same token, a closer look into Peruvian migrant associations
reveals that although these often gather numerous migrants for social, cultural, or religious reasons they are also ridden by internal conflicts not only
between migrants from different social and ethnic groups in Peru but also between those who arrived first and already have obtained legal status and those
who have arrived later and still are undocumented. Hence, rather than assuming that Peruvians share a common sense of belonging and automatically
form homogeneous collectivities on the basis of their national origin I explore
such identities as categories that are constructed, imposed and appropriated;
likewise, I study migrant communities and identities not merely in terms of
how they are attributed meaning but also how this meaning is negotiated and
contested by different groups of migrants.

TRANSNATIONALITY AND DIASPORA

My study of Peruvian migration has been triggered by an interest in global
connectedness. Two concepts in particular are useful in this context: transnationality and diaspora. The former has been introduced "to explore flows and
movements that extend beyond national borders and entail global linkages between people and institutions in different parts of the world. It is defined as

the processes by which immigrants forge and sustain multi-stranded social relations that link together their societies of origin and settlement" (Basch,
Glick Schiller, and Szanton Blanc 1994: 7). In a similar vein, the term "trans-
migrants" has been suggested to denote "immigrants who develop and maintain multiple relationships—familial, economic, social, organizational, religious, and political—that span borders" (Basch, Glick Schiller, and Szanton
Blanc 1994: 7). Some scholars, however, express concerns about the broad
use of these terms. Thus Portes, Guarnizo, and Landolt contend that "if all or
most things that immigrants do are defined as 'transnationalism,' then none is
because the term becomes synonymous with the total set of experiences of
this population" (1999: 219). In a similar vein, Smith and Guarnizo (1998: 5)
criticize the concept for its emancipatory connotation and deplore the
counter-hegemonic import of the term transmigrant. Indeed, a close inspection of the definition of transnationalism reveals that it fails to account for migrants' creation of new identities and their efforts to be recognized as immigrants in the host society. It also lacks sensitivity to the everyday life of
transnational migrants and their interaction with the social and cultural environment of the receiving country.

More recent research, however, documents that transnationality can serve as
a useful tool to understand processes of exclusion and inclusion that shape migration flows. In a study of immigrants in the United States Guarnizo and Portes
found that, "transnational entrepreneurs are *more* likely to be U.S. citizens and
to have resided in the country for longer periods of time than the sample average" (Portes 2001: 188). A parallel analysis of political transnationalism based
on the same study indicates similar trends (Portes 2001: 188), which leads Portes
to conclude: "The cultivation of strong networks with the country of origin and
the implementation of economic and political initiatives based on these networks
may help immigrants solidify their position in the receiving society and cope
more effectively with its barriers" (Portes 2001: 189). In other words, contrary
to what has so far been assumed by the theories of transnationality, assimilation,
and incorporation in the receiving society may go hand in hand with transnational practices and projects. Waldinger and Fitzgerald even go as far as to claim
that, "the standard depiction of assimilation and transnationalism as competing
theoretical perspectives or analytic concepts is misleading" (2004: 1179). These
observations suggest that insofar as transnationality is properly contextualized in
relation to migration pattern, immigration policies, and migrants' legal status and
the specific forms of practices and activities that migrants engage in the concept
may help us differentiate better between those forms of transnational engagement that prompt social mobility and those that merely strengthen migrants' ties
to the country of origin at the cost of migrants' incorporation in the labor market
and integration in the receiving society.

Although it is common for Peruvians to sustain multiple relationships with Peru and their home region or village and extend their networks beyond Peru's national borders, the impact of these links on their everyday lives is limited. To the majority, monthly or bimonthly remittances sent to relatives back home make up the principal, and in some cases the only, transnational link with Peru. While transnationality thus makes up an important point of reference in their sense of belonging, their daily struggle to make a living, deal with the local authorities, and find a place to live is shaped by economic and social forces in the host society rather than by transnational relationships with their country of origin and must therefore be analyzed within this context. Moreover, as a large proportion of Peruvian migrants have previous experiences of rural-urban migration in Peru, their transnational experience grows out of already existing networks and migrant practices. To them, leaving Peru is just another challenge in a lifelong struggle to *progresar* (make progress).

Unlike transnationality, the concept of diaspora has roots in European literature, referring originally to the exile of the Jews from their historic homeland (Safran 1991). It currently reflects the ambivalent space that all displaced people occupy as cultural minorities whose national loyalties are divided between their country of origin (whether mythical or real) and the host country, a position that implies a potential tension between belonging and travel, or, as Clifford phrases it, between roots and routes (1997: 251). In the early 1990s the term began to resonate among scholars of global migration, refugeeism, and related issues, to whom it evokes the image of people who either are on the move or located in places other than their homeland (Mallki 1992). Tölölyan suggests that the concept's renaissance was caused by a belief among academics that "the term that once described Jewish, Greek, and Armenian dispersion now shares meanings with a larger semantic domain that includes words like immigrant, expatriate, refugee, guest worker, exile community, overseas community, ethnic community" (1996: 4). Clifford goes a step further in asserting that, "In the late twentieth century, all or most communities have diasporic dimensions (moments, tactics, practices, articulations). Some are more diasporic than others" (1997: 254).

As in the discussion of transnationality, the extensive reference to diasporas by migration scholars creates confusion about its meaning. Vertovec claims that "the current over-use and under-theoretization of the notion of 'diaspora' among academics, transnational intellectuals, and community leaders alike . . . threatens the term's descriptive usefulness" (1997: 301) while Brubaker states, "If everyone is diasporic, then no one is distinctively so" (2005: 3).[6] Indeed, there are several reasons why a study of Peruvian migration should refrain from essentializing the term "diaspora" by giving it a specific meaning. First, Peruvians outside Peru constitute an extremely heterogeneous population divided by class, ethnicity, education, gender, and age and, second, "diaspora" is not a native term in the world of Peruvians, nor have I heard migrants employ similar terms or expressions to articulate the idea of an exiled people united by a dream of returning to their homeland. While some think of themselves as exiled in the sense that they have escaped political violence or otherwise been forced to leave Peru, most agree that the principal motive in emigrating is economic and a wish to achieve social mobility. The only exception is a small group of trained professionals and economically well-off Peruvians for whom the idea of diaspora exists in the form of a cosmopolitan identity (cf. Hannerz 1996: 102–11). However, this notion of a dispersed ethnic community united by a shared loyalty to the homeland is based on the exclusion of the vast majority of fellow migrants. It is the identity of an urban elite from upper-class neighborhoods in Lima, who often claim descent from European or American immigrants. Similar forms of fragmented diasporic identities can be observed among Peruvian of Japanese descent in Los Angeles, who have formed an association exclusively for so-called *nikkei* migrants, or among migrants from rural Andean areas, who often form regional associations and establish ties with their home villages.

There are, however, a few exceptions. A small group of economically well-off Peruvians are directly involved in transnational practices and diasporic networking on a major scale. They participate or work in institutions with transnational links, travel frequently to Peru, communicate (such as by e-mail and the Internet) with Peruvians in other places, or otherwise engage in activities that are contingent on or imply a transnational connection. They belong to a small elite of Peruvians who either play the role of migrant leader or exploit the market that is emerging among migrants for Peruvian products, courier and remittance services, legal counseling, visa and travel arrangements, video conferences, and so on. Another group of less privileged migrants practice transnationality in a quite different way. In Europe, Argentina and to some extent in the United States, a growing number of female but recently also male Peruvians are seeking employment as domestic servants and carers for old people. Because many of these migrants do not have legal papers and work as live-in domestics, their physical mobility is highly constrained and their life-worlds confined to the homes of their employers. Similarly, their contact with the host society and participation in migrant associations and networks are sporadic. Although these migrants often establish long-term relationships with the people they take care of, their precarious legal situation and social isolation prevent them from creating bonds with other migrants or the surrounding society. Rather than forming new identities as immigrants or future citizens in the countries where they have taken up residence, they continue to feel strongly attached to their country of origin, and in particular to their relatives in Peru.

Perhaps because the meaning and use of the two concepts are so slippery, migration scholars tend to use transnationalism and diaspora rather indiscriminately. What is transnational may as well be diasporic and vice versa. Moreover, as both terms convey a counter-hegemonic imaginary, they entail the same danger of romanticizing the people under study and essentializing their practice and identities. The semantic intersection of transnationalism and diaspora also induces scholars studying contemporary processes of globalization to use the two concepts uncritically. Thus they may use either or both to refer to the multifocality that molds the identity formation of migrant populations, as well as the communities and the networks and multi-stranded ties that these forge both with migrant groups in other parts of the world and with their home country. Rather than employing the notion of transnationality and diaspora indiscriminately to all kinds of migrant networks and communities I follow Butler's suggestion to identify and isolate a set of categories of analysis that are applicable to all migrant populations and that can help us to distinguish between those aspects of the migration process that rightly may be labeled transnational or diasporic and those that do not (Butler 2001). Further, I concur with Brubaker who proposes that we treat diaspora "as a category of practice, project, claim and stance, rather than as a bounded group" (Brubaker 2005: 13). More specifically, I draw on transnationality and diaspora as complementary analytical categories to explore how the relations of inclusion and exclusion that tie migrants to their country or region of origin and that tie migrants in one location to migrants in other locations in the world shape their practices and imaginaries. Whereas I call the former transnational I label the latter diasporic. Metaphorically, the difference between the two concepts is one between rain pouring down from above and plants cropping up from the ground. Thus, transnationality conveys the elusive nature of contemporary processes of migration and the mobile character of modern lifestyles through reference to the economic, social political forces that forge migrants' links with Peru and their home region or community. Diaspora, on the other hand, expresses the multifocality that shapes their global awareness and leads them to challenge the status they are ascribed as immigrants by the receiving societies. The concept thus reflects the social relations and cultural imaginaries that emerge from migrants' grounding in already existing localities and their engagement with the dominant native population and other ethnic minorities.

RESEARCH DESIGN

I am visiting a restaurant called Ninoska in Barcelona, which I know is owned by a Peruvian couple from the city of Huancayo. From the outside it seems no different from other restaurants in Barcelona and inside the bartender looks like any other Catalan. Yet as I venture to ask whether the man is Peruvian, he first stares at me with distrustful eyes and then replies stoically "Yes, I am." I'm just about to continue my faltering attempt to establish contact when a woman appears from the kitchen crying "Melvin, where are you?" As if a light suddenly hits the three of us at the same time, we all take a close look at each other. The woman called Ninoska then exclaims, "I know you; you used to live in Huancayo. You are . . . Karsten. Yes, that's it—Karsten." Then it is Melvin's turn "Yeah, I know you too." Within a few minutes time we're all engaged in an intense conversation about the old days in Huancayo.

Because anthropologists have traditionally conducted fieldwork among people in small rural places, they often thought of their informants as being part of the local habitat. They also regarded culture as a territorially confined and discrete unit that could be examined without paying attention to interference from the outside world (Gupta and Ferguson 1997). Moreover, in the classical monographs the ethnographic field was uncritically identified with political and administrative units such as the village, district, peasant community, tribal territory, or native reservation. In effect, many fieldworkers felt little need to distinguish their own definitions of the field from the native notion of place, mistakenly assuming that the political boundaries delimited by the colonial or national state were congruent with the local population's geographical and cultural identities and their own sense of belonging.

This confusion concerning the definition of the ethnographic field have prompted modern researchers to question the relevance of ethnography in the study of current globalization processes. Thus Burawoy asks, "How can ethnography be global? How can ethnography be anything but micro and ahistorical?" (2000: 1). More bluntly, is a global ethnography possible? In this book I argue that ethnography indeed provides the researcher with a highly relevant tool to study global processes. However, I also suggest that the study of migrant communities in different parts of the world raises new and very different research questions compared to traditional ethnographic research. How do we study a dispersed population of more than one million as one people? How do we localize it in physical settings and examine the relationship between these localities? How do we explore people's attachments to different sites and their sense of belonging to places? How do we analyze people's movements between different places while observing their social practice and identity constructions in particular locations? The scope of these questions is reflected in my notebooks: a mess of names, words, and numbers bear witness to the analytical problems of making the countless parts of this global puzzle fit together.

In order to provide answers to these questions, I had to explore the political and cultural processes that connect this diversity of events, relations, and actions across countries and continents. My study attempts to do this by combining fine-grained, in-depth studies of local life-worlds with general analyses of immigration politics, multiculturalism, and global migration. I distinguish between three different domains of data collection: (1) *study sites*, or the physical, social, and political settings of Peruvian emigration; (2) *relations of belonging*, or Peruvians' own sense of belonging to place; and (3) *research fields*, or the geographical and social terrain within which I move as a researcher. By keeping separate the three domains of research, I hope to elicit the methodology that guided my field research and produce analytical transparency in exploring the interaction between migrants and their social and political surroundings. This also allows me to position myself as researcher in relation to social actors, political institutions, and cultural identities in the arena of global migration.

STUDY SITES

I am standing with Miguel eating arroz con pollo *and drinking Peruvian beer in La Chopera, which is the southwest corner of Madrid's famous Parque de Retiro. Up to recently respectable Spanish citizens used to promenade in this park with their families on quiet Sunday afternoons. Well, they still do, but now the local Madrileños are difficult to spot among hundreds of Third World immigrants performing art shows, selling folklore items, playing exotic music and, as in La Chopera, playing soccer. Every Sunday afternoon Peruvian women sell homemade food and Latin American beer outside the soccer fields, where hundreds of fellow countrymen, together with Bolivians, Ecuadorians, and Colombians, are all eager to get a taste of home. Then four police cars suddenly appear. The street sellers seem to know the game and remain calm. Miguel and I rapidly throw away the rest of our delicious* arroz con pollo, *hide behind a couple of trees, and watch the scene from a distance. Five police officers approach the street sellers to confiscate their products. After a lot of shouting and yelling in Spanish, the woman who sold us the food throws a big pot with* ceviche *after one of the police officers. In a few minutes the incident is over and the four police cars leave La Chopera, packed with pots, dishes, glasses, and enough Latin American food to feed the entire police station. We all think it is over and the atmosphere seems normal again. I hear people saying, "They got the food, but we've still got the beer." Then the four cars appear again. This time the officers must have been tipped off by someone. They search for beer everywhere: they remove the manhole covers of the sewage, they look in the trees, everywhere. Once again they fill the cars with confiscated goods and leave. We are left with nothing and everybody is upset.*

The study sites of my research consist of those places, both urban and rural, in the United States, Spain, Italy, Japan, and Argentina where Peruvians settle and establish immigrant communities (see figure 1.1). These sites constitute the points of impact of contemporary Peruvian emigration, the historical junctions around which migrant routes are organized, and the physical localities in which Peruvians create new livelihoods and identities. They also make up the milieu that shapes Peruvians' encounters with the host society, their relation to other immigrant minorities, and their inclusion in (or exclusion from) the dominant politics of identity and integration.

My study draws on ten months of fieldwork among Peruvian migrants over a three-year period. It encompasses two months of field research in Barcelona and one week in Madrid in 1997; two months each in Miami and Los Angeles, and two weeks in Paterson, New Jersey, in 1998; one month in Isesaki and other cities in Japan in 1999; and one month in Buenos Aires in Argentina in 2000 (see figure 1.2). The study also includes brief trips to Toronto in 1998 and Milan in 1999 and a stay of a month and a half in Peru in 2000 (see figure 1.3). Field sites were selected with the aim of gathering information on Peruvian emigration on a worldwide basis, combined with a number of indepth studies of particular migrant communities in the United States, the European Union, Japan, and South America. Although a few countries and cities with important Peruvian populations were not included in my global odyssey due to limitations in research time and travel funding, the field sites of my

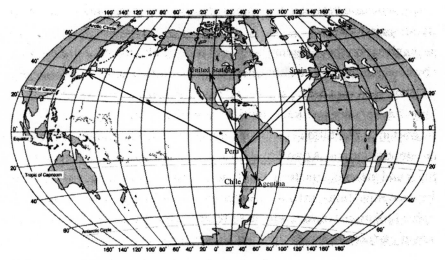

Figure 1.1. Main Destinations of Peruvian Emigration

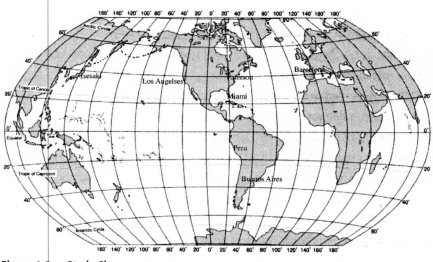

Figure 1.2.   Study Sites

study are fairly representative of Peru's migrant population in terms of most favored points of departure and arrival. Field data were gathered by mapping out migrant institutions and practices in each country and city, interviewing community leaders (editors of Peruvian newspapers, leaders of cultural, regional, and religious associations, consulate officials, representatives of business communities, etc.), collecting the life stories of individual migrants (of both sexes and from different social strata), and examining the networks, livelihood strategies, and transnational engagements that migrants draw on to reach their goals and participate in social, political, and religious activities. Although the conditions of conducting research vary considerably in the United States, Spain, Japan, and Argentina I attempted, and partly succeeded, to gather samples of more or less the same size and composition in the principal sites of my study (Miami, Los Angeles, Paterson, Barcelona, Isesaki, and Buenos Aires) thus allowing for cross-city and cross-country comparisons.

Figure 1.3.   Map of Peru

Peruvian culture and language are strongly influenced by three hundred years of Spanish colonization. This makes Spain one of the preferred destinations in the European Union for Peruvian migrants (see figure 1.5). In 1950s and 1960s, large numbers of young middle- and upper-class Peruvians emigrated to study medicine and law or settle in Spain. However, the traditional image of Peruvians as educated and well-off foreigners

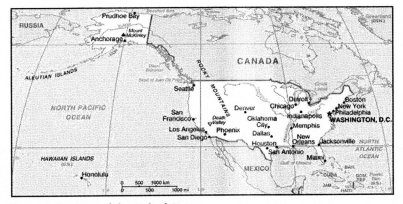

Figure 1.4.   Map of the United States

stands in sharp contrast to Peruvian immigrants of today, who make their living primarily as caretakers of old Spaniards and who live on the margins of modern Spanish society. The impact of Third World immigration on Spain is particularly evident in Catalonia and its capital Barcelona, the main site of my fieldwork in Spain, because of the province's national revival and economic bonanza since the introduction of democracy in 1975. The other European Union country I visited was Italy, which unlike Spain where immigrants predominantly come from Morocco and Latin America, is the destination of a broad variety of foreign immigration (including Albanians, North Africans, Filipinos, and others).[7]

The United States has the largest Peruvian population outside Peru by far (see figure 1.4). However, unlike Mexicans, Cubans, Puerto Ricans, Dominicans, Salvadorans, and other Hispanics, who tend to concentrate in one or two cities, Peruvians live dispersed in many urban centers. This, of course, made it much more difficult to select the locations in the United States for my study.[8] While most sectors of Peruvian society are represented in Miami, making this city a particularly interesting case study, I chose Los Angeles because of the size of the Peruvian migrant population there. Similarly, I found the city's medley of ethnic minorities to be a perfect context in which to study the multicultural environment that shapes Peruvian immigration in North America. I also used Los Angeles as a base to study social and political problems related to the recruitment of Peruvians to work as sheepherders in the Californian desert. Finally, I decided to explore Paterson, a city in

Figure 1.5.   Map of Spain

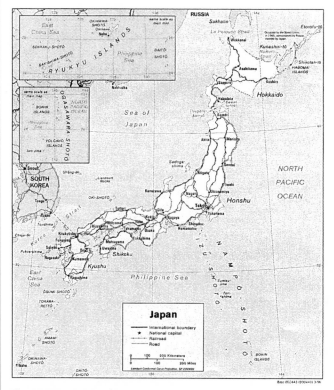

Figure 1.6.   Map of Japan

New Jersey where Peruvians established a strong immigrant community several decades ago. The place has its own peculiar atmosphere due to its pioneering role in U.S. industrial history and offers a unique opportunity to observe how a particular group of Peruvians (from Lima and its port, Callao)
recreate a microcosms of their home society abroad.[9]

Any study of Peruvian emigration is bound to include Japan on its research
itinerary (see figure 1.6). From the early 1990s this country became the favorite
destination for Peruvians who belong to Peru's Japanese minority. The members of this community descend from Japanese who emigrated to Peru in the
first half of the twentieth century.[10] While many claim to be of Japanese descent, others identify themselves as Peruvians. Together with immigrants from
other Third World countries (including a large group of Brazilians who are also
of Japanese descent), they make up a highly visible and distinct minority group
in Japan's emerging multicultural society. The majority of Peruvians works as
factory workers and live dispersed in the central part of the country.[11]

Figure 1.7. Map of Argentina

Neighboring countries of Peru in South America are another major destination of Peruvian emigration. Argentina is particularly interesting because it emerged as one of the preferred destinations of Peruvian emigration in the early 1990s along with the European Union and Japan, at a time when the United States was tightening up its immigration policy (see figure 1.7). As in the case of Spain and Italy, Peruvian women who work as domestic workers dominate emigration to Argentina. At first glance South America seems the most convenient choice for Peruvians because most Latin American countries share the same cultural and linguistic history. Yet in recent years Peruvians and immigrants from other Andean countries in Argentina have experienced similar forms of racial discrimination and social exclusion as their fellow countrymen in other parts of the world. This, of course, makes comparative studies of immigration in countries not only of the First World but also the Third World highly relevant.[12]

RELATIONS OF BELONGING

The karaoke party at Fortaleza Latina in Isesaki is now at its peak. Apart from a couple of Paraguayans and Argentineans and myself, all the customers are Peruvians. If it hadn't been for the karaoke show, one would believe that we were in Peru. I'm sitting in a corner drinking beer with Antonio. He recounts that his parents were Japanese who migrated to Peru in 1934 on the same boat as the parents of former president Fujimori. Antonio, who is a widower, left for Japan in 1990 leaving his four children behind in Peru. Later a couple of them joined him. Yet they do not want to stay in Japan. While Antonio feels partly Japanese and wants to stay, his children identify themselves as Peruvians and have little desire to live in Japan. Antonio deplores their inability to understand his situation, which he says is because their mother was not of Japanese descent.

Migrants' sense of belonging is shaped by their mobility and multifocal activities. At the heart of most Peruvian migrants is a strong feeling of belonging to Peru. Despite decades of living in foreign lands, they usually maintain a firm loyalty to their country of origin, home region, or native village. Even when they change legal status and become residents or citizens in their host country, their identification with their place of origin usually remains intact.

Notwithstanding their own self-identification, however, Peruvians are assigned legal or political categories and attributed new social identities and
cultural labels as immigrants along with other minority groups. These em-
blems vary from one host country to another, depending on the latter's immigration and integration policies.

Spanish immigration policy grants work permits according to immigrants'
regional and national origins. This means that all Latin Americans are classified in the same category. Similarly, Moroccans are lumped together with
Algerians and other North Africans as "Maghrebies." In the labor market, on
the other hand, Peruvians occupy a special niche as the carers of old people,
and in the public media they have a reputation for being more astute but also
more delinquent than other Latin American immigrants. Similarly, in the
United States Peruvians are placed in the dominant multicultural categories
along with other ethnic minorities. While the general label for Latin Americans is "Hispanic" (Oboler 1995), Peruvians tend to be categorized with any
of the dominant Spanish-speaking immigrant groups in the United States.
Thus in Miami Peruvians are often mistaken as Cubans, in Los Angeles as
Mexicans, and in New York and New Jersey as Puerto Ricans. In Japan most
non-Japanese are classified as *gaijin* (foreigners), including Peruvian *nikkeijin*, that is, Peruvians of Japanese descent (Takenaka 1999). Although it is
common to distinguish between different groups of *gaijin*, Latin Americans
including Peruvians are generally classified as Brazilians, the major Latin
American immigrant group in Japan (Linger 2001; Tsuda 1999).

Depending on their economic status and social position in Peruvian society
before migrating, migrants respond in different ways to these politics of identification and mechanisms of exclusion and inclusion. While rural Peruvians
often fashion their new identities as an immigrant minority in the host country with a strong focus on their native village or home district, migrants from
urban areas stress their loyalty to the nation state. However, the meaning they
attach to these identities varies greatly among different groups of migrants
and changes during an individual's lifetime. National identities are more significant to middle-class migrants from an urban background than to those
from rural areas. Since the latter tend to identify with their regional rather
than their national origins, they are less reluctant to adopt new social and political identities, which they regard as complementing rather than competing
with former feelings of belonging. Whereas migrants from the Andean hinterland with previous experiences of migration within their home country are
particularly skillful in negotiating identities because of their hybrid lifestyles,
Peruvians of mixed national backgrounds, such as Antonio, who is of Japanese descent, face the more difficult task of remolding one form of national
minority identity in Peru to another in the host country. This puzzle of coa-

lescing national, geographical, and ethnic forms of belonging is further complicated by such variables as gender, class, occupation, and age.

The fluidity of Peruvians' feelings of belonging has yet another dimension. The loyalty that many migrants feel to their place of origin does not coexist only with legal classifications and the popular labeling of immigrants in the host countries, but also with temporary notions of locality that migrants develop outside Peru. This sense of belonging may be the locality of dwelling, of work, of cultural activities, of religious worship, of public performance, or other forms of social practice. As many migrants are constantly on the move changing homes, shifting jobs, attending meetings, and participating in organizations, these temporary resorts of diasporic identities in the host countries seldom supplant their sense of belonging in Peru. Rather than becoming the incubators of more permanent identities based on loyalty to the receiving country, migrants' attachments to these new settings tend to be temporary. Because Peruvian migrants are almost habitually mobile, their sense of belonging in the receiving country often conflates with the networks they create across different cities, nations, and continents, and the social relationships they establish with other migrants in the neighborhoods where they live and the places where they work. This more transient notion of place differs from migrants' loyalties to Peru because it is inscribed into localities that are already inhabited and to which meaning is also ascribed. In Appadurai's terminology, Peruvians try to produce locality in "actually existing social forms in which locality, as a dimension or value, is variably realized" (1991: 179).

The attachments that migrants create to the places where they live and work express a very localized sense of belonging, but at the same time they are highly relational and contextual. Wherever Peruvians travel, they arrange soccer matches and drinking parties in public parks, organize religious processions on the streets, open shops and restaurants, create immigrant institutions, and form networks in shopping centers and other places to assist new migrants to find jobs, for instance. Yet these activities are constantly changing localities, and with a few exceptions the significance that migrants assign to these settings tends to be incidental and temporary.[13] Rather than establishing new and more permanent forms of attachment to the different localities they inhabit that, over time, would replace their original sense of belonging to Peru, migrants think of these as mere junctions for the social networks they create and the chains of information in which they participate. Or, as I shall demonstrate in chapter 6, they contest the meaning attributed to these localities by the host society by using them as platforms to make themselves visible in a public space in order to claim civil and legal rights along with other minority groups.

Migrants' divided sense of locality is reflected in my research design, through which, on the one hand, I examine their economic and social links to relatives, institutions, and activities in Peru, and on the other, explore the formation of new migrant networks and identities in the multicultural milieu of the host societies. Hence, I include a broad spectrum of social life-worlds, geographical locations, and national borders in my study, which raises critical questions concerning the delimitation of the research field.[14] How broadly should this be defined? Should the field be constituted by the sum of all the settings with a Peruvian population (Miami, Los Angeles, Madrid)? Should it also include Peru and the many regional and local sites that migrants regard as their place of origin? Furthermore, as migrants often spend considerable amounts of time traveling between destinations in widely different places in the world, should the many routes, stopping places, conjunctions, and other geographical localities and circuits that become part of Peruvians' global itinerancy also be included in the field?

RESEARCH FIELDS

It is one of those long dreary periods of waiting during field research that fill you with despair because the people you are looking for do not appear. I am sitting in Ventura Mall in northeast Miami sipping my third cup of coffee while watching the crowd of people who either walk by, stand in line at one of the many restaurants, or sit eating the fast food they have just bought. The faces I am looking at are those of a multicultural society—a spectacular medley of colors and races. Here Spanish is heard as often as English; in fact, to many, "Spanglish" is the most natural way of communicating. I wonder whether the place I have picked to make field observations is the transit point for just about everybody in Dade County.

The object of my visit to Ventura Mall that day in February 1998 was to meet a young Peruvian woman. Silvia was employed as a waitress at an espresso bar in the mall's eating lounge and had promised to introduce me to the Peruvians working there. I had been waiting for almost two hours and was starting to doubt whether this was the right way to study Peruvian migrants in Miami. How would I identify the object of my study among this huge crowd of people, and to what extent should I include the surrounding milieu in order to contextualize my observations? It occurred to me that the study site I had chosen was perhaps too large to serve as a suitable field of research or to catch more than a glimpse of Peruvians' construction of a locale. I could not see the forest for all the trees.

My spirits rose considerably when Silvia eventually appeared and introduced me to several fellow countrymen and women working in the mall. She also explained to me how the Peruvian network of family relations was established in the mall. Initially, almost two years ago, a couple of migrants got jobs as table cleaners; today more than twenty Peruvians work as shop assistants, car-park attendants, and security personnel. I also learned that the threads that knit these migrants together into a Peruvian sub-world within the mall provide them with a sense of belonging. Yet this feeling is radically different from their loyalty to their place of origin. Rather than conveying the meaning of a locality, Ventura Mall incarnates the fluid and mobile identity that emerges from being part of the same network of family relations or the sharing of an ethnic or minority identity. This sense of belonging materializes in shifting localities depending on migrants' livelihood strategies, the extension of their networks, and their integration into the host society. Ventura Mall, then, was only one of many points of impact of Peruvians' diasporic identity.

Recent attempts to study contemporary processes of globalization and localization have spurred anthropologists to revise their notion of the ethnographic research field and propose new approaches in examining flows of people, things, and ideas in the world. One scholar has proposed multi-sited ethnography as a methodology that operates in "multiple sites of observation and participation that crosscut dichotomies such as the 'local' and the 'global,' the 'life-world' and the 'system'" (Marcus 1995: 95). He continues, "For ethnography this means that the world system is not the theoretically constituted holistic frame that gives context to the contemporary study of peoples or local subjects closely observed by ethnographers, but it becomes, in a piecemeal way, integral to and embedded in discontinuous, multi-sited objects of study" (Marcus 1995: 97).

The idea of multi-sitedness is implicit in my research into the Peruvian diaspora. Indeed, my despair in Ventura Mall reflects the methodological predicament inherent in the strategy of following Peruvians around the world and thus constantly moving in and out of geographical and political sites and positioning oneself in new environments. Apart from drinking coffee in Ventura Mall while waiting for Silvia and other migrants, these movements and positions include crossing the Californian desert in a rented car in a search for Peruvian sheepherders, driving around in Japan's Gunma province in the van of a Peruvian tradesman to interview migrants, listening to Andean music and talking to Peruvian musicians in Plaza de Catalunya in Barcelona, and participating in the religious procession of Peruvians in the central streets of Buenos Aires to honor the Lord of the Miracles—my odyssey seemed eternal.

While Marcus's concept of multi-sitedness correctly expresses the idea of selected study sites in different parts of the world and thus evokes the notion of a discontinuous and fragmented research field it is less accurate in describing how global migrants construct their sense of belonging and thus convey the meaning of locality that is embodied in their diasporic identity. In order to understand the cultural import of migrants' notions of place, we must extend the definition of our research field beyond the confines of the particular study sites selected to inspect more closely[15] and mold our field in the same way that migrants forge their networks and shape their notions of place. More bluntly, we must follow in the footsteps of those we study. Hence, instead of imagining the research domain of diasporic studies as a "multi-sited" field, I prefer to think of it as an "extended" field. Rather than the mere sum of several single-sited ethnographies, the extended field is constituted by the interlocking of a number of brief in-depth studies of specific aspects of migrant lives (movements, networks, livelihoods, identities, institutions, collective activities) in many different places. Thus, while the term encompasses the idea of locality, it also reminds us of the mobility and interconnectedness that link migrants together in and between the many settings they inhabit.

The notion of an extended field not merely emphasizes the importance of analyzing migrant communities in terms of their global networks but recognizes that diasporic populations are grounded in particular places at particular times and that it is in these settings that migrants remold old identities and create new ones, as well as forms of belonging in and interacting with the surrounding world. These localities of migrant activities and interchange constitute the study sites for ethnographic research in which the researcher may observe the everyday life of particular groups of migrants and explore how immigration and labor market policies shape their strategies and identities. Such studies belong to what Marcus calls "strategically situated ethnographies." In contrast to the notion of global processes as the macro frame that contextualizes the study of local people (as conveyed by conventional single-site ethnographies), the strategically situated ethnography "attempts to understand something broadly about the system in ethnographic terms as much as it does its local subjects: It is only local circumstantially, thus situating itself in a context or field quite differently than do other single-site ethnographies" (Marcus 1995: 111).

The situating context that Marcus is referring to here is essential to the design of diasporic studies. Yet unlike Marcus's strategically situated, single-sited ethnography, which examines local life-worlds as a model of macro processes, and his multi-sited ethnography, which applies the "follow the object" approach and explores how cultural phenomena are constructed through global processes, the extended field research approach situates the researcher in not merely one but a series of strategically selected study sites that each becomes the setting for in-depth ethnographic studies. Thus, the sites are discrete yet connected, their selection being the outcome of a research strategy that not only intends to explore global linkages, but also allows the researcher to zoom in on the face-to-face relations of migrants' everyday lives in particular settings. By including elements of both of Marcus's two research strate-gies, the extended field approach constitutes a complex research domain made up of a whole series of vantage points in different parts of the world, which are the objects of ethnographic studies. This allows the researcher to explore the macro processes that frame Peruvians' migration practices and global networks (like, therefore, multi-sited ethnography), while at the same time investigating ethnographically the local life-worlds and identities that Peruvians create at each vantage point (like single-sited ethnography).

GLOBAL CONTEXTUALIZING

I'm interviewing Goyo at his office in Los Angeles about his migrant experi-ences. Goyo is a Chinese Peruvian whose father came from Canton. He runs a business together with his twin brother importing food articles from Peru and exporting them to Japan, where they are sold to Peruvian immigrants. Our conversation suddenly changes direction as we both take up our note-books to exchange information. Goyo is looking for the phone number of a Peruvian customer he wants me to meet, while I'm looking for the name of a Peruvian migrant in Los Angeles whom Goyo might want to contact. At one point I get a look at Goyo's notebook and discover that it looks very much like mine. Of course his is bound in an expensive-looking skin and looks much more fancy than mine, which was bought for fifty cents in the supermarket. Yet inside both look the same: names of persons and places, telephone numbers and addresses are written pell-mell. Instinctively I exclaim, "Goyo, it looks like we're into the same business." And he replies with a wry smile, "You're right, we both collect names and gossip."

Population movements have been the topic of my research for a number of years. In a previous study, I explored the cultural complexity of rural-urban mi-gration flows in Peru and discussed the analytical and methodological implica-tions of contemporary processes of deterritorialization for anthropological the-ory (Paerregaard 1997a, 1997b, 1998). The object of the study was a remote village in the Peruvian Andes and its migrant communities in the country's ma-jor cities. After conducting a census of the villagers and migrants, I mapped the economic, social, and cultural ties that link the village to the migrant commu-nities. My intention was to use ethnographic in-depth studies in several loca-tions to understand more general processes of identity creation within the Pe-ruvian nation. Metaphorically speaking, my approach could be described as one of observing the formation of the concentric circles that emerge when a stone is dropped into a pond. Migrant networks are created in the same way, whether one starts in a small village or a large nation. Indeed, circles formed by rural migrants are often the roots of larger international networks, as I shall describe in chapter 4. The design of this book, then, is fashioned in the same manner as my earlier work, though on a larger scale. While previously I examined the modest circles generated by rural-urban migration within one nation, I now explore the currents produced by diasporic movements across the globe.

Despite these similarities, the scope and implications of the study in this book are radically different from my former research experiences in Peru. Obviously the methodological and conceptual tools required to examine a population of more than two million migrants are different from those applied in studying a tiny rural population of less than two thousand. Moreover, the very nature of the topics inspected in the two studies differs in a number of respects. Whereas Andean migrants cross the social and cultural borders that have divided Peruvian society since colonial times, international migrants of the contemporary world face obstacles of another kind, like that featured in the opening scene of this book. Nation-states are separated by political boundaries (whether the walls protecting their diplomatic embassies or the borders defining their territories) intended to regulate the physical movement of their citizens. The regulatory mechanisms employed in doing this include not merely the actual control of movement across national borders, but also the identification and surveillance of foreign subjects within the national territory. Because migration beyond national borders normally implies traveling long distances, with considerable costs of transportation, international migrants are often pushed into the hands of rapacious moneylenders and cynical people smugglers. Similarly, difficulties of communication with relatives at home, combined with the cultural and linguistic problems of adapting to foreign countries, put international migrants under great personal pressure and make their attempts to create new livelihoods abroad highly demanding.

In contrast to the notebooks from my previous fieldwork on rural people in Peru, which contained detailed and vivid observations of the social events, agricultural activities, ritual celebrations, and incidents that occurred in the field, the notes I made during my research on the Peruvian diaspora were remarkably prosaic. Rather than recording the peculiarities of a local life-world, these data consist of an array of person names, addresses, telephone numbers, dates, meeting places, and other kinds of "hard core" local knowledge. The matter-of-fact and condensed character of these field notes is evidence of the mobile nature of my object and the extended field approach that I have designed in order to map the movements of the people I study. Throughout the book I crisscross between various cities, countries, and continents, drawing on data gathered and observations made in different places at different times. The glue that binds all these activities, institutions, and events together is the relationships and networks that Peruvians establish across the settings they live in or move between. As Gille and Ó Riain point out, "Conceiving of ethnographic sites as internally heterogeneous and connected to other places by a myriad of social relations requires that the extension of fieldwork to several sites be dictated not by the logic of the ethnographer but by the character of these social relations themselves, both within and between sites" (2002: 287).

At first glance, the conspicuous lack of coherence and consistency in my field data seems at odds with anthropology's holistic approach, which purports to understand social life as an integral whole and encourages the anthropologist to contextualize local "name and number" knowledge within a broader framework of information derived from his or her general observation. As long as the anthropological object was confined to small-scale rural societies and the research field was congruent with the geographical and political setting and people's own notions of locality, holism was understood as coherence in the functionalist sense, so that efforts at contextualization stopped at the local bus station when the ethnographer headed for home.

In this book I shall argue that the meaning of holism changes as anthropology searches for new objects. In contrast to the implicit assumptions of the conventional (usually functionalist) ethnography of isolated rural populations, to the effect that culture is physically confined and that people's life-worlds must therefore be understood within the narrow geographical and social context of the location they inhabit, anthropologists who study social life in the modern world need to find new ways of contextualizing their ethnographic data. Hence, holism is no longer inherent in the study site or the object of research, but must be argued and accounted for in the research design. Moreover, because people are becoming more mobile and culture more deterritorialized, ethnographers must devise new approaches in identifying the objects of their research and invent appropriate methods to follow the movements of the people they study. This, of course, makes it more difficult to identify specific situations, relations, or structures in people's life-worlds within which the ethnographic data can be contextualized. The predicament in modern research design, therefore, is to examine the field material within a context that is neither too broad (e.g., the world system or other macro processes) nor too narrow (e.g., the individual life stories of one or two informants). In other words, the art is to fashion a research field that generates precisely the amount of knowledge and information required to contextualize the data within a framework that is relevant to the study.

Despite modern anthropologists designing their research in new and innovative ways the discipline's traditional holistic approach to social life has not lost ground. Quite the contrary, as anthropologists we must still draw on the experiences and wisdom we acquire in the field to interpret native perspectives, analyze how they interact with other local/global viewpoints, and account for the processes that generate diasporic identities. Likewise, we must still participate in migrants' everyday lives and institutional activities, observe the local social and political milieu in which they engage and explore the macro processes that cause and control migratory movements, and facilitate an awareness of global connectedness. We still need a "somewhere" to contextualize and generate anthropological knowledge, whether a street corner, a neighborhood, a workplace, or an institution, that is, a study site in the global world. It is in how field data are contextualized, not in the means by which they are gathered or in the places where this happens, that the strategically situated single-site ethnography is set apart from conventional single-sited ethnography. Rather than new research tools and field methods, global holism implies alternative ways of viewing the world, defining the field, and approaching the anthropological object.

The seed of holistic thinking in modern anthropology lies in the extended field, which uses interconnectedness as a global frame to juxtapose the findings from different in-depth ethnographies. The analytical challenge of such an approach consists of generalizations across the various single-site research settings and particular pieces of fieldwork. For instance, my conversation with Goyo provided me with the "hard core" local knowledge to do this: not only did the information he gave me expand my research field and connect me with new informants, it also provided me with insights into how his and other migrants form and use their networks to expand geographical and social spaces for their livelihood activities and strengthen their economic and legal status in the host society.

Marcus points out that the broader, more universal dimensions of ethnographic research were always present in anthropological thinking, yet often ignored or not fully explored (1995: 86). By juxtaposing several in-depth ethnographies of migrants in different settings, global holism offers new strategies for inquiring into larger political processes, such as national immigration and integration policies, and racial and multicultural relations in the industrialized world. While anthropology conventionally compared cultural phenomena in societies that were studied and analyzed independent of each other, comparison is an integral dimension of the extended research field.

Two kinds of comparisons are particularly relevant for this study. One concerns Peruvian migration practice as a historical phenomenon. Here comparisons are made across time (e.g., between Japanese immigration into Peru in the first half of the twentieth century and Peruvian emigration to Japan in the 1990s), space (e.g., between the formation of Peruvian immigrant communities in the United States and in the European Union), and identities and polities (e.g., between Peruvian and other diasporas). The other kind of comparison deals with the economic, political, and cultural processes that are propelling international migration in the contemporary world. Peruvian migration, which extends to the three major industrialized centers in the contemporary world, the European Union, the United States, and Japan (as well as Argentina, Chile, and Venezuela, all three of which are among the dominant economies of South America), is a particularly instructive case for, first, examining the relationship between poverty and emigration in Third World countries and labor market policies and processes of social exclusion in the industrialized world; and second, for comparing the development of migrant networks in response to shifting immigration control in different First World countries.

RESEARCH TOOLS

Although the sound of cumbia *can be heard from far away, it comes as a surprise to discover the secret world of Cuoco Rota Mayo on the outskirts of Milan. Few would imagine the Fellini-like ambience inside this junkyard for old cars, with Peruvian immigrants eating* ceviche, *drinking Cuzco beer, and dancing* cumbia. *It is not precisely what you expect to meet on a Sunday evening in northern Italy. While entering Cuoco Rota Mayo together with Carla and Raúl I try to take a photo, but a man speaking Italian with a strong Arabic accent immediately approached us. He says that he owns the place and does not want journalists snooping around. My Peruvian friends explain to the man who I am and why we have come and he gives us permission to stay and join the party. Once inside the Cuoco Rota Mayo, we take a look at the people and the surroundings and order food and beer. I say, "So this is Rota Mayo, which everybody talks about" and Raúl replies, "Yes, this is where we meet every Sunday to forget our sorrows. I know it doesn't look so nice, but it makes me feel as if I was in Peru."*

Despite the recent rethinking of the anthropological construct of cultural boundedness, Geertz's assertion that anthropologists make ethnographies in small places still holds true (1973: 22). Not only is the junkyard of Cuoco in Milan as marginal to modern European society as Geertz's village was remote to Indonesia at the time of his field research, but it also offered me a place to be in, just as the village has done to so many other anthropologists. Indeed, much of the personal wisdom required to contextualize the local "name and number" knowledge that Goyo and other informants provided me with was obtained through my presence in activities such as the *cumbia* party in Cuoco Rota Mayo and Peruvians' weekly gatherings at La Chopera. Participatory observation at these events allowed me to investigate the particular and complex conditions in which migrants produce localities, create social activities, and form immigrant communities. Observing body language, listening to conversations, sensing the atmosphere, and tasting the food gave me a different perspective on migrant life. As Geertz claims, "The important thing about the anthropologist's findings is their complex specificness, their circumstantiality" (1973: 23).

Other events that became the focus of participatory observation in my research were religious processions, charity concerts, collections of emergency aid for the victims of the natural disaster caused by el Niño in 1998, folklore performances, soccer matches, and public events and private parties organized by different types of Peruvian organization. I also spent a considerable amount of time at Peruvian consulates, restaurants, shops, and other public places. Finally, I followed the lives of migrants more closely in the homes of the Peruvian families with whom I stayed while in the field.

My presence at such events was enriched by more systematic extended case studies of selected migrant families in different locations at different times to explore the strategic organization of migration within sibling groups and family networks. I also conducted interviews with officials from Peruvian consulates and migrant leaders, as well as with pioneers in Peruvian emigration, and obtained information from local Peruvian newspapers and home pages. Finally, I collected data on immigration policies in the contemporary world and on the historical development of international migration systems.

Another important source of information in my research was migration histories. These often took the form of life stories, with a strong emphasis on movement from one location to another. A life story is "simply the story of someone's life," which, unlike a life history, "does not connote that the narration is true, that the events narrated necessarily happened, or that it matters whether they did or not" (Peacock and Holland 1993: 368). They contain a rich body of information on migrants' everyday life, their collective activities, and the institutions they create. Life histories, on the other hand, are accounts of individuals' lives guided by the anthropologist's questions (Linde 1993: 47). In this study, I make particular use of life stories because they provide more scope for expression and are less susceptible to the researcher's own subjectivities.

However, in order to turn the collection of life stories into an effective method for revealing migrants' attempts to create new lives and livelihoods, I suggest an approach that analyzes migrant lives as a trajectory. Unlike the chronicle, the recounting of events temporally (e.g., "in 1950 I got married and moved to the city"), or the history, the recounting of events not only in time but also by theme (e.g., a migration record listed year by year), such a trajectory presents a life story as a sequence of events, actions, or intentions leading to specific goals. Thus, telling life stories could be considered an attempt by the narrator to present his or her past as a coherent life trajectory and to relate this reconstruction to present and future prospects. Analyzing migrants' life stories as a trajectory makes it possible to observe how the narrator reconstructs his or her life as if it had been a planned or intended project.[16] Yet, the trajectory does more than account for the narrator's intended performance: it also discloses the motivating and strategic considerations that inspired the narrator to engage in these events and actions in the first place, as well as informing us about the experiences and reflections that these strategic maneuvers gave rise to. Indeed, narrativity may even become a motivating force in itself. Or, as Ochs and Capps put it, "Personal narrative simultaneously is born out of experience and gives shape to experience" (1996: 20). Apart from portraying the narrator as a social actor, the interpretation of migrants' life stories as a trajectory helps us understand the optional landscape within which he or she operates. Moreover, it sheds light on the acquired dispositions, social capital, and cultural knowledge that the narrator commands, as well as showing how he or she mobilizes these resources in order to achieve the goals being pursued. Finally, it offers information on crucial incidents in the narrator's life, such as natural disasters, political changes, or other dramatic occurrences that have had an important impact on the rest of the community or region being studied.

The life stories that this study draws on were collected among a broad spectrum of migrants in Miami, Los Angeles, Paterson, Barcelona, Isesaki, and Buenos Aires. I conducted informal interviews with women as well as men, young as well as old, migrants from almost all parts of Peru (Lima and other coastal cities, the northern, central, and southern highlands, and the jungle), from different social classes (Lima's middle and upper class, migrants from the working class living in shantytowns on the outskirts of the major cities, and migrants with a peasant background), and those from different minority groups (Peruvians with an Andean background, Peruvians of Japanese, Chinese, or European origin, and members of the country's African population). The trajectories differ significantly in content as well as structure, depending on migrants' social status before migrating and their personal migration experiences. To many of them it is the particular act of traveling that is the focus of their narrating. Thus people who migrated illegally spent days, weeks, or even months moving from one location to another, often exposed to harsh conditions and hazardous adventures. Their sense of traveling sometimes continues long after they arrive at their final destination because they live in fear of being sent back. Others stress the events that preceded and led up to the act of traveling. This may be a traumatic experience, such as the death of a family member or political persecution. In other cases the sudden loss of a job and livelihood has triggered the decision to migrate. Yet others emphasize the events that followed the migration. For some the social and cultural encounter with a foreign country implies a radical change in lifestyle and sense of identity: they narrate the migration experience as a transformation of their sense of self and the start of a new life. While some associate this with a feeling of personal liberation, others think of it as the cause of suffering and decay. Still others recount their life stories with few or no references to the actual act of migrating. Rather, they regard migration as a mere physical movement between geographical localities that are attributed meaning in the narrative only in relation to major events in the migrant's lifecycle, such as contracting a marriage, graduating from school, accidents, or diseases.

Combined with participatory observation, migrants' trajectories can be used as a methodological tool to explore their livelihood strategies, their networks and collective activities, their links to and relationships with their place of origin, and the institutions they form in the host countries. Moreover, they serve as an important source of information in contextualizing the "name and number" local knowledge gathered in different study sites within a broader framework of information on migrants' lifecycles. Such information includes observation of the conditions that encourage migrants to move, the circumstances that determine the routes and destinations of their migrancy, and the events that make them settle and establish new lives in other parts of the world. Together with other field data and observations, migrants' own narratives shed light on their individual experiences, aspirations, and concerns, revealing the motives that drive them to embark on global travel, and illuminating the personal predicaments and identity transformations they go through when trying to establish a new life in faraway places.

THE ORGANIZATION OF THE BOOK

The organization of this book reflects my wish to describe the processes of exclusion and inclusion that shape Peruvian migration. My aim is to examine the diversity of relations and practices that constitute migrants' networks and organizations and understand how these are embedded in national and global economic and political structures.

In chapter 2 I offer an introduction to the history of Peruvian migration and present a chronology of the waves of immigration and emigration that Peru has experienced in the twentieth century. I also discuss the economic and political contexts of the emigration waves that Peru has experienced in the past fifty years and suggest that this exodus needs to be examined as a geographical hierarchy of potential destinations available to Peruvians.

In chapter 3 I address immigration policies in the First World, and in particular how these control mechanisms affect Peruvian emigration. In addition,

I offer a brief introduction to the migration histories of Spain, the United States, Japan, and Argentina and examine the different contexts of reception that shape Peruvians' adaptations to the countries and cities where they settle.

The role of migrant networks in Peruvian emigration is the theme of chapter 4. Here I discuss different types of network and examine how they develop, change direction and form in response to shifting immigration policies and labor markets in the industrialized countries. On the basis of the case studies in the five selected countries of emigration, I distinguish the different phases through which migrant networks develop and spread. I also explore the relationship between internal migration processes in Peru and the emergence of a global migrant population in the past two decades.

In chapter 5 I study the events, processes, and institutions that stimulate Peruvians' engagement in transnational practices and that prompt their awareness that they constitute a separate population, in other words their diasporic consciousness. Analytically, the chapter focuses on the relationships of exchange that migrants create and the conflicts and contestations that occur when they organize social, political, and cultural activities and establish links to their country and regions of origin.

Throughout the world, migrants establish institutions and organize processions to celebrate Peruvian national and regional religious icons. The internal conflicts between migrants within these institutions are the subject of chapter 6; likewise, the different meanings that Peruvians in the United States, Europe, Japan, and South America ascribe to the icons are analyzed, pointing to the possibility that, by recreating former religious practices and organizing processions in honor of their icons, migrants are conquering public spaces in the host societies and challenging the dominant stereotypes of Third World migrants.

What impact does global itinerancy have on individual migrants' notions of belonging and on their life courses, and how do the control mechanisms that First World countries employ to restrict immigration influence their sense of self? These questions, among others, are raised in chapter 7, where I also ask how migrants from different social classes and ethnic groups in Peru create new notions of belonging and alter their ideas of social inequality in response to the context of their reception and their migration experiences.

In chapter 8 I discuss the meaning of "illegality" and how illegal traveling affects the lives of individual migrants. I also examine how the politics of identity practiced by the receiving countries and the forms of inclusion and exclusion that these policies give rise to shape the lives of immigrants and explore how migrants respond to the classification as "illegal." Finally, I compare the strategies and room for maneuver that different immigration policies allow undocumented immigrants, and examine the networks that they draw in finding work and somewhere to live.

In the concluding chapter, I sum up the theoretical and analytical findings of the study and explore the future options available to Peruvians in engaging in transnational activities, creating diasporic identities, and seeking adaptation in the United States, Spain, Japan, and Argentina.

NOTES

1. Altamirano uses data from Peru's Dirección General de Migración y Naturalización based on routine counting of the number of Peruvians who leave and enter the country. According to the 2005 census, Peru's population is currently 26.1 million (INEI 2005).

2. On Cubans in Miami, see Pérez 1992; on Mexicans in Los Angeles, see Ortiz 1996; on Puerto Ricans in New York, see Duany 2002; Flores, Attinasi, and Pedraza 1987; on Jamaicans in London, see Foner 1978.

3. On Moroccans in Spain, see Bodega et al. 1995; on Algerians in France, see Wadia 1999, Holifield 1999; on Turks in Germany, see Chapin 1996; on Pakistanis and Bangladeshis in England, see Ballard 1987, Gardener 1992, Werbner 2002a; on Sikhs in Europe, see Axel 2001; on the Filipinos, see Salazar Parreñas 2001.

4. On Asia, see Shah 1995 and Vertovec 2000; on Africa, see Adepoju 1995; on Latin America, see Castillo 1994, Balán 1992.

5. For a critical discussion of Agamben's ideas of the state of exception, see Das and Poole (2004: 11–13).

6. Stratton (1997) suggests that we distinguish between several forms of diaspora on the basis of the Jewish experience. In the pre-modern version, the concept is linked not only to colonial capitalism, which demanded the movement of workers between the colonies, but also the Greek, Jewish, and Armenian dispersions. These classic diasporas implied the ideas of displacement, exile, and return (Safran 1991: 83–84), which gave rise to the strong collective identification of an ethnic group with its homeland (in some diasporas such as the Jewish, this identity even converges with religion). The post-modern import of the term derives from the massive population flows that took place in the western world when the modern nation state was formed in the nineteenth century, and later when it started to come under pressure in the late twentieth century (Stratton 1997: 307–10). In both periods, diasporas were central to the conceptualization and imagination of a confined and homogenous national population, acting as a catalyst in, as well as a barrier to, the development of the nation-state. Paradoxically, nationalism and transnationality are both inherent in diasporic identities (Tölölyan 1996: 5).

7. With a Peruvian immigrant population of almost 60,000 (Peruvian Consulate in Milan, 2006), Milan is particularly interesting because it attracts a blend of very different categories of Peruvians: while a large portion of migrants come from the Andean hinterland (Junín and Ancash), the city has also become the global center for Peruvian gay males and transvestites. Other countries of major Peruvian immigration in the European Union are France and Germany, while countries such as Switzerland,

Holland, and England have somewhat smaller Peruvian communities (see Altamirano 1996). Sweden, on the other hand, was the haven of Peruvian political refugees until less than ten years ago.

8. Peruvian communities are also represented in large numbers in such cities as Chicago, San Francisco, Austin, Dallas, and Washington, D.C. The latter is a particularly interesting place to study migrants from Peru's Andean highlands. Paul Gelles reports (personal communication) that there are currently more than five hundred migrants from the village of Cabanaconde, located in the Department of Arequipa, in Washington, D.C.

9. Canada also has a large Peruvian community, though not as large as that of the United States. In 1998 I spent five days in Toronto. Apart from visiting Peruvian restaurants, I had the opportunity to participate in a public event organized by the Peruvian association in Toronto on Mother's Day.

10. Fujimori, Peru's former president, is the son of Japanese immigrants who came to Peru in the 1930s.

11. Japan is the only Asian country with a large Peruvian immigrant community. In recent years, however, a growing number of Peruvians have migrated to South Korea. In the Pacific Rim, Australia also has an important community of Peruvian immigrants (Altamirano 1996: 277–93).

12. Up to twenty years ago, Venezuela was the main destination of Peruvian emigration in South America. However, as falling oil prices and political crises crippled the economy of this country in the late 1980s, Peruvian migrants started to look elsewhere. In the late 1990s Chile emerged as the principal center of Peruvian emigration along with Argentina. In both countries, immigrants from Bolivia, Peru, and other neighboring states are marginalized socially and in some cases discriminated against because of their ethnic background. In 2002 and 2005 I spent ten days in Santiago, Chile's capital, visiting Peruvian migrants.

13. Miami's Kendall district is an interesting exception to this pattern. Here the Peruvian community has negotiated an agreement with the local authorities and the owner of a local shopping center to put up a statue of Miguel Grau (one of Peru's maritime war heroes from the nineteenth century) and to create what is known as the Plaza del Perú with a statue of an Amazon Indian and shields from several Peruvian cities. Employees from the Peruvian consulate participate in weekly gatherings on the Plaza to hoist the Peruvian (and American) flag and sing Peru's national anthem. The plaza also serves as the setting for the celebration of Peru's independence day and other events (such as the collection of cloth, food, and money for the victims of the El Niño disaster in Peru in 1998).

14. Studying a diasporic population implies researching not only a wide spectrum of social actors in the modern world, but also social and ethnic groups that in anthropology have conventionally been considered opposed and to a certain extent exclusive. While diasporic communities are labeled immigrant minorities in the host countries and thus classified in opposition to the local and indigenous population, many Peruvians living outside Peru continue to conceive of themselves as Peruvian natives. Indeed, many migrants belong to the country's indigenous population and maintain close ties with their native region or home village in the Andean highlands. Some of

these migrants even draw on this image as the descendants of Peru's pre-Columbian ancestors when creating new livelihoods in Europe, North America, and Japan, making a living by either playing so-called Andean music, selling folklore handicrafts, or making native art. Hence local and global perspectives on immigrant and native tend to conflate in the diasporic context, and terms and categories that were formerly regarded as opposed take on a less exclusive and more situational meaning.

15. Marcus prefers to call this "strategically situated ethnography."

16. Methodologically, the researcher plays an active role in choosing and framing the issues and concerns to be dealt with in the trajectory. If possible, the field-worker starts by asking the narrator to give a brief historical account of his or her life in order to map out the major topics to be addressed in the trajectory. The most significant occurrences in the narrator's life history can be clarified at this point (education, migration, inheritance, marriage, deaths within the family, droughts, civil wars, economic booms, etc.), which often serve as important points of reference in the thematic organization of the narrative.

Part I

FLOWS AND CONTEXTS

Chapter Two

Coming and Going

The present chapter explores two dimensions of Peruvian migrant history. First, I examine the main waves of immigration during the colonial and republican periods, which initially brought European conquerors and settlers and enslaved Africans to Peru, and later Chinese and Japanese as contract workers. Second, I explore the economic and political contexts that have generated the recent exodus of Peruvians to the United States, Spain, Japan, and Argentina and examine how this emigration has developed in waves over the past fifty years. Third, I use the term geographical hierarchy to analyze the social and cultural meaning that Peruvians attribute to the cities and countries they migrate to.

PERUVIAN IMMIGRATION HISTORY

Before the arrival of the Europeans population movements were common within the Inca Empire (Saignes 1985: 10–21), and ever since the Spanish conquest a constant flow of people has been moving in and out of the country. Not surprisingly, a major concern of Peru's rulers has been how to control and, if possible, benefit from these migration flows economically and politically. It is therefore essential to any study of Peru's history to understand the importance of migration. By the same token, Peruvian society and culture cannot be studied without taking into consideration processes of the hybridization of languages and cultures that the intense population movements in and out of the country have entailed. To use a proverb of José María Arguedas (1980), Peru's famous novelist and anthropologist, contemporary Peru is the product of an astonishing mixture of "all the bloods" (*todas las sangres*). Indeed, due to massive immigration from

Europe, Africa, Asia, and the rest of South America, Peru's contemporary population can trace its cultural and ethnic roots to almost every corner of the world.

Historically, Peru has received two kinds of immigrants. On the one hand, Spanish conquerors, fortune-hunters, settlers, administrators, traders, and missionaries have left their home country voluntarily to start a new life, with the expectation that their status as *peninsulares*, or individuals born in Spain, would assure them access to the upper strata of Peru's colonial society. After Peru won its independence in 1821, other Europeans followed the Spanish and became a part of Peru's upper-class society, a population flow that continued through the twentieth century. Today, the descendants of this influx still exert a strong influence on Peru's economic and political development.

Conversely, enslaved Africans, Chinese coolies, and Japanese contract workers have migrated to Peru to work in the cotton and sugar plantations, the mines, the railroads, and the *guano* (bird manure) industry. As enslaved workers the Africans were forced to migrate during the colonial and early republican periods. Cut off from maintaining their ties to their home regions and countries, they were left with no other alternative than to adopt their employers' language and religion and eventually identify with Spanish settler culture. The Chinese and Japanese came as voluntary migrants, at least on paper, during the late nineteenth and early twentieth centuries, having been induced to sign labor contracts that obliged them to migrate to Peru and work for a definite period of time. Often poor and uneducated, however, these contract workers were in no position to imagine the working and living conditions that were being offered to them in their new country of residence. Indeed, once in Peru many of them realized that their situation in many ways recalled that of the former slaves from Africa.

THE COLONIAL PERIOD

The society that grew out of the Spanish conquest of Peru in 1532 was from the beginning multiethnic. The main reason for this development was the dramatic fall in population, which the native population of the former Inca Empire experienced in the years that preceded and followed the conquest. Fifty years after Pizarro and his men had defeated the Incas only 1.1 million of an estimated pre-Columbian population of nine million were alive (Cook 1981: 94, 114).[1] The rest died primarily because of the contagious diseases the conquerors brought with them. In effect, the Inca Empire was reduced to small, isolated political units struggling to reproduce themselves socially as well as physically. The conquerors, on the other hand, were primarily men who had left their home country to look for gold and adventure, but later found themselves short of concubines and marriage partners, a need satisfied by indigenous women. In effect, as the servants or mistresses and occasionally wives of Spaniards, Indian women occupied a central role in the Hispanic world in contrast to their male counterparts, who lived on the margins of the colonial society (Lockhart 1968: 220). The outcome was a predominantly mestizo population and a society blended by both indigenous and European culture and religion.[2]

The process of ethnic differentiation and cultural hybridization was also promoted by the presence of enslaved Africans and so-called *moriscos*, that is, Spaniards of African ancestry who accompanied the Spanish conquerors (Lockhart 1968: 171–98).[3] In the early days of the conquest, the main function of these Africans was to serve as valuable military auxiliaries. In the words of Lockhart, Africans "were an organic part of the enterprise of occupying Peru from its inception" (Lockhart 1968: 198). Some got to Peru by various means of their own accord. Others came with their permanent owners or with Spaniards hoping to make a profit by selling a couple of extra slaves. Most Africans served as domestic servants in the homes of the Spanish conquerors, but as time passed they were also used in the mining industry in the highlands and the plantations on the coast (Aguirre 2005: 49–71). Once the Spanish had founded their own cities, however, the Africans were assigned other tasks as well and became part of Peru's colonial population.[4] Some even obtained their freedom and became hacienda owners themselves (Lockhart 1968: 192–93). Their contribution to the emergence of a multiethnic society was significant in that the Spaniards sometimes mixed with their enslaved female Africans and *morisca* servants, who, on the other hand, occasionally had offspring with the indigenous population. Moreover, because the Spaniards rarely kept track of the geographical origin of the slaves they brought with them to Peru, and because the latter were prevented from having any contact with their home regions, most Africans adopted Spanish and the Hispanic religion and identified themselves with the conquerors' culture (Aguirre 2005: 101–26). However, as I shall demonstrate in chapter 6, Afro-Peruvians created their own interpretations of Spanish culture and religion.

During the colonial period, while Spaniards and enslaved Africans continued to immigrate to Peru, the presence of other nationalities was limited (Altamirano 1996: 24–25). The indigenous population, on the other hand, grew very slowly, and it was not until the end of the seventeenth century that it regained its pre-conquest level. However, under Spanish rule physical mobility between indigenous communities in the Andean highlands in general was high, making it difficult for the Spanish to prevent the Indians from mixing with the rest of the population and thus maintaining the categorical distinction between the ethnic groups (Wightman 1990). Consequently, when Peru gained its independence in 1821 it was a multiethnic society consisting of elements of Spanish, African, and Indian cultures. The society of "all the bloods" heralded by José María Arguedas was already in process of formation.

THE REPUBLICAN PERIOD

Throughout the colonial and early republican period, slavery was the most popular form of labor recruitment in Peru. However, when the importation of enslaved Africans was stopped in 1836 and slavery itself abolished in 1854, the need for labor in the plantations, on the railroads, and in the *guano* industry encouraged employers and the dominant political classes to introduce labor contracts in order to recruit workers (Trazegnies 1995a: 23–24). In effect, in the second half of the nineteenth and the early twentieth centuries, a new Pacific migration link was established, which, over a period of almost a century, was to bring hundreds of thousands of Chinese and Japanese to Peru.[5] Although the influx of Asian labor migrants in the republican period differed in a number of ways from the importation of enslaved Africans in the colonial period, the similarities between the two processes of migration are hard to ignore. In essence, Africans and Asians both came to Peru because their labor was needed, whether as domestic servants, plantation, mine or railroad workers, or collectors of *guano*. The only difference between the two groups of immigrants was the means of recruitment. Slaves were forced to migrate against their own will, while contract workers migrated because they were led into debt, which obliged them to work in conditions they had no knowledge of before migrating (Rodríguez Pastor 2000: 37–43).

The first ships to leave with contract workers came from ports in China proper (Trazegnies 1995b: 104–5). However, Hong Kong, by then a British colony, and neighboring ports controlled by the British Crown soon became the principal cities shipping out Chinese workers. When the British authorities forbad the embarkation of emigrants from its ports in China, Macao, which was controlled by the Portuguese, became the main port of emigration (Trazegnies 1995b: 249). In fact, the migration link that emerged between China and Peru in the nineteenth century developed as an extension of an already existing population movement from China to different destinations in the Pacific. As early as 1802 Chinese migrants settled in Hawaii, and by the 1830s Chinese workers were being recruited more systematically to the islands' sugar plantations (McKeown 2001: 33). Later the migratory chain was extended to California, where Chinese men participated in the gold rush in the 1850s.[6] However, the Chinese Exclusion Act of 1882 brought immigration from China to the United States to a temporary halt, driving Chinese emigrants in search of work to other destinations such as Peru (McKeown 2001: 26–30).

Although an Asian presence in Peru can be traced back to 1613, when thirty-eight Chinese, probably from the Philippines, were recorded as living in Lima, it was not until slavery was abolished that Chinese immigration to Peru started on a larger scale (Dobyns and Doughty 1976: 172–73). This influx gained momentum in 1849, when the so-called Chinese Law was passed to provide for the importation of indentured workers from China (Trazegnies 1995b: 85–86), and it increased still further when slaves in Peru were emancipated in 1854 (McKeown 2001: 44). As a result, between 1848 and 1874 a total of 90,000 Chinese, mainly from the Canton area, the closest Chinese city to Hong Kong and Macao, migrated to Peru,[7] where they found work in the cotton and sugar plantations and the *guano* industry on the coast and in railroad construction in the highlands (Pastor Rodríguez 2005: 47–54; Trazegnies 1995a: 26).

Chinese immigration to Peru blossomed again when the first direct steamship lines between Hong Kong and Callao, Lima's port, were established in 1904. Thus between 1905 and 1909 it is estimated that as many as three thousand Chinese a year arrived in Callao (Trazegnies 1995a: 45), a population movement that, unlike previous waves of Chinese immigration into Peru in the nineteenth century, was free. However, the fact that the Chinese and Peruvian governments signed an agreement in 1874 to end contract labor and allow the free movement of people and goods between the two countries did not alter ordinary people's prejudices against Chinese immigrants in Peru, and in 1909 anti-Chinese riots broke out in Lima. In effect, in the following two decades Chinese migration to Peru became increasingly unpredictable and never reached pre-1909 levels. In 1930 it was eventually brought to an end when the populist government lead by Sánchez Cerro that came to power in a coup banned all Chinese immigration (Trazegnies 1995a: 46–47).

Just as the abolition of slavery in 1854 forced Peru's plantation owners to look for labor on the other side of the Pacific, so the decision to end the importation of Chinese contract workers in 1874 prompted employers and politicians to search for cheap labor in other places, from which people could be persuaded to migrate and work on the Peruvian coast. In fact, a surplus of labor was already available in Peru's highlands, where the owners of haciendas and mines traditionally recruited workers through a patron-client system. Such relationships, which are common throughout Latin America (Wolf and Hansen 1972: 200–204), are based on "a reciprocal arrangement tying members of various social strata together, in terms not of social or economic equality, but of reciprocal obligations of an unequal sort" (Gillin 1960: 36).[8] They were widespread in Peru's rural highlands into the twentieth century and did not end until the land reform dissolved the hacienda system in the 1970s (Tullis 1970: 39–45; Alberti and Fuenzalida 1969; Trazegnies 1995b: 201–15; Klaren 1970: 72–86). Often these patron-client relationships were established through a form of labor recruitment called *enganche*, which ensured hacienda and mine owners in the Peruvian highlands of a reliable source of labor. Davies explains that "agents sent to the Sierran Indian *comunidades*, usually after the harvest, offered large initial sums to idle Indians and those Indians who were deeply in debt because of crop failure or fiesta expenditures. In return, the Indians signed a labor contract which usually bore no relation to the terms offered orally" (1974: 54).[9] In 1910 *enganche* was legalized by the Peruvian government and used on a large scale to recruit Indian labor to the mines and sheep ranches in the central highlands, some of which were owned by American companies (Davies 1974: 71; Mallon 1983: 186–205).

However, the *enganche* system did not satisfy the demand for labor that emerged in the plantations after the importation of Chinese workers was ended. The owners complained that *enganche* brokers failed to provide sufficient Indian workers from the Andes, and that those they recruited either ran away or returned to their home regions as soon as they had completed their contracts (Morimoto 1999: 47–48). They wanted workers from more remote areas or countries that had no previous knowledge about Peru and could not escape or go home once their labor contracts expired. Consequently, a similar recruitment practice was introduced to contract labor from Japan (Sakuda 1999: 94–105). Here a system called *dekasegi* had been in use since the eighteenth century, which allowed the rural population to take temporary work in other parts of the country.[10] In 1868 the Meiji restoration legalized *kaigai dekasegi* (migration outside Japan), which triggered the large-scale migration of contract workers to the Americas in the second half of the nineteenth and first half of the twentieth centuries (Fukumoto 1997: 44–50; Takenaka 2004: 78). Hence, when Peru's hacienda owners started to look for new *enganche* workers in the late nineteenth century, the *kaigai dekasegi* system had already reached Hawaii and California and was about to expand into South America, where the Peruvian and other national governments had signed agreements with Japan to encourage the import of Japanese labor. In 1899 the first boat arrived in Peru with 790 Japanese male workers, who were sent off to the waiting hacienda owners on different parts of the Peruvian coast (Fukumoto 1997: 120–22; Gardiner 1981: 3). Further shipments of contract workers arrived in the following years, but as the Japanese established their own migrant networks in Peru in the first decades of the twentieth century, the newcomers made use of other ways of migrating. Japanese emigration to Peru and other

Latin American countries continued throughout the first half of the twentieth century, leading to the establishment of large Japanese communities in Brazil (1.28 million) and Peru (between 80 and 90,000), and somewhat smaller communities in Argentina, Paraguay, and Bolivia (Yamanaka 1996: 71; Takenaka 1999: 1460).

Japanese immigration to Peru ceased when World War II broke out and Peru and Japan suddenly faced each other as enemies (Yamawaki 2002: 113–34). During the War rioters targeted many Japanese-owned shops and farms, and between 1942 and 1944 1,393 Japanese nationals were deported to the United States and detained together with the Japanese population living in North America (Gardiner 1981: 95).[11] Although this experience is still recalled with bitterness among *issei* (first-generation Japanese immigrants), it reminds many *nisei* and *sansei* (second- and third-generation Japanese immigrants) that the ties their parents and grandparents maintained with Japan and the exclusive identity as an ethnic minority that they claimed before World War II jeopardized their position in Peru, and that their own future lies in the country where they were born (Takenaka 2004: 93–95). This shift in orientation away from their country of origin toward their country of residence is reflected in the fact that, since 1945, Japanese immigrants to Peru have married outside their own ethnic group to a much greater extent than Brazilians of Japanese descent. Moreover, the image that many Peruvians have of the descendants of Japanese immigrants as a closed ethnic community has changed dramatically since Alberto Fujimori, a Peruvian of Japanese descent, was elected president of Peru in 1990. Finally, the discrimination that Latin American *nikkeijin* (descendants of Japanese immigrants of all generations) living in Japan as foreign workers have experienced in recent years has further urged Peru's Japanese minority to alter their self-identification as Japanese (Tsuda 1999; Takenaka 1999).

Although transpacific population movements contributed significantly to Peru's economic and political development in the late nineteenth and early twentieth centuries, the country continued to receive immigrants from other parts of the world. During the nineteenth century it attracted about 50,000 immigrants from Spain, Italy, France, Germany, Portugal, England, Ireland, and, to a lesser extent, North America. Under the colonial system, the Spanish were the largest immigrant group and the Italians were the second. According to Ciccarelli, however, the latter passed the Spanish in the 1860s and became the largest European colony in Peru, reaching a peak of 13,000 in 1906 (1988: 369).[12] Moreover, Italian immigrants left their home country on an individual basis and spontaneously, rather than as a result of government initiatives. Most of them came from northwestern Italy and were reasonably well educated (Ciccarelli 1988: 370).[13] The French occupied third place among European immigrants in Peru, accounting in 1876 for 9 percent of Lima's foreign population. Another national group whose presence in Peru has been felt since the mid-nineteenth century are the Germans, who arrived both in groups for settlement and individually as immigrants. Some stayed in Lima, while others settled in the foothills of Huallaga and in Tarapoto, Moyobamba, and Pozuzo. Working in import-export businesses, shipping, manufacturing, and mining companies, English and Irish immigrants also constituted a large foreign colony until the mid-nineteenth century. Other European nationals arrived too, though in smaller numbers (M. Vásquez 1970: 81–82).

Throughout the colonial period, the mixing of immigrant ethnic groups with native-born Peruvians and their integration into the social and cultural life of Peru was fostered by the high proportion of male immigrants and the existence of a large, mostly Indian, local population of rural and urban workers. This development continued during the early republic. According to the 1876 census, almost 85 percent of all foreigners in Peru were males, while among the native born women formed a clear majority, mainly as a result of wars (M. Vásquez 1970: 85). The combination of the continuous immigration of foreign males and the presence of a large group of working-class women facilitated ethnic mixing, and today Peru, like many other Latin American countries, is a highly diversified society characterized by a *mestizaje* ideology claiming Peruvian language and culture to be the product of the European culture inherited from the Spanish conquerors. Although contemporary processes of modernization and globalization increasingly have challenged the idea that the nation's identity has been forged solely by its colonial inheritance, the *mestizaje* ideology continues to dominate political thinking and practice in Peru.

CONTEMPORARY PERUVIAN EMIGRATION

While Peru was for centuries the destination of conquistadors, slaves, refugees, and fortune hunters from Europe, Africa, Asia, and North America, about thirty years ago it became a source of out-migration. The racial and cultural mixture that the country experienced during the years of immigration produced the diversity of today's emigrant population. Spaniards, Italians, Argentineans, North Americans, and Japanese who came to work or settle in Peru up to the mid 1950s created economic, political, and cultural connections between their new country of residence and their place of origin that Peruvians have used to spread across the world in the second half of the twentieth century.[14] Today Peruvian migration takes the form of a global spider's web, in which people from the same part of Peru tend to migrate to the same destinations (Altamirano 1990, 1992, 1996, 2000, 2006) (see figure 1.1). Spain has become the preferred destination of Peruvian migration from the coastal cities of northern Peru, in particular Trujillo (Escrivá 1997, 1999, 2000, 2003, 2005; Merino Hernando 2002, 2004; Tornos et. al 1997). American cities such as New York, Paterson, New Jersey, Chicago, and Los Angeles, together with Japan, Argentina, and Chile, attract Peruvians primarily from Lima and other coastal cities of central Peru (Avila 2003, 2005; Berg 2005; Bernasconi 1999; Julca 2001; León 2001; Nuñez 2002, 2005; Pacecca 2000; Paerregaard 2005b, 2005c; Ruiz Bahía 1999; Sabogal 2005; Stefoni 2002, 2005; Takenaka 1999, 2003, 2004, 2005; Torales 1993; Walker 1988); Milan, Rome, and Turin in Italy, and Miami, Florida, and, to a lesser extent; Hartford, Connecticut; Washington, D.C.; and Dallas and Houston, Texas, in the United States have been the chief destinations of migrants from the Peruvian highlands for a number of years (Gelles 2005; Paerregaard 2002a, 2003, 2005a,b,c, in review; Tamagno 2002a, 2002b, 2003a, 2003b, 2005). Although this mapping of migrants' regional origins and global destinations fails to convey the specifics of the geographical and cultural dynamics that propel Peruvian emigration, it does indicate broad trends on the basis of which substantive conclusions may be drawn.

The United States makes up the main destination of Peruvian emigration (Altamirano 2000: 31). The first important wave (although relatively small in terms of numbers of migrants) occurred in the early 1930s when small groups of political refugees particularly belonging to the APRA party went into exile and settled in U.S. cities as Chicago and New York.[15] After World War II Peru experienced an economic bonanza and in the 1950s and 1960s it became common among the country's middle- and upper-class families to send their sons to Spain and Argentina to study medicine, law, and other academic professions. Many of these young men formed migrant associations in the cities where they settled and quite a few married local women, established families, and stayed. In the same period, women from Quechua-speaking rural areas in the Andean highland who were working as domestic servants in Lima started to emigrate to South Florida and other places in the United States and in the late 1950s to do domestic work there, while males from Lima's working-class neighborhoods (Surquillo, La Victoria, and Callao) began to travel to Paterson and other cities in New Jersey to work in the booming textile industry (Altamirano 1990).[16] Simultaneously, New York and Chicago emerged as the center of immigration of a growing number of Peruvians (Walker 1988) and when many factory workers in New Jersey are laid off in the 1970s, Los Angeles and other Californian cities also became a magnet for Peruvian migration. During the 1970s and 1980s, Miami received large numbers of migrants from Peru's Andean rural areas particularly the departments of Ancash, Junín, and Ayacucho and by the end of the 1980s the city emerged as the preferred destination for middle- and upper-class Peruvians mostly from Lima, who fled the economic and political crisis in Peru of the 1980s. This exodus continued under the Fujimori government between 1990 and 2001, spreading to other U.S. cities such as Dallas, Houston, Washington, D.C., and San Francisco. According to Altamirano, the total number of Peruvians in the United States amounted to 500,000 in 1992 (2000: 26). Today, this number is likely to have reached one million, which makes it the largest concentration of Peruvians outside Peru (Altamirano 2006: 124–25).

Since the late 1980s and early 1990s, Peruvian emigration has changed direction and in the past fifteen years a number of new destinations have emerged. A survey carried out by the Latin American Migration Project at Princeton University in 2001 identified twenty-five countries as destinations of Peruvian migration (Takenaka 2003). This explosion in alternative destinations has been triggered by two factors. On the one hand, Peru experienced an explosion in the unemployment rate in the late 1980s and early 1990s due to the economic and political crisis that haunted the country during the government of Alan García (1985–1990) and the neoliberal policies introduced by the Fujimori government (1990–2001) causing further impoverishment of the population and growing emigration rates. On the other hand, in this same period, the United States tightened its immigration policy and border control making it more difficult for Peruvians and other immigrant groups to enter and remain in the country. This has only become worse since the post 9/11 general crackdown on the U.S. immigrant population.

Almost simultaneously the Spanish, Italian, and Japanese governments passed new immigration laws (Escrivá 1997; Merino 2004; Takenaka 2004; Tamagno 2003) that encouraged the importation of foreign unskilled workers in order to satisfy the growing need for labor in the domestic servant sector and manufacturing industry in these countries (Paerregaard 2003). Spain and Japan in particular have favored Peruvian immigration. Thus, since 1990 Latin Americans have been allowed to apply for work permits within specific occupations in Spain; likewise, the same year Japan allowed descendants of Japanese emigrants living in Peru (and Brazil) to take temporary work in the country in order to satisfy the demand for labor in the manufacturing industry. Subsequently, large numbers of Peruvian males have migrated to Japan to do factory work whereas Peruvian females have gone to Spain (and Italy) to do domestic work. Whereas the number of migrants in Japan has remained relatively stable since the Japanese government began to require tourist visas from Peruvians in 1992 currently making up 65,000 (Peruvian Consulate, Tokyo, 2005), Spain and Italy continue to attract large numbers of Peruvians who either migrate through family reunification, obtain one of the annual work permits that the Spanish or Italian governments grant to foreigners, or benefit from the amnesties that these government recurrently offer undocumented immigrants.[17] Today, the Peruvian populations in Spain and Italy amount to almost 100,000 in each country (Escrivá 2004: 155; Tamagno 2003: 14).[18]

In a similar vein, Argentina (from 1994) and Chile (from 1997) have become magnets for Peruvian emigration in the second half of the 1990s, partly in response to the difficulties of finding work in the Spanish, Italian, and Japanese labor markets and partly because of the growing demand for unskilled labor in the two countries.[19] There are currently 100,000 and 62,000 Peruvians in the two countries respectively (Peruvian Consulate, Buenos Aires, 2000; Stefoni 2002: 56). From a gender perspective this more recent migration flux toward Argentina and Chile resembles the sudden inflow of Peruvians that Spain and Italy experienced in the early 1990s. Thus women who take work as domestic servants for either Argentinean and Chilean or Spanish and Italian families have spearheaded both waves. However, from a class perspective the two migration waves differ in a number of respects. Because Peruvians can reach Argentina and Chile by bus in two to three days and are allowed to enter the two countries on a tourist visa Argentina and Chile primarily attract migrants from Peru's impoverished urban shantytowns who cannot afford to travel to Spain and Italy (or other destinations). Indeed, to these migrants Argentina and Chile represent a last resort in a situation where all other migratory options have been ruled out.[20] In the past fifteen years, then, Peruvian emigration has constantly changed directions toward new destinations in Europe, Asia, and the Americas in response to shifting immigration policies and demands for unskilled labor in these settings.

MIGRATION AS A GEOGRAPHICAL HIERARCHY

In both the colonial and early republican periods Peru was the target of mass immigration of conquerors, slaves, contract workers, and businessmen from Africa, Europe, Asia, and other parts of the Americas. It is from the connections that these migrations established that Peru's contemporary population benefits when seeking new horizons to find work and create new lives in response to the country's economic and political crisis. This continuity becomes evident by looking at migrants' choice of destination and the co-relation between their global dispersal countrywide and citywide and their social status and regional origin in Peru. Thus Peruvians who come from the same regions or belong to particular ethnic groups and immigrant minorities in Peru tend to concentrate in the same places in the world. In other words, the social diversity and geographical dispersal that make contemporary Peruvian emigration so unique are the outcome of Peru's political and cultural history and previous population movements.

Insofar as migrants come from very different social strata in Peruvian society their strategies to migrate, adapt, and find work vary; likewise, in as much as they settle in a variety of cities and countries the contexts of reception in the host societies differ. Whereas Peruvians in such U.S. cities as Miami, Los Angeles, and Paterson are inserted into already existing multicultural environments that encompass a broad range of minority groups of which some have a long migration history in the country. In Spain, Japan, and Argentina they are viewed as a visible example of the increasing immigration of people from the Third World and therefore often objects of cultural and racial prejudices and xenophobic sentiments. Although this creates barriers for migrants' integration and possibilities of achieving social mobility in all three countries the context of reception in Spain, Japan, and Argentina varies significantly. Whereas the Spanish and Japanese populations up to recently were relatively homogeneous, massive European immigration during the nineteenth and twentieth centuries transformed Argentina into a culturally very diverse society. Nevertheless, rather than regarding the recent influx of immigrants from Peru, Bolivia, and other neighboring countries as a continuity of this migration history the growing presence of Peruvians and other South Americans is viewed by many as a threat to the social order. Similar variations may be observed when comparing the Spanish and Japanese context of reception. In Spain Peruvians and Spaniards not merely share the same cultural history but speak the same language (except for Peruvians residing in Catalonia), which facilitate their adaptation to Spanish society. Conversely, although the bulk of Peruvians who migrate to Japan descend from Japanese emigrants their lack of proficiency and skills in Japanese language and culture limit their opportunities to achieve social mobility.

Many Peruvians read the range of possible migration connections and the varying contexts of reception as well as economic and social opportunities in the receiving countries as a geographical hierarchy that indicates future possibilities. In this hierarchy the United States represents a unique opportunity to study, do business, or in other ways make fast money because of its open immigration policy, liberal labor market, and multicultural environment. Similarly, Japan is regarded a haven by many because salaries are higher than in other countries while Spain and Italy are preferred destinations because Peruvians find it easy to adapt to the local language and culture. By reverse, Argentina and, in particular, Chile, are thought of as the last option because salaries are lower and migrants' prospects of improving the living conditions for themselves and their children are less prosperous in these countries. The choice of destination is also read as an indicator of migrants' economic and social status in Peruvian society. Thus, only Peruvians of Japanese descent and their spouses are allowed to obtain working visa to Japan. Similarly, migration to the United States, Spain, and Italy requires that migrants already have relatives in these countries that either invite them to come through a family reunification program or lend them money to pay people smugglers to arrange for the trip. In contrast, Argentina and Chile are viewed as discount destinations used by migrants who neither have the connections in the United States, Japan, Spain, or Italy to "pull" them nor the economic means to pay for illegal traveling to these countries. However, as I shall discuss in the following chapter, within this migration hierarchy there is also room for maneuver. Thus, migrants often migrate to Argentina and Chile in order to save money to go to Spain or Italy at a later point of time; likewise, some *nikkeijin* migrate to Japan with the aim to obtain tourist visa or work permit in the United States.

NOTES

1. The infectious diseases brought by the Spaniards from Europe had disastrous consequences for the native population. The extent of the depopulation as well as the size of the original population is a matter of controversy. Rowe (1963: 184–85) estimates the total native population in the Andean region before contact with the Spaniards to have been 6 million, Dobyns (1966: 415) says 30–37 million, C. T. Smith (1970: 453) 12 million (only the Central Andes), Wachtel (1977: 90) 10 million (in the Inca Empire) and Cook (1981: 114) 9 million (just Peru).

2. Lockhart laconically notes, "Without undue cynicism, it is safe to say that practically all Spaniards had Indian mistresses" (Lockhart 1968: 215).

3. The vast majority of *moriscos* were women (Lockhart 1968: 197). These were for the most part Caucasian, Spanish-born slave women of Muslim descent who had converted to Christianity and spoke Spanish as their native language. As a transitional phenomenon, *moriscas* satisfied the need for Spanish women in the very early period of the conquest, when free Spanish women were still extremely scarce. However, the gradual immigration of more Spanish women led to the almost complete eclipse of *moriscas* as a category by the 1550s (Lockhart 1968: 151). Most of them were granted freedom and assumed the status of Spanish women, among whom they disappeared as an ethnic group (Lockhart 1968: 197).

4. The exact number of Peru's African population in the early colonial period is difficult to estimate. Lockhart asserts that on the Peruvian coast there were as many Africans as Spaniards. He points out that in the first coastal censuses of around 1570, Africans had even overtaken Spaniards, and that although less numerous than on the coast, they were also present in the highlands in substantial numbers (Lockhart 1968: 180). In fact, Lima was almost half African from the 1590s to the end of the seventeenth century, and the same can be said of both coastal and highland towns in northern and central Peru (Bakewell 1997: 165).

5. Population groups from other parts of the Pacific also migrated to Peru during the nineteenth century. Thus 1,680 Polynesians (called *canacas*) arrived in Peru in 1862 to work on the coastal plantations (Vásquez 1970: 85).

6. The gold rush in California attracted men of many nationalities, among them a considerable number of Peruvians (Monaghan 1973).

7. McKeown states that the vast majority of Chinese migrants to the western hemisphere came from one of the many villages within a small area of about ten thousand square kilometers on the west side of the Pearl River Delta in Guangdong province. The coastal regions of Fujian province and the Chaozhou and Jiaying areas of eastern Guandong also supported strong traditions of overseas migration (2001: 62).

8. Wolf finds patron-client relations to be a universal aspect of peasant societies in not only Latin America but also other parts of the world (1966: 86–87).

9. The *enganche* (literally, the "hook") is a centuries-old labor recruitment system in Peru. Mallon writes "*enganche* was a form of labor acquisition in which owners of haciendas or mines would advance money to merchants with connections in the area's peasant villages. These merchants would then advance cash to peasants in exchange for the obligation to work off the debt, at a set daily 'wage,' at the hacienda or mine whose owner had provided the money" (1983: 3).

10. *Dekasegi* is the Japanese term for a temporary migrant worker (Tsuda 1999: 146).

11. The 1940 census showed that there were a total of 17,583 Japanese in Peru. Apart from 1,393 Japanese nationals, 643 Germans and 49 Italians were also deported from Peru to the United States during World War II (Gardiner 1981: 95). Axis nationals living in other South American countries were also shipped to the United States from Bolivia, Ecuador, and Columbia (Gardiner 1981: 23).

12. Most of the Italians arrived during the ten years from 1891 to 1901, during which period they constituted 45 percent of the total in Peru (Vásquez 1970: 78–82).

13. Taking advantage of the country's booming *guano*- and nitrate-based economy before the War of the Pacific (1879–1883), the Italians had become the third-richest foreign community in Peru, after the English and the French. Between 1890 and 1930 they continued to enjoy the benefits of Peru's economic expansion, and by 1936 the Italian mission in Lima estimated that 30 percent of Peru's economic activity was in the hands of Italian nationals (Ciccarelli 1988: 370).

14. The correlation between immigration and emigration in Peru is evident from the following list of the country's six largest immigrant groups up to 1981: North Americans, Chileans, Argentineans, Spaniards, Japanese, and Italians (Altamirano 1996: 29; see also Naciones Unidas/SIMICA 1998: 13). It is precisely the countries of origin of these six emigrant groups that have been the primary destination of Peruvian migrants during the past twenty years.

15. This emigration was triggered by the failed coup by the APRA party in 1931.

16. Altamirano asserts that Paterson and other cities in New Jersey became the destination of Peruvian factory workers as early as the 1920s (2000: 32) but provides no sources to document this claim.

17. In 2005 the Spanish government offered yet another amnesty to the undocumented immigrants currently living in the country. Almost 700,000 migrants applied and of these 89 percent were granted amnesty (*El País* July 28, 2005, p. 20). How-

ever, undocumented immigrants continue to enter Spain. In 2006, one year after the amnesty, the total number of undocumented immigrant (or "foreigners in a irregular situation" as the Spanish government prefers to call them) in the country was estimated to be one million (*El País* July 26, 2006, p. 17).

18. Escrivá claims that the number of Peruvians in Madrid is 50,000 and in Barcelona 30,000 (2004: 155). Somewhat smaller Peruvian communities are found in Valencia, Seville, and other cities. Officially, 86,900 individuals are registered as Peruvians who have taken residence in Spain (*El País* July 26, 2006, p. 17) but the actual number of Peruvians living in the country is estimated to almost 100,000 (*El País* July 19, 2006, p. 22).

19. It is important to notice that other South American countries such as Venezuela and Bolivia have received thousands of Peruvian emigrants in the 1970s, 1980s, and 1990s (Altamirano 2006: 113–37). Today 150,000 Peruvians live in Venezuela (*La República* May 3, 2006, p. 5) and 30,000 in Bolivia (*La República* June 5, 2005, p. 4).

20. In fact, in the past five years one more even closer destination has emerged. Thus a growing number of Peruvians are migrating to Ecuador where they take over the houses and fields left behind by Ecuadorians who migrate abroad (Jokisch and Kyle 2005: 65–66).

Chapter Three

Strangers at the Gate

So far I have been concerned with the major trends of Peru's migration history. But how does Peruvian emigration look from the point of view of the receiving countries? In other words, what are the receiving contexts? How have the immigration policies and labor markets of the United States, Spain, Japan, and Argentina evolved historically? In what ways do such structural changes influence Peruvian emigration? Moreover, precisely where do Peruvians who emigrate settle in these countries? Do they cluster together in the same cities or neighborhoods, or do they live scattered in many places? And in what ways do the local environments where Peruvians settle shape their adaptations to the host society? These are the questions I address in this chapter, which is divided into country and city sections. In each section I first discuss the development of the receiving country's immigration policy and labor market, second examine for the local immigration history of the city or area of Peruvian settlement, and third describe how Peruvians have arrived. However, before describing the receiving context of the four countries I briefly discuss the political economy of the immigration policies that the industrialized countries pursue.

IMMIGRATION POLICIES AS A CONTROL MECHANISM

Historically, immigration control has developed very differently in America, Europe, and Japan. While the United States, Canada, and many South American countries such as Argentina have until recently pursued an open door policy, European and Japanese immigration control is and always has been stricter. This difference is, of course, partly due to the mass movements of population from the Old to the New Worlds in the nineteenth and twentieth centuries, when the Americas received millions of European and Japanese (and other Asian) immigrants. While European and Japanese immigration declined considerably into the twentieth century, North America continued to receive foreign immigrants, who now came from Latin America and Asia. In a similar vein, the southern cone countries of South America (in particular Argentina) attracted migrant workers from the neighboring countries throughout the second half of the twentieth century. Conversely, most European countries and partly also Japan remained emigrant societies up to the 1960s and 1970s, making little or no effort to promote the immigration of foreign labor.

The different forms of immigration control employed by governments in North America, Europe, Japan, and Argentina in recent times must be understood in the light of these countries' population and labor market policies, which have stimulated the need for foreign workers. Whereas for many years the governments of Argentina considered European immigration as a means to populate the country. In the United States certain economic activities have traditionally been open to immigrants from different parts of the world (agricultural and domestic work, jobs in the service and high tech industries, etc.). Conversely, European countries and Japan tend to regard labor as a privilege reserved for their own citizens. Only for shorter periods of time, when national labor was scarce, have European governments allowed the importation of foreign workers to fill the shortage. This happened for the first time in the late 1960s and early 1970s, when northern Europe opened its borders to so-called guest workers to satisfy the growing demand for labor in industry. A similar move was made by southern Europe twenty years later, when Latin Americans, Filipinos, and other Third World migrants entered Spain and Italy to work as domestic servants and take care of the sick and elderly, as well as by the Japanese government in 1990, when it allowed the descendants of Japanese emigrants to take temporary work in the country's factories.

Despite different historical developments, immigration control in America, Europe, Japan, and the southern cone countries of South America is designed to serve the same political purposes, among which the regulation of the demand for labor and the protection of jobs occupied by the country's own citizens is one of the most important (Brochman 1999b: 323–27). Hence entry and resident permits, whether for tourism, study, entertainment, business, research, or family visits, are of two kinds: they either allow foreigners to take work or prohibit them from doing so. The notion of immigration policy as a control mechanism in the service of not merely of the labor market is further reflected in the rules concerning the contracting of marriages with foreigners or reunification with foreign relatives, a legal right in immigration policy that has played an important role in the development of Peruvians' migrant networks. In North America, Europe, and Japan, such rights are only granted provided that a national subject supports the immigrant economically and as long as immigration does not jeopardize the employment of the domestic population.

THE UNITED STATES

Until 1965 immigration policy in the United States was based on the 1921 and 1924 Quota Acts, which set quotas for different nationalities according to the demands for skilled and unskilled workers on the labor market (Bernard 1998: 63–70). While these acts reduced European immigration, which had dominated migrant flows to North America for centuries and barred Asian immigration (except for the Filipinos) (J. Smith and Edmonston 1997: 26), they made it easier for Mexicans and the populations of other western hemisphere countries to immigrate (Calavita 1992: 58–59). A door was thus left open for what was to become one of the fastest growing immigrant groups in contemporary United States, the Latin Americans. Among those who benefited from the national-origin quota system were a rather small number of young Andean women who went to Miami to work as domestic workers for middle- or upper-class American or Peruvian families in 1950s.

In the second half of the 1960s, a new migration policy was introduced after the Immigration and Nationality Act (Amendments) was passed in 1965 (Ueda 1998). The act replaced the national-origin quota system with a visa system based on job skills and family reunification, which enhanced the possibilities for legal immigrants to bring relatives from their home country to the United States (J. Smith and Edmonston 1997: 22–31). The 1965 Act was introduced to find a solution to the problems of illegal migrants crossing the border from Mexico, which began to concern American society in the late 1940s and early 1950s (Calavita 1992: 59–60; Heyman 1998: 22–32). However, although the new act tried to limit the entry of Mexican and other immigrants, it did little to prevent employers from hiring undocumented immigrants already inside the United States. Likewise, the liberalization of the family reunification regulation for immigrants became a crucial tool for Latin American immigrants in the United States to help relatives in their home regions to emigrate. Ironically, therefore, the act was later blamed for causing the explosive growth in illegal immigration in the 1970s and 1980s (Portes and Rumbaut 1996: 8).

Because of rapidly growing immigration in the 1970s and early 1980s, the Immigration Reform and Control Act was passed in 1986 with the aim of halting illegal immigration, particularly over the U.S.-Mexican border. At the same time, the act legalized about 2.7 million individuals already residing in the United States as undocumented migrants (J. Smith and Edmonston 1997: 29). The 1990 Immigration Act continued the policy of family reunification by allowing an unlimited number of visas for the immediate relatives of U.S. citizens. It also addressed labor issues by reducing the number of visas for unskilled workers, thus making it more difficult for rural women in Peru and other Latin American countries to enter the United States on special work permits. The most recent step in controlling immigration in the United States is the Illegal Immigration Act, which was passed in 1996 and continues along the same lines as the 1990 Act by tightening up the rules for family-preference admissions and thus reducing the possibilities of family reunification for immigrant groups. The 1996 Act should be understood in light of the fact that in 1995 relatives accounted for almost two-thirds of total admissions by immigrants applying for a visa to enter the United States (J. Smith and Edmonston: 41). Although the Bush administration has expressed its wish to adjust the immigration policy to the growing demand for foreign labor in the country's economy and, in this context, offer temporary work permit to some of the millions of undocumented immigrants that currently live in the United States, its attempts to pass a new reform have so far been unsuccessful (*New York Sun* Nov. 2004).

Peruvians who emigrate to the United States settle in the major cities in states such as New York, Connecticut, New Jersey, Illinois, Washington, D.C., Florida, California, and Texas. This study focuses on Miami, Los Angeles, and Paterson, New Jersey, three cities that have received the bulk of Peruvians in the United States.

Miami

In the second half of the twentieth century Miami became a significant city because its geographical location in the tropical southeast United States favored tourism and agriculture. At this time, the city's dominant ethnic communities were Blacks, Anglo Saxons, and Jews (Dunn and Stepick 1992: 41–56; Portes and Stepick 1993: 70–88). Today Miami continues to be a distinct phenomenon in the urban landscape of North America but for other reasons than a hundred years ago. Thus Portes and Stepick state that "Nowhere has the social and economic weight of the newcomers or their political significance been greater than in South Florida," which lead them to conclude that, "Miami is not a microcosm of the American city" (1993: xi). Rather, one could rightly add, the city is a microcosm of contemporary Latin American diasporic cultures. Indeed, comparing Miami to other U.S. cities, it is mostly known as a center of attraction for its Caribbean and Latin American immigrants, who in the past forty-five years have arrived in large numbers. As a result, Miami has the largest proportion (35 percent) of foreign-born residents of any city in the United States (Grenier and Stepick 1992: 2), of whom the vast majority is of Latin American origin, although other national groups such as Haitians also make up a significant immigrant population. This influx has not only contributed to the emergence of Miami's modern multicultural society, it has also transformed the city into the economic, social and, to a certain extent, even political capital of the Caribbean and Latin America (Grenier and Stepick 1992: 2). In 1990 the metropolis had nearly one million inhabitants of Latin origin, making up about a half of the population of Greater Miami of approximately two million (Grenier and Stepick 1992: 5).

Miami's main immigrant group are the Cubans, who account for 56 percent of Greater Miami's foreign-born population and 70 percent of all Hispanics in the area (Pérez 1992: 83). Indeed, in the eyes of many, Anglo-Saxons as well as Hispanics, Cubans are almost synonymous with the city. Their impact on Miami is difficult to underestimate. Not only do they put their stamp on the city culturally, but the Cuban community heavily influences Miami's economic activities and political life. The Cuban presence dates back to before Fidel Castro's revolution, but it was not until 1959 that the city experienced immigration from the island in large numbers, and it was not until the early 1960s that Miami emerged as the main Cuban community in the United States.

Other Latin Americans and people from the Caribbean have followed the Cubans. In the 1980s Nicaraguans started to migrate to south Florida, similarly because their country was also affected by civil war. In fact, the growth and consolidation of Miami's Nicaraguan community can be compared to the pattern established by the Cubans in several respects. In both migrations, a wave of landholders, industrialists, and company managers first fled the country, then one of professionals and white-collar workers, and finally, one of primarily urban blue-collar workers. Miami had some 70,000 Nicaraguans in the late 1980s (Maingot 1992: 35). Another important influx occurred between 1977 and 1981, when 70,000 Haitians, who have come to be known as "America's boat people" (Stepick 1992: 57), arrived by boat in south Florida. By the mid-1980s they made up a community of approximately 80,000 (Stepick 1992: 65). Just as in the Cuban and Nicaraguan cases, the Haitian exodus has taken the form of waves of migration that reflect the country's economic and social classes.[1]

The first Peruvians to settle in Miami were a group of young women originating from rural areas in the Andean departments of Ayacucho, Huancayo, and Ancash who had been working as domestic servants for Peruvian or American families in Lima and were brought to Miami by their employers.

These women became the spearhead of a mass flow of migration that started in the 1960s and gained momentum in the 1980s and 1990s. Initially, it was dominated by migrants of Andean origin who were brought to the United States by female relatives or fellow villagers working as domestic servants in Miami. Later Peruvians from the country's middle and upper classes followed. Thus during the Vietnam War a group of medical doctors who had studied at universities in Lima migrated to Miami, where they found work in hospitals or opened their own private clinics. In the aftermath of the military regimes of Velasco Alvarado (1968–1975) and Morales Bermúdez (1975–1980) and the second democratic government of Belaúnde Terry (1980–1985), many ex-politicians, retired military officers, and members of Peru's upper classes, who felt that the state and those in power could no longer protect the privileged positions they had traditionally enjoyed in Peruvian society, settled in residential areas such as Coral Cable and Key Biscayne. Similarly, in the late 1980s, during the government of Alan García Perez (1985–1990), Miami's Kendall district became a popular site of residence for Lima's middle-class families escaping from Peru's economic and political crises.

Because the Peruvian migrant community in Miami consists of such a variety of social and ethnic groups, it can be regarded as a microcosm of Peruvian society, to use Portes's and Stepick's term. With a population of approximately 50,000, the Peruvian community in Miami's Dade County is one of the largest groups of Peruvians outside Peru (Peruvian Consulate, Miami, 1998). It is also one of the most active such communities. Peruvians in Miami are organized in different kinds of institutions, embracing Andean regional organizations, urban *mestizo* religious brotherhoods, cultural organizations recreating Peruvian dance, music, and indigenous traditions, private clubs for middle- and upper-class Peruvians, professional associations for medical doctors and businessmen, and political movements promoting migrant participation in national politics in both Peru and the United States. These institutions arrange a wide variety of activities, including folklore shows, art exhibitions, carnival parties, Catholic processions, sports competitions, and charity events in favor of the victims of natural disasters in Peru and the celebration of Peru's national day (July 28). Further, five weekly newspapers published in Spanish by Peruvians provide the community with the latest news from Peru and information about local activities in Miami, while approximately twenty-five Peruvian restaurants and shops offer migrants the smell and taste of food from their country of origin or home region. Similarly, a number of Peruvian agencies provide services such as money transfer, travel arrangements to Peru, and immigration consultation.

Los Angeles

Just like the rest of California, Los Angeles was under Spanish influence until the U.S.-Mexican war of 1848, when the area was taken over by the United States. By 1880 the Spanish-speaking inhabitants of Southern California had been outnumbered by English speakers, and after Los Angeles was connected by rail with the rest of America in 1886, the influx of white Anglo-Saxons skyrocketed. Although the area experienced immigration from China, Japan, and Mexico in the late nineteenth and early twentieth centuries, Anglo-Saxon control over the city remained unchallenged for more than a century, and it is only since the 1960s, when Southern California became a major recipient of immigrants from especially Asia and Latin America, that this ethnic pattern and the underlying power structure started to change (Allen and Turner 1997: 10).[2] Today Los Angeles is the incarnation of what many imagine as a future multicultural metropolis, with representations of just about every national and ethnic group in the world. In 1990 the 14.5 million residents of the five counties (Los Angeles, Orange, Riverside, San Bernardino, and Ventura) that constitute the Greater Los Angeles area and make up the heart of Southern California represented 49 percent of California's population and contained one-fifth of all the foreign-born population of the United States (Allen and Turner 1997: xii).

Mexicans represent the fastest growing immigrant group by far. Whereas in 1960 they made up only 2 percent of the area's population, the 1990 census counted as many as 3.7 million, that is, one-fourth of the total population, of whom 46 percent were born abroad (Waldinger and Bozorgmehr 1996: 8). Mass immigration from Mexico has transformed Los Angeles and made the Hispanic presence highly visible in most parts of the city. It has also had a significant impact on the labor market and the economy, as well as on interethnic relations and the articulation of multicultural identities. Other Latin American nationalities have also contributed to the influx of immigrants, and today Los Angeles is home to immigrants from throughout America. Most non-Mexican immigrants from south of the border are Central Americans, who make up 12 percent of the area's Hispanic population.[3] Among these the Salvadorans and Guatemalans are the largest communities, the former counting 302,000 individuals and the latter almost 150,000 according the 1990 census (Waldinger and Bozorgmehr 1996: 281), thus outnumbering such communities as the Puerto Ricans, Cubans, and Dominicans, who dominate the ethnic landscape of other U.S. cities with big immigrant populations such as New York and Miami. Unlike Mexicans, who have historically been in close contact with the United States and who mainly emigrate to their northern neighbor for economic reasons, most Salvadorans and Guatemalans in Los Angeles left their country of origin because of political violence and civil war in the 1980s. This difference in migration patterns is reflected in the high number of Salvadorans and Guatemalans who live in Los Angeles as undocumented immigrants (between 40 and 50 percent) and the relatively low number of undocumented Mexicans (less then 10 percent) (Waldinger and Bozorgmehr 1996: 281–87).

With a population of more than 50,000 Peruvians, Los Angeles has received more migrants from Peru than has Miami. However, because they are scattered over such a huge area, Peruvians in Southern California make up not one but many dispersed communities. Indeed, many migrants in this city do not think of themselves as part of a distinct Peruvian community but as Hispanics or Latinos or, more frequently, simply as individual immigrants trying to adapt to North America's multicultural society. This dispersal and lack of unity is reflected in Peruvians' immigration histories and settlement patterns in California. Thus in the 1960s and 1970s Los Angeles served as hub for Peruvian immigrants heading for New York and Paterson, New Jersey. While some of these eventually stayed in or later returned to Los Angeles, most continued on to the East Coast and ended up settling there. However, during the 1980s and 1990s California became the target of more permanent Peruvian settlement on a large scale, and today Los Angeles is the home of one of the largest Peruvian immigrant colonies in the world.

Unlike Miami, which in the past fifty years has experienced a steady influx of migrants, initially from Peru's Andean highlands, looking for jobs in the domestic industry and the service sector, followed by Lima's upper and middle classes, who either invest their savings in business or make a living as professionals, the majority of Peruvians in Los Angeles belong to Peru's urban working class and originate from the country's coastal cities, primarily Lima. This again makes the population extremely heterogeneous and difficult to identify in terms of class and ethnicity. While a small group of Peruvians have managed to create professional careers or to establish themselves as successful businessmen, the majority belong to America's growing proletariat of unskilled, immigrant, blue-collar workers. Most toil as factory workers, waiters, cleaners, domestic servants, gardeners, or car-park attendants, earning the minimum wage and in many cases even less. Moreover, many spend their first years in the United States as undocumented immigrants facing different forms of cultural discrimination and social exclusion. To them, the hardships of adapting to North American society become synonymous with those of being a migrant.

Paterson

When you turn off New Jersey's Garden State Parkway and drive into Paterson, for a brief moment you might believe that you are in Peru and not the

United States. The city is home to 29,000 Peruvians (Peruvian Consulate, Paterson, 1998), who together with the African-Americans, Puerto Ricans, and Dominicans constitute the majority of its population. Somewhat smaller Peruvian migrant communities live in neighboring cities such as Newark, Elisabeth, Morris Town, Passaic, Dobber, and Bergen, while New York City, where between 50,000 and 100,000 Peruvians live, is within an hour's drive. Evidently, in the eyes of the newly arrived, Paterson appears to be yet another American city that has become the center of settlement of Latin American immigrants. Yet a closer look at the history of Paterson reveals that the city has been a chief recipient of migrants of changing nationality for more than a century. The main reason for the population influx has been the constant demand for unskilled labor in the city's manufacturing industry, which represents a unique chapter in North American economic and political history.

When Alexander Hamilton formed the Society for Establishing Useful Manufactures in New Jersey in 1791, he took the first organized step to propel the United States' dawning industrial revolution. The Society chose Paterson as the center for New Jersey's manufacturing operations because of its location next to the Great Falls of the Passaic (Bebout and Grele 1964: 19–20). One and a half centuries later, the city once again became the object of national attention when William Carlos Williams, North America's famous poet, wrote *Paterson*.[4] According to Williams "Paterson has a definite history associated with the beginnings of the United States" (1992: xiii). He declares that he chose Paterson as the site for his renowned book not merely because of its natural beauty and forces, but because he found it ideal to demonstrate "the resemblance between the mind of modern man and a city" (Williams 1992: xiii). Just as Williams felt intrigued by the intricacy of Paterson's urban life, the city's history of migration attracts the eye of the scholar. Since its formation two hundred years ago, the city has been the destination for thousands of foreign immigrants in search for work and a better life. In the beginning these were first and foremost of northern European descent, but in the last half of the nineteenth century and the first part of the twentieth southern Europeans, particularly of Italian descent, started to immigrate in large numbers too. Indeed, immigration constituted the major contributor to the rapid population growth that the area experienced during this period (Bebout and Grele 1964: 32), and it only started to decline after the restrictive immigration laws were introduced in the aftermath of World War I (Bebout and Grele 1964: 30). Thus in only ten years, from 1880 to 1890, the population of Paterson went up by more than 50 percent, a growth that continued from 1920 to 1960, though in far smaller numbers (Bebout and Grele 1964: 54).[5]

Altamirano states that Peruvian migration to Paterson goes back to the first and second decades of the twentieth century, when the manufacturing industry in New Jersey experienced an economic boom and started to import Peruvian textile workers (2000: 24). The Peruvian consulate in Paterson, on the other hand, asserts that immigration to the city started around World War II, when Grey, a North American textile manufacturing company producing and exporting cotton to Peru, brought some of its Peruvian workers to work in its factory at Paterson. However, as already noted, no written documentation exists for this migration flow, nor do migrants' oral testimonies substantiate the assertion that Paterson has been the destination for Peruvian emigration for more than half a century. The interviews I conducted with Peruvians in Paterson suggest that contemporary Peruvian migration to the city began in the late 1950s and gained momentum in the 1960s. The migrants who spearheaded this migration chain were men from Lima's working-class neighborhoods, such as La Victoria, Surquillo, and Callao, searching for work in Paterson's factories. These pioneers later brought their wives, children, and other relatives to join them. Thus Guillermo, who arrived in 1962 and whom I interviewed in 1998, claims that the cousin of two brothers he worked with in Lima left for Paterson in the late 1950s.[6] Soon afterwards the brothers followed him. Guillermo says, "The cousin's surname was Bazurco. The brothers' surname was Balta. They were the first Peruvians in Paterson."

The migration chain to Paterson peaked in the 1970s, when economic crisis hit the city's industry and left many Peruvians unemployed and forced them to move to neighboring cities such as Elisabeth, Morris, and Bergen or more remote destinations such New York or Los Angeles to find work. For a number of years the social problems caused by the economic crisis gave Paterson a reputation for moral decay and a bad lifestyle that, according to many migrants, led Peruvians into criminality and drug abuse and turned the city into a magnet for Peru's urban proletariat. Jorge, who I met in Los Angeles in 1998, told me that he spent two years in Paterson before moving to California in 1995. He recalls, "When I arrived I got a job as waiter, but most of the time I was either drunk or on drugs. In Paterson you could really fall into the worst. Thanks to a friend I got out of drugs and moved to Los Angeles."

In the late 1990s Paterson recovered from the economic crisis, and today Peruvian community is represented by a broad variety of migrant institutions, supported by a Peruvian consulate that was opened in 1987. These institutions include several soccer leagues, an umbrella organization for the Peruvian Catholic brotherhoods in the northeastern United States (OHCAPERUSA; see chapter 6), a political institution that encourages migrants to seek American citizenship and tries to influence the political process in the United States (Congreso Peruano Americano; see chapter 5), and an association that organizes an annual parade from Passaic to Paterson on Peru's national holiday (Peruvian Parade Inc.; see chapter 5). The parade, which so far stands out as a unique event in Peruvian emigration history, was initiated by migrants in the early 1990s under the influence of other Latin American communities in Paterson such the Puerto Ricans who have organized national parades in New York and other American cities for a number of years (Berg 2005).

SPAIN

Migration has shaped the history of the Mediterranean countries in many ways. Jews, Lebanese, Greeks, Maltese, and Corsicans in particular have migrated in this region, thus connecting its many economic and cultural centers. In the sixteenth, seventeenth, and eighteenth centuries, Spain and Portugal orchestrated colonial emigrations to Latin America that by the nineteenth century became a mass phenomenon for southern Europeans in general, also now including Italians. This development continued after the war with the United States in 1898 and the loss of the last colonies (Cuba, Puerto Rico, and others) and has only been brought to an end since democracy was reintroduced in Spain thirty years ago. By the same token, Spaniards traveled to central European countries to look for work in great numbers up to Franco's death, and it was not until the late 1980s when emigration rapidly decreased and Spaniards (together with Italians and Portuguese) working in northern Europe had returned (King 2000: 4–7) that the country became a net importer of immigrants and thus has had to face the social and political problems involved in being a member of the European Union and representing a "pull" factor for labor migrants from poorer countries. As a result, the foreign-born sector now represents more than 7 percent of Spain's population.[7]

In Spain the change from being an emigrant society to a host country for foreign immigration began in the mid-1980s, thus triggering the first legislation concerning immigration with the La Ley de Extranjería in 1985 (Dirección General de Ordenación de las Migraciones). This law primarily dealt with the civil rights of *comunitarios*, that is other European Union citizens residing in Spain (Izquierdo 1996: 133–39),[8] but it also reflects the country's strong historical links with its ex-colonies by granting Latin Americans and citizens of other countries that have a Spanish colonial past special rights to apply for residence and work permits (Escrivá 2000: 202). However, it was not until 1991 that the problem of Third World immigration was addressed by the Spanish government, with the proposal known as Lineas Básicas de la Política Española de Extranjería (Escrivá 2000: 133). The aim of this policy was to control the growing immigration of foreign workers who began entering the Spanish labor market in the mid-1980s and increased in numbers in the late 1980s, with Latin Americans and North

Africans being the two dominant immigrant groups (Dirección General de Ordenación de las Migraciones). An important political instrument in this proposal was the *proceso de regularización* (the regulation process), allocating a limited number of annual *cupos* or *contingentes* (work permits) to foreigners. In 1991, the year the policy was introduced, an extraordinary *regularización* offered more than 100,000 undocumented immigrants residence and work permits in Spain. Arguably, the proposal can be compared to the act passed by the U.S. government in 1985 to put an end to the presence of undocumented immigrants by simply offering them status as legal residents.[9] Initially, these permits were restricted to specific occupations and geographical areas and mainly reserved for Moroccan workers to satisfy the need for seasonal labor in agriculture. A similar quota system has been applied by different Spanish governments since 1993, who have granted a growing number of work permits to the domestic industry (Arango 2000: 264–73). This development has confirmed the privileged status of Dominicans, Ecuadorians, and Peruvians in particular in Spanish immigration policy.[10]

Since 1991 the Spanish government has continued the policy of *regularización* with a quota system of work permits to assure the regular and controlled immigration of foreign workers who are required in certain sectors of the labor market (Arango 2000: 259–61). The allocation of these *cupos* is based on a division of labor between the principal national immigrant groups. Thus North Africans are allocated work in agriculture, while Latin Americans and Filipinos are offered *cupos* in the service sector or as domestic workers (Dirección General de Ordenación de las Migraciones 1996: 224). However, as *cupos* only are allocated for one year at the time and as the number of annual quotas is around 30,000,[11] the policy has far from achieved its objective of bringing illegal immigration to a halt. Quite the contrary, not only do many foreign workers overstay once their *cupo* expires and thus become undocumented, but an even greater number of relatives and fellow countrymen have followed in the footsteps of these pioneer immigrants by entering Spain on a tourist visa or by crossing the border from France after entering another European Union country illegally from eastern Europe.

Because of its policy of *regularización* and labor *cupos* combined with frequent amnesties the country's foreign labor force is today concentrated on just a few national groups (Arango 2000: 259–61; Driessen 1998) composed to a large extent, of Moroccans, who mostly work in agriculture and construction (Apap 1997; Bodega et al. 1995), Latin Americans, primarily Ecuadorians, Dominicans, and Peruvians working in Madrid and Barcelona as domestic servants, and to a lesser extent other African and Asian nationals (Martínez Veiga 1997: 21–118, 167–220; Merino Hernando 2002: xxxvi,

2004). This specialization in livelihoods within the migrant labor force is clearly reflected in the gender composition of the three dominant immigrant groups: 83 percent of the Moroccans are men, while 80 percent of the Dominicans and 65 percent of the Peruvians are women (King and Rodríguez-Melguizo 1999; Ribas-Mateos 2000: 177, 181).[12] Until recently many of these were undocumented but in the past four years shifting governments have tried to reform La Ley de Extranjería in order to control the growing immigration in the country. In 2000 the Aznar administration announced its plan to introduce a reform that seeked to not only thwart illegal immigration but also reduce the rights of legal immigrants already living in Spain (*El País* June 2000). Subsequently, the Zapatero administration, which came into power in 2004, has introduced another reform more favorable of Spain's immigrant population and granted amnesty to 700,000 undocumented immigrants (*El País* July 28, 2005).

Although the presence of Peruvians in Spain is far from new, their role in the country's recent transformation from an emigrant to an immigrant society demands attention. During the 1950s and 1960s it was mostly the sons of Lima's middle- and upper-class families who traveled to Spain to study medicine and law at the country's universities.[13] Since the late 1980s, however, women from Peru's urban shantytowns (mostly in Lima and the northern coast towns such as Trujillo), who have migrated in search of work, have dominated the flow of migration toward Spain and other countries in southern Europe. In the late 1980s and early 1990s many of these female immigrants took over the positions that Filipino and Portuguese workers had previously occupied as domestic servants in upper-class Spanish families. More recently this immigration has been fueled by an urgent need for imported female workers to replace the younger generations of Spanish women, who increasingly prefer to take work outside the home. In effect, in 2000 Peruvians constituted the second largest immigrant group in Spain (Escrivá 2000: 207), and Peruvian women "are preferred to other foreigners because they often have training or knowledge of the health professions, they behave respectfully toward the elderly and they have Spanish skills" (Escrivá 1997: 54).[14]

The recent migration to Spain, then, has induced these young semi-professional urban women to engage in livelihoods conventionally reserved for rural uneducated women and to assume the pioneer role formerly occupied by female migrants from Peru's Andean hinterlands. It has also pushed them into an occupation that still is dominated by clientelistic relationships, not only in Peru but also in the Mediterranean countries. Thus, the domestic servant industry in Spain "is a sector without the same legal rights enjoyed by other workers," where live-in servants are submitted to "quasi-servile relationships" (Escrivá 2000: 216) and "suffer isolation in the work place" (2000: 209). The vulnerable position of many Peruvian women in Spain is underscored by their lack of legal rights as temporary migrant workers and thus dependence on their employers to renew their work permits. As Anthias points out, "Few domestic maids have a migration status separate from their work entitlement on entry as domestic workers, and they are therefore vulnerable; if they leave their employer they could be deported" (2000: 26).

Most Peruvians in Spain live in Madrid and Barcelona, the country's two major cities (Merino 2004: 245). To the immigrant they make up two very different settings. Due to its size and status as the country's capital, there are more jobs available in Madrid than in Barcelona, though salaries are generally slightly higher in the latter. However, because of Catalan nationalism, migrants often feel that cultural and language barriers are stronger in Barcelona than in Madrid. The situation in the two cities is also influenced by the fact that while Barcelona mainly attracts immigrants from Morocco, Madrid is mainly the target of immigrants from the Philippines, the Dominican Republic and various African countries. Notwithstanding these differences, Peruvian settlement in Spain is to large degree determined by regional origins in Peru. Thus migrants who come from the northern coastal cities of Trujillo and Chimbote tend to settle in Barcelona, whereas Peruvians who live in Madrid come mainly from Lima.

JAPAN

Prior to 1859 Japan was a relatively isolated country with little or no contact with the outside world. However, in 1859 when the Japanese government reopened some ports to foreign trade, and in particular after the Meiji government was formed in 1868, the country became the object of foreign settlement. Its immigration policy prior to and during World War II can be divided into three periods (Yamawaki 2000: 40). The first period was from 1859 to 1899, when there were foreign settlements in Japan to which foreigners were restricted. The only exception were the Koreans, who were free to live and work outside the settlements. A second period lasted from 1899 to 1939, during which Westerners were free to immigrate and take work anywhere in the country, while Chinese workers were imported to do forced labor in the former foreign settlements. This policy was changed in 1939, when the Japanese government allowed companies in Japan to recruit Koreans in Korea and Japan on a larger scale to work in the country (Yamawaki 2000: 41–49).[15]

World War II represents a crossroad in Japan's migration history. Before the war more than two million foreigners were living in Japan proper, mostly people from the Korean Peninsula, Taiwan, and other areas under Japanese domination who were treated as Japanese (Mori 1997: 3). After 1945 many of the foreign workers who were brought to Japan as cheap labor in the decades preceding World War II returned home. Thus of the roughly 2.3 million Koreans who were living in Japan in 1945, about 1.7 returned (Sugimoto 1997: 178), while the remaining 600,000 chose to stay.[16] When Japan won back its independence in 1952 these individuals lost their Japanese nationality, and today their descendants comprise the country's largest minority group of foreign origin. Although they were born in Japan, their native language is Japanese and their parents or grandparents were regarded Japanese before the war, an overwhelming majority of them do not have Japanese citizenship. As second-class residents in Japan, they are subject to discrimination in many spheres of civil rights (Sugimoto 1997: 178).

Until the 1960s, Japan remained a net international exporter of low-wage migrants. This trend began to reverse by the 1970s and 1980s, when more foreign labor entered Japan than Japanese workers left the country (Douglass and Roberts 2000: 6–7). The first foreigners to look for work in Japan were South Asian women, who began to appear in the sex industry as undocumented immigrants in the 1970 (Douglass 2000; Sellek 1997: 179–82).[17] In addition to this influx, since the mid-1980s there has been larger scale, irregular migration of male "working tourists," who enter the country as tourists and remain illegally when their visas expire, a development which caused much concern among politicians and within the Japanese population (Sellek 1997: 182–83). The "pull" factors in Japan of this immigration of foreign workers are the ageing of the Japanese workforce and the accompanying shortage of labor in unskilled, manual, and physically demanding areas (Sugimoto 1997: 2–5). Furthermore, the changing work ethic of Japanese youth has made it difficult for employers to recruit them for this type of work, which is described in terms of the three undesirable Ks (in English the three Ds): *kitanai* (dirty), *kitsui* (difficult), *kiken* (dangerous) (Fukumoto 1997: 355; Sellek 1997: 182; Sugimoto 1997: 187). Among the "push" factors, on the other hand, are low salaries, overpopulation, and unemployment in the migrants' home countries (Herbert 1996: 5–9). In fact, the number of undocumented workers in Japan was between 200,000 and 300,000 in 1990 (Herbert 1996: 60), and in 1995 Japan's total foreign population was estimated at 1.4 million (Weiner 2000: 65).[18] Given that Japan's population is almost 124 million, these numbers can hardly be described as alarming. Yet, in the eyes of many Japanese, the very fact that a growing number of *gaijin* (foreigners), particularly from Third World countries, are choosing to settle and work in Japan represents a treat to their notion of a homogenous Japanese society (Lie 2000).

The ambivalent legal status of Japan's foreign subjects after 1945 prompted the country's legislators to provide a new framework to execute an immigration control policy in post-war Japan. As a result, an Immigration Control and Refugee Recognition Act, a Special Law on Immigration Control directed toward the foreigners who had lost Japanese nationality after World War II and an Alien Registration Law were enacted on the threshold of the country's independence. The effect of these acts is that today Japan is a country that maintains remarkably strict migration controls, not only at the border, but also during the stay, a control that is exercised on the basis on the law in force (Mori 1997: 1). The Immigration Control and Refugee Recognition Act has undergone revision a number of times since its inception without radically altering Japan's immigration policy. However, due to the growing need for labor in the industry in the late 1980s and the recognition that undocumented immigrants were increasingly entering the labor market, the government promulgated an amendment to the Immigration Act from 1952 in June 1990 allowing a limited number of unskilled foreigners to take work in Japan (Mori 1997: 99–103; Sellek 1997: 182–86; Shimada 1994: 61–68).

Before 1990, second-generation *nikkeijin*, that is the descendants of Japanese emigrants,[19] were admitted to reside in Japan for up to three years as the children of Japanese nationals. After the amendment not merely second-generation but also third-generation descendants of Japanese emigrants (including their spouses) were offered special status as "residents," which allows them to work without restrictions (Matsumoto and Gashu 1998; Sellek 1997: 121, 184, 189). The rationale of this policy was that *nikkeijin* are better prepared to adapt to Japanese society than other foreigners because of their ancestry. In order to encourage immigration the Ministry of Labor established an official agency for *nikkeijin* from Brazil, the country with the largest number of immigrants of Japanese descent in the world (Herbert 1996: 121). As a result, Brazil and Peru, which host the second largest population of Japanese ancestry outside Japan, have become the two main suppliers of so-called U-turn (or return) migrants (Yamanaka 2000). Sellek reports: "As a result of the revised law, in Sao Paulo between 1988 and 1991, the number of visas jumped from 8,602 to 61,500, and in Peru about 15 percent of Peruvian *nikkeijin* are thought to have gone through the formalities of emigration" (Sellek 1997: 189).

In the wake of the 1990 law non-Japanese Peruvians have also migrated in large numbers to Japan to work in factories. Until the visa exemption for Peruvians was abolished in 1994 many entered as tourists; later others traveled with forged papers or as adopted relatives of *nikkeijin*.[20] Initially, migrants were mostly males (79 percent of all Peruvians migrating to Japan in 1991 were men), many single and with university degrees (Fukumoto 1997: 357). However, in the mid-1990s many foreign workers were laid off because of the economic crisis, and although Japan's economy is slowly recovering, unemployment is still high by Japanese standards. Moreover, as female labor is traditionally paid less than male labor in Japan, the industry now prefers to hire women instead of men, prompting a growing number of Peruvian female *nikkeijin* to migrate. Currently, the number of Peruvians in Japan is 65,000 (Peruvian Consulate 2005), of whom approximately 11,000 are undocumented immigrants, an immigrant community only surpassed in numbers by the Koreans, Chinese, Brazilians, and Filipinos (Foreign Press Center, Japan 1999: 7; Mori 1997: 113–14).[21]

A decade after the *nikkeijin* migration to Japan began, most Peruvians still have little interaction with Japanese society, partly due to language and cultural barriers and partly due to their marginal position on the job market. Because brokers often hire Peruvians, they can lose their jobs with very short notice. This again means that many are continuously on the move in order to find new contracts. Naturally, this makes it extremely difficult to create stable and enduring communities in the places where they reside, causing a strong feeling of isolation and solitude among Peruvians in Japan. Moreover, many foreign workers, including *nikkeijin*, complain of discrimination and prejudices against them. One Japanese Peruvian explained to me, "Here all Peruvians are *gaijin* ['foreigners' in Japanese], whether *cholos*, *negros* or *niseis* [urbanized Indians, Blacks or *nikkeijin*]." Indeed, the encounter with the country of their ancestors and the experience of being *gaijin* in Japanese society have radically altered the ideas that many Peruvian *nikkeijin* had of being Japanese and Peruvian before migrating. As Takenaka points out, "The transformation of Japanese Peruvians' ethnic identity first involved the denial of their Japanese identity in return for migrating to Japan" (1999: 1466). Or as one Peruvian told me, "I came to Japan in 1989. At that time we *nisei* felt different and somehow more privileged than all the illegal Peruvians. Today we feel much more the same."[22]

Over the last decade, many *nikkeijin* households have extended their close kinship and marriage ties across the Pacific to embrace relatives living scattered in Peru as well as Japan. In effect, relatives who are already in Japan, who offer them economic support to travel and help them arrange the necessary paperwork, now summon most newcomers. Transnational networks have also been created between *nikkeijin* organizations in Peru and the emerging community of Peruvians in Japan, which make it possible for immigrants to acquire Peruvian products, renting video copies of films with Spanish subtitles and Peruvian television programs, and sending remittances to relatives in

Peru. Moreover, the fact that *nikkeijin* are increasingly replacing Japanese as brokers has improved the ability of migrants to negotiate their work contracts.[23] However, because of the strict immigration policy of the Japanese government and the lack of alternative job opportunities for immigrants, the emergence of transnational networks and the formation of a Peruvian community in Japan are not likely to alter immigrants' position in the Japanese labor market or to change the clientelistic relationship between Peruvians (particularly those of non-Japanese descent who are undocumented) and the contractors.

ARGENTINA

Most Latin American countries adopted liberal immigration policies after the colonial period. However, only Brazil, Argentina, Uruguay, and to a lesser extent, Chile and Cuba actively recruited immigrants. During the mid- to late eighteenth century, immigration was seen by these countries as a mechanism for obtaining rural settlers and cheap labor for plantations, but by the early nineteenth century immigrants were settling in urban areas as well entering manufacturing jobs (Kritz and Gurak 1979: 409–10). As a result, South America experienced mass immigration of particular Europeans that became the prelude to the continent's demographic explosion of the twentieth century (Sarramone 1999). Among these countries was Argentina, which absorbed 10 percent of all European emigrants to the Americas between 1830 and 1950 (Mera 1998: 30). In fact, the country had one of the highest demographic growth rates in the New World in the early twentieth century, when its population was growing by 3.1 percent annually (Bakewell 1997: 413).

By 1950 European immigration to Argentina had lost impetus and a new migration pattern had emerged. Instead of receiving immigrants from the Old World, the country experienced an increasing influx of foreign workers from the neighboring region, mainly Paraguay, Chile, and Bolivia (Balán 1988: 221–23; Benencia and Karasik 1995: 7–17; Mera 1998: 32). This immigration has been largely spontaneous and uncontrolled and has in gross terms coincided with the migration flow of native Argentineans, who moved from rural areas to Buenos Aires and other cities in the same period (Marshall 1979: 488). Between 1970 and 1980 this population flow decreased, but it began to increase again at the end of the 1980s. Overall, since World War II Argentina has experienced the same trends in migration as the rest of Latin America: immigration has progressively been Americanized (Carrón 1979). However, by 1990 Argentina was the only country that was still serving as an important magnet for immigration to South America. Thus strong job growth in Argentinean cities, particularly in metropolitan Buenos Aires, combined with low domestic fertility, yielded a strong demand for immigrant labor during the 1950s, 1960s, and 1970s. Despite difficulties in the Argentinean economy, this demand continued up through the 1980s, attracting large numbers of working-class and agrarian immigrants from neighboring countries (Massey et al. 1998: 198–204), and from 1990 yet another national group was added to the list of Argentina's South American immigrants, namely the Peruvians (Pacecca 2000: 3; Bernasconi 1999: 640–41; Torales 1993).

Since Argentina became independent in 1810, immigration has been a matter of fundamental importance to policymakers. Hence, the country adopted "grand" policies aimed at attracting European immigrants. The 1853 Constitution established an open-door policy by explicitly favoring European immigrants and granted all civil rights to foreign residents. This policy was confirmed by the so-called Avellaneda Law of 1876, which served as a legal framework for the mass immigration that took place between 1890 and 1914, and it remained in place until the 1920s, when the great depression prompted Argentina to establish restrictions on admission based on employment considerations (Mera 1998: 29–31; Plataforma sudamericana de derechos humanos, democracia y desarrollo 2000: 117–19). However, by the end of World War II Argentina had lifted these restrictions and opened the doors to European immigration again. As a result, more than half a million Italian immigrants arrived in Argentina (Balán 1992: 119).

In response to the decrease in European immigration in the 1950s and the growing demand for foreign labor, Argentina and Bolivia entered into a bilateral labor agreement in 1958 to regulate the admission of migrant workers from the latter country. Argentina signed similar agreements with Chile and Paraguay. However, because these agreements were mainly aimed at satisfying the need for labor in Argentinean agriculture and because the expansion of job opportunities in the urban labor market grew rapidly during the 1960s and 1970s, the country experienced an increase in the number of illegal entries (Balán 1992: 121). In 1963 the government promulgated a new Immigration Law (regarded as complementary to the Avellaneda Law of 1876) to regulate the growing presence of undocumented immigrants, and in 1967 yet another law was passed to tighten the government's control over foreign workers from neighboring countries (Mera 1998: 32). Argentina's current immigration policy is based on the Migration Law of 1981, which replaced the Avellaneda Law. The 1981 Law, which established different categories of immigrants, who may be transitory, temporary, or permanent, was designed to satisfy the country's growing need for cheap foreign labor (Pereyra 1999: 16). However, in 1998 the government entered a bilateral labor agreement with Peru similar to those previously signed with Bolivia, Chile, and Paraguay to control the growing influx of Peruvians in the 1990s (Plataforma sudameri-cana de derechos humanos, democracia y desarrollo 2000: 138–39).

Since the 1940s amnesties have become an integral part of immigration policy in Argentina. The government has passed regularization acts in 1949, 1958, 1964, 1974, 1984, and 1993 with the explicit goal of regularizing the status of those foreigners who had arrived in violation of established admis-sion policies (Balán 1992: 122; Casaravilla 1999: 48). While the beneficiar-ies of these regulations were initially Europeans who arrived in Argentina during and after World War II, later amnesties explicitly covered immigrants from neighboring countries, in particular Bolivia (Casaravilla 1999: 50; Grimson 1999: 30–34). These amnesties reflect the difficulties that Argen-tinean governments have faced in the past five decades in meeting the many goals achieved by immigration. Despite a wish to control the growing influx from neighboring countries for political and ideological reasons, the Argen-tinean economy needs cheap foreign labor. Hence, immigration policies have been notable for their lack of consistence, and different government offices often implement diametrically opposed policies during the same administra-tion (Balán 1992: 124). In effect, Argentina has continued to attract South American immigrants, who either enter the country illegally or overstay their entry visa and then wait for the government to grant a further amnesty. Since 2000, however, Argentina's economic and political crisis has dramatically re-duced the demand for labor, and a growing number of undocumented migrant workers in particular have either returned home or re-migrated to new desti-nations.

Peruvian immigration in Argentina goes back to the 1930s, when Apristas (members of Apra, the party that governed Peru between 1985 and 1990) sought refugee in the country early in the decade. In the 1950s, 1960s, and 1970s, middle-class families from Lima and other cities sent their sons to Ar-gentina to study medicine, veterinary science, agronomy, architecture, or law at universities in La Plata, Rosario, Mendoza, Bahía Blanca, and Cordova. Like their fellow countrymen, who went to Spain to study in the same period, many of these men married local Argentinean women and stayed after they had finished their studies. Angel, sixty-eight, originally from the city of Tru-jillo, says, "I traveled to Argentina in 1959 by train to study architecture. However, I never returned because I met my wife, who is Argentinean." Al-though these immigrants adapted to Argentinean society, they continued to celebrate events such as Peru's national holiday (28 of July) together and to organize social and cultural events to remember their country of origin. As a result, in 1979 Peruvians in Buenos Aires created the Centro Cultural Peru-ano, which aims to help newly arrived migrants get established and find work. The president of the organization, Juan, originates from Cerro de Pasco in Peru's central highlands. He recalls, "My father sent me to study agronomy in Argentina in 1954 because it was cheaper than studying in Peru. I remember that when we formed the Centro there were only 2–3,000 Peruvians in Buenos Aires, and the only activities we arranged were soccer and debates for students. At that time we were well received by the Argentineans, and Peruvians had a very good reputation."[24] Migrants also created other institutions, including the Peru Club Privado (Private Peruvian Club), the Centro de Estudiantes Peruanos (Center for Peruvian Students), Debate Político (Political Debate), Manco Cápac (named after an Inca), and the Asociación de Damas Peruanas (Association of Peruvian Ladies).

The pattern of Peruvian emigration to Argentina changed dramatically in the early 1990s, particularly after 1994, when the country became an important magnet for migrants from Peru's urban working class. This influx, which increased throughout the 1990s until Argentina's financial crisis at the beginning of 2001, was dominated by women from the shantytowns of Lima and Peru's northern coastal cities, such as Trujillo, Chimbote, and Piura, who mainly found work as domestic servants and as the carers of children, the disabled, and old people. Pacecca estimates that in 1998 the number of Peruvians in Argentina was between 50,000 and 65,000, of whom three quarters lived in Buenos Aires, 53 percent being women (2000: 7), 74 percent single, 51 percent from the department of Lima, and almost 50 percent between 21 and 30 years of age. Two years later, in 2000, the number was estimated to be 100,000, of whom 80,000 were believed to live in Buenos Aires, 75 percent being without documents (Peruvian Consulate, Buenos Aires, 2000). The response of Argentinean society to this sudden immigration has been mixed and in some sectors of the population negative, generating a xenophobic image of Peruvians (together with other Latin American immigrants) as invaders (La Primera de la Semana 2000), very much in contrast to the conventional perception of former European immigrants (Oteiza, Novick, and Aruj 1996: 1–2).[25] After the economic crisis in 2001 many Peruvians in Argentina lost their jobs, and today a growing number are either returning to Peru or emigrating to the neighboring country of Chile and other destinations.

CONCLUSION

Whereas the development of North American society and Argentina (and Chile) has depended on the continuous influx of immigrants, it is only recently that immigration has become a political issue in Europe and Japan. Indeed, it was precisely because of European and Japanese immigrants to North America that the first immigration laws were passed in the United States more than a hundred years ago. Today, the same countries that shipped off the vast majority of international immigrants before and around the turn of the nineteenth century are struggling to come to terms with the growing global mobility of people and thus the emergence of immigrant populations within their own borders. This development is particularly conspicuous in southern Europe and Japan, where the number of emigrants still exceeded the numbers of immigrants less than twenty years ago (Cornelius 1992: 331–35).

Peruvian migration forms part of today's population movements from the less developed countries in Asia, Africa, and Latin America to the industrialized countries. Just like the Europeans and Japanese who migrated to the Americas in the late nineteenth and early twentieth century they are economic migrants in the search for a more prosperous future for themselves and their children. Moreover, as discussed in the previous chapter, it is the very connections that the former immigrants in Peru created to their countries of origin that Peruvians today make use of when emigrating. In other words, Spain, Italy, Japan, Argentina, and partly also the United States, which have been the main producers of immigrants in Peru in the past five hundred years, are now the main receivers of the country's current emigration flow. The importance of these connections is evident in the immigration policies of several of these countries. Thus, since 1990 Japan has exempted certain groups of Peruvians from its strict immigration control; likewise, in 1989 the Spanish government introduced an immigration program that favors Peruvians together with other Latin Americans on the labor market. In addition, the government of Spain recurrently grant amnesty to the country's undocumented immigrant population. Yet, from the point of view of the millions of Peruvians who wish to emigrate these are exceptions from a more general pattern of immigration control that makes it almost impossible for many to enter and take work in the industrialized world. To them, the only way to do this is to either enter the United States, Spain, Japan, and Argentina on a tourist or student visa, which they later overstay and become unauthorized immigrants, travel illegally and to take residence and find work in as undocumented immigrants, contract marriage to someone who already is a legal resident or citizen in the receiving country or simply wait until a close relative is allowed to ask for family reunification. In the following chapter I use ethnographic research to demonstrate how Peruvians make use of these strategies.

NOTES

1. Unlike the Cubans, who are concentrated in Miami, the largest Haitian community (300,000) in the United States is in New York (Stepick 1992: 58).

2. The multi-ethnic composition of Los Angeles is unique because of its immigration history. Up to the 1980s immigration of non-Europeans in the city was low compared to other U.S. cities such as New York and Miami (Waldinger and Lichter 1996: 419). This picture changed radically after 1980, when the city experienced an explosive immigration of other national groups, particularly Latin Americans and Asians.

3. Four-fifths of the Los Angeles area's Hispanic population is Mexican (Lopez, Popkin, and Telles 1996: 280–81).

4. In an author's note Williams writes, "*Paterson* is a long poem in four parts—that a man in himself is a city, beginning, seeking, achieving and concluding his life in ways which the various aspects of a city may embody—if imaginatively conceived—any city, all the details of which many be made to voice his most intimate convictions" (1992: xiv).

5. In fact, Paterson was the only major city in New Jersey that grew between 1920 and 1960. All other cities over 100,000 experienced a population decline (Bebout and Grele 1964: 54).

6. Guillermo recounts, "The man was a renowned soccer player and he was looking for a place where he could make a living playing soccer. In the United States he chose Paterson because there were a lot of Italians."

7. The major immigrant groups are Moroccans (often referred to as Maghrebies), Filipinos, and Latin Americans. In 2006 more than one million of Spain's foreign population of 2.8 million were Latin Americans. Of these 400,000 were Ecuadorians, 200,000 Colombians, and 100,00 Peruvians (*El País* 2006: 22).

8. During the Franco regime, government legislation on migration focused on the problem of Spanish emigration. In 1984, one year before the Ley de Extranjería was introduced, the democratically elected government passed La Ley de Asilo y Refugio to address the problem of political refugees, particularly from Argentina and other Latin American countries troubled by political violence and rightist dictatorships (Izquierdo 1996: 37). The situation of these political refugees, which was regarded sympathetically by many Spaniards in the post-Franco era of the late 1970s and early 1980s, was very different from that of the undocumented immigrants of the 1990s.

9. A similar development to that of Spain occurred in Italy in 1998–1999, where the northern cities of Milan and Turin in particular have experienced an explosive increase in immigration from Third World countries, including Peru and other Latin American countries. As a result, in 1999, the Italian government decided to offer a so-called *sanatorio*, or amnesty granting the country's illegal immigrants legal residence. For more details on Italian immigration policy, see Sciortino 1999.

10. In 1998 the total of permits granted by the Spanish government to immigrants from non-EU countries was 28,000, with 9,154 in agriculture and catering, 1,069 in construction, 16,836 in services, and 941 in others (Escrivá 2000: 205). In 2002 the government issued a total of 32,079 permits (Dirección General de Ordenación de las Migraciones 2002: 550).

11. Latin Americans are not the only foreigners to be privileged by the Spanish labor quota system. Other former colonial subjects of the Spanish Crown such as Filipinos and Equatorial Guineans are also given priority when allocating the annual *cupos* (Escrivá 2000: 202).

12. A similar feminization of Peruvian immigration can be observed in Italy, where 70 percent of Peruvians are women (Campani 2000: 150).

13. One of the oldest Peruvian organizations in Spain is the Centro Peruano in Barcelona, which was formed in 1963 on the initiative of Peruvian migrants who had come to Spain to study and later decided to stay. It still plays a dominant role within the Peruvian community in Barcelona. The current president is a lawyer who migrated to Spain in 1978. His father, who came to Spain to study medicine in the 1950s, was also president of the organization for a number of years.

14. In recent years, a growing number of Peruvian migrant men have also been hired to nurse elderly Spaniards and Catalans.

15. In fact, Koreans migrated to Japan in great numbers before the Japanese government began to force them into labor. Thus in 1920 there were over 30,000 Korean workers in Japan, increasing to 300,000 in 1930 and reaching 800,000 in 1938, a year before the forced labor began (Yamawaki 2000: 38).

16. Apart from the Korean immigrant population there were 28,000 Taiwanese in Japan, of whom 14,000 elected to remain. Together with the Chinese who remained, they numbered 34,000 in 1948 (Douglass and Roberts 2000: 5).

17. The importation of foreign so-called comfort women is not new in Japanese history. During World War II, as many as 200,000 foreign women were forced to prostitute themselves for Japanese troops in different parts of the territories conquered by Japan (Douglass and Roberts 2000: 11).

18. The official figures for undocumented workers are much lower. In 1983 the number of foreigners found to be working without proper ID documentation in Japan was 2,239. In 1987 the number had risen to 10,000 and in 1990 to almost 30,000, a tiny proportion of Japan's total workforce of over 65 million (Shimada 1993: 24–25). In 1999 the number of foreign workers was estimated to be 271,000 (Foreign Press Center of Japan 1999: 59).

19. Generally, *nikkeijin* refers to all descendants of Japanese who emigrated abroad between 1968 and 1973. However according to Sellek, "in the context of the issue of foreign migrant workers in Japan, the term *Nikkeijin* refers specifically to South American Japanese descendants up to the third generation and their spouses, mainly those from Brazil and Peru" (Sellek 1997: 178).

20. Peruvian *nikkeijin* recall that in the heyday of immigration in the early 1990s, flights arrived at Tokyo's airport full of Peruvians, who all happened to be "brothers or sisters." Many entered with forged passports or *koseki*, Japanese family registers, which they purchased from Japanese families in Peru (Takenaka 1999: 1461). Some non-*nikkeijin* have even undergone eye surgery before leaving Peru in order to look more Japanese and thus avoid being detected as illegal immigrants in Japan (Fukumoto 1997: 358). Fukumoto estimates that more than 50 percent of all Peruvians in Japan are "falsos *nikkei*"; that is, fake *nikkei* (Fukumoto 1997: 358).

21. Other immigrant groups come from Pakistan, Bangladesh, Iran, Thailand, and Malaysia (Sellek 1997: 182).

22. Takenaka reports that the "ethnic denial" experienced by Peruvian *nikkeijin* in Japan has been transmitted to Lima through personal communication and the ethnic media. As a result, "Japanese Peruvians in Lima, regardless of their migratory expe-

rience, have come to perceive a greater distance from the Japanese. They have learned that the image of 'good, old Japan' that has served as the principal identity of the community no longer exists. The Japanese simply have ceased to be the reference group for the community" (1999: 1466).

23. To lay off migrant workers in times of crisis, however, many employers exploit the replacement of Japanese by *nikkeijin* brokers.

24. In 1980 the total number of Peruvians in Argentina was 8,561 (Pacecca 1998: 3).

25. One way in which these xenophobic sentiments are being expressed is though the racial classification of immigrants from other Latin American countries as *bolitas* (Bolivians), *chilotes* (Chileans), *paraguas* (Paraguayans), and *peruchos* (Peruvians) (Oteiza, Novick, and Aruj 1996: 10–12).

Part II

NETWORKS AND PROCESSES

Chapter Four

The Cat and the Mouse

Elvira was only twenty-four years old when the American family she was working for in Lima asked her whether she wanted to go with them to the United States. The family had lived in Peru for a couple of years for work-related reasons and was now returning to Miami, their hometown. They had been so pleased with Elvira's nursing of their children that they wanted her to continue working for them. Although Elvira's knowledge of the United States and for that matter the rest of the world was very limited, she did not hesitate to say yes. To this young woman, who had left her native Andean village when she turned eighteen to look for work as a domestic servant in Lima, the offer to travel with the American family to Miami represented just another step in her search for new and better livelihoods. Along with many of her female relatives and fellow villagers, Elvira regarded migrating as an essential activity in the struggle of a poor peasant woman to earn a living. Accordingly, she left her home country for what turned out to be a lifelong transnational experience. That was in 1954; today, fifty years later, Elvira still lives in Miami, now enjoying her retirement. However, she is not alone in Miami. Indeed, over the past four decades more than twenty-five relatives of hers have migrated to the United States, and currently more than thirty of her relatives are living in Miami. They include Peruvian-born sisters, brothers, in-laws, cousins, nieces, and nephews, as well as their American-born offspring. Apart from these family members, many of whom live in Elvira's neighborhood in the city of West Miami, a large number of *paisanos*, that is, people originating from Elvira's Peruvian home region of Ayacucho, live in the Miami area.[1]

In this chapter, I discuss the formation of six migrant networks that link Peruvians in the United States, Spain, Argentina, and Japan to their home villages and towns in Peru. For several decades the four countries have experienced a significant influx of Peruvian and other Latin American immigrants. The aim of my analysis is to clarify three aspects of Peruvian migration. First, I explore the social and cultural contexts within which Peruvian migrant networks are created and reproduced. While my material suggests that Peruvians often initiate their networks by drawing on already existing social relations, it also indicates that the relations constituting these networks vary significantly, depending on migrants' geographical origins and previous migration experiences. Three of the six networks that I shall examine were initiated by female migrants in the 1950s and 1960s, who all come from rural districts in Peru's Andean highlands and who established their emigration chains by extending already existing rural-urban migration networks. Women from squatter areas in the country's major cities established the fourth and fifth networks in the 1990s. In contrast to Andean migrants who use their long-distance ties inside Peru to initiate new networks outside the country, these urban-based migrants form their international networks by drawing on close kin ties and friendships based on neighborhood, work, etc. Finally, men looking for blue-collar jobs in factories, workshops, construction, and other traditional male-dominated industries have spearheaded the sixth network.

Second, I scrutinize the dialectic relationship between migrant networks and the power structures that try to contain them. My analysis is focused on how migrants change migration strategies and migration routes in order to adapt their networks to shifting immigration policies and livelihood opportunities in the United States, Spain, Japan, and Argentina. In particular, I am interested in understanding why the shift in immigration policies of the United States, Spain, and Japan in the late 1980s and early 1990s prompted some migrant networks to change strategy and direction (from the United States toward Spain, Italy, and Japan), while others continued unchanged. Similarly, I explore why some networks in the mid-1990s changed direction from southern Europe and Japan toward Argentina and later Chile. To illustrate the intricate relationship between immigration policies and migrant networks, I identify six phases through which Peruvian emigration has passed during the past five decades. The different strategies and routes that migrants create to draw newcomers and exploit job opportunities in the United States, Spain, Japan, and Argentina define these phases. These are

1. *Regional and rural-urban migratory processes*, which historically formed part of the mobile livelihood strategies of Peru's rural population.
2. *The pioneer emigration phase*, in which Peruvians initiated emigration based on existing rural-urban networks and mobile livelihood strategies developed by Andean migrants in Peru.
3. *The family reunification phase*, which emerged in response not only to the tightening of U.S. immigration policy toward the growing influx of Third-

World immigrants in the 1960s, but also because Peruvian men wish to join their female relatives and wives in the United States.

4. *The wetback phase* started when U.S. immigration policy tightened the rules for family reunification in the mid-1980s and thus forced an increasing number of Peruvian migrants to look for alternative routes to enter the United States.

5. *The transatlantic and transpacific phases* were ones in which, on the one hand, women migrating to southern Europe once again assumed the pioneer role in Peruvian emigration, while on the other, *nikkeijin* males spearheaded a return migration wave to Japan.[2]

6. *The regional migration phase* was directed toward Argentina from 1993 and Chile from 1997, triggered by Peru's continuous economic and political crisis and the tightening of immigration policies by Spain, Italy, and Japan in response to the first waves of Peruvian immigration to these countries between 1989 and 1992.

Third, I discuss the implications of my data on Peruvian networks in the United States, Spain, Japan, and Argentina for the recent attempts by migration scholars to theoretize transnationality. My data demonstrate that the first Peruvians to initiate migrant networks outside the country were domestics working in Lima who were brought to the United States by their employers. They also suggest that migrants' lives are embedded in the power structures that try to hamper their movements and exploit their labor force, and, more importantly, that migrants contribute to the reproduction of these power structures through their own agency. These observations imply that the current trend toward presenting "transnationalism from below" as a movement of people that takes place independently of "transnationalism from above" runs the danger of ignoring important relations of domination between the two kinds of transnationality. However, by arguing that the forces of "below" and "above" in contemporary Peruvian emigration practice are closely linked, I am not suggesting that migrant networks are entirely controlled by the dominating power structures. Rather, I argue that networks make up important tools for migrants to cross borders and create new livelihoods, but always in negotiation with the forces that are trying to dominate them.

THE ROLE OF NETWORKS IN MIGRATION

Conventionally, anthropologists have used the concept of the network to explore the creation and reproduction of informal relations in everyday life. Barnes, one of the first social scientists to use the term, stated that, "the notion of network has been developed in anthropology to analyze and describe those social processes involving links across, rather than within, group and category limits" (Barnes 1969: 54). In contrast to institutionalized and formally defined social relations, the network is essentially a field of interpersonal ties between individuals. Moreover, unlike studies of institutions and structures, network analyses are conducted at a fairly low level of abstraction that requires an intimate knowledge of the content of the network under study and the meanings that social actors attribute to the interaction that shapes it (Mitchell 1974: 284, 296). A distinction can be made between networks constituted by an unbounded group of people and a bounded group centered on an individual (Noble 1973: 4–5). Another distinction can be made between networks that are constituted by close-knit relations (called "effective" networks) and loose-knit social relations (called "extended" networks) respectively (Epstein 1969: 109–13).

In anthropology the concept of a network has often been linked to urbanization and modernization. Given the crucial role that migrant networks play in processes of migration, this is hardly surprising. As Tilly points out, "the vast majority of potential long-distance migrants anywhere in the world draw their chief information for migration decisions (including the decision to stay put) from members of their interpersonal networks, and rely on those networks for assistance both in moving and in settling at the destination" (1990: 84). Scholars who examined labor migration and urbanization processes in southern Africa in the 1950s and 1960s were among the first social scientists to make use of the concept of the network in ethnographic studies (Epstein 1969; Mitchell 1969). Migration scholars later applied the concept in other parts of the world too. Most of these studies use the notion of a network to examine the social organization of rural-urban migration (Banerjee 1983; Lomnitz 1977; Ross and Weisner 1977), but in recent years a growing number of scholars have also examined migrants' use of networks in migration processes between different countries (Balán 1992; Massey et al. 1987: 139–71; Singhanetra-Renard 1992; Tilly 1998: 147–69; Wilpert 1992). These studies suggest that networks play a different role in the two kinds of migration process due to their different determinants and consequences. Thus Gurak and Caces observe that "the key distinction between them [internal and international migration] stems from government efforts to control the entry and exit of both foreigners and citizens. Few governments, on the other hand, attempt to regulate internal migration directly. Inasmuch as these two forms of migration differ in their policy context, they may also generate distinct network configurations" (1992: 152–53). In other words, international networks differ from other migrant networks because of the policies that national governments draw up to regulate population movements (an issue dealt with in length in chapter 3).[3]

Although international networks are formed under the influence of policies that national governments design in order to contain them, so that, in effect, "immigration and immigration law are almost inseparable" (Coutin 2000: 10), this does not mean that immigration policies always succeed in controlling them. In fact, such policies are rarely effective or consistent because the economic and political interests that lead the receiving countries to regulate immigration tend to be conflicting (Brochmann 1999a; Martin 1992). Moreover, as migrant networks are constituted by informal relations based on kinship, neighborhood, friendship, and migrants' sense of belonging to their place of origin, they can easily change form and direction and, in a context of international migration, adapt to shifting immigration and labor market policies (Balán 1992; Singhanetra-Renard 1992: 198–201). As Gurak and Caces point out, "Because networks are not normatively defined, at least at their inception, they can take on a range of forms, as conditions warrant, more readily than more institutionalized structures such as families and formal organizations" (1992: 152).[4]

Indeed, rather than preventing Third World migration, First World immigration control sometimes does the opposite by actually promoting the development of migrant networks. Wilpert, who has studied the immigration of Turkish so-called guest workers in Germany in the 1960s and 1970s, explains that, "to recruit and control guest-worker entries, Germany set up a government-to-government recruitment programme" (1992: 178). However, "about a third of those registered as using official auspices were not drawn from the waiting lists of the joint Turkish-German labour offices but were nominated by firms in Germany based on recommendations of relatives or friends already employed there" (Wilpert 1992: 184). This recruitment practice particularly favored migrants from Turkey's rural areas, who "have more effective social networks at their disposal than do residents of large urban areas for the organization of chain migration" (Wilpert 1992: 179). Wilpert's analysis reveals that migrant networks that initially were encouraged by Germany's guest worker policy and used by German companies to recruit labor continued to pull in new migrants after Turkish migration was banned in 1973. It also suggests that "the increase in Turkish migration that followed the 1973 ban has been largely due to the migration of family members joining migrants workers in Germany" (Wilpert 1992: 178).

Wilpert's study indicates that structural imbalances between the supply and demand for labor in different regions or countries are playing a major role in providing the initial impetus for the formation of migrant networks (see also Gurak and Caces 1992: 154). This is also evidence that once migrant networks have been initiated they often develop into enduring entities, or as Tilly asserts, "social networks used and transformed by migration endure far be-

yond the time of displacement" (1992: 90). One of the most important roles
of social networks in such long-lasting migration chains is to act as cost-re-
ducing mechanisms to pull new migrants and to facilitate a continuous flow
of information and resources between the host country and migrants' places
of origin (Massey et al. 1987: 147–53). In order to do this the networks must
constantly adapt to changing immigration and labor market policies of the receiving countries by changing direction and migration strategies (Balán 1992;
Singhanetra-Renard 1992). Thus, while shifting immigration policies may
hamper mobility in one part of the world they may prompt the formation of
new networks in other parts. As I shall try to demonstrate, this was what happened when Peruvian emigration began to change course and direction from
the United States towards Spain, Italy, Japan, and Argentina in the late 1980s
and early 1990s.

ELVIRA'S U.S.-BOUND NETWORK:
THE LONG-TERM PERSPECTIVE

Let us go back to the anecdote introducing this chapter and see how Elvira
and her family organized their transnational migration chain and managed to
solve their legal problems and establish a new life in Miami. In 1954, when
Elvira's American employer brought her to Miami, there were only a few Peruvians in south Florida. However, over the coming decades the number
steadily increased, partly due to Elvira's family network. In 1958 she succeeded in finding an American family who agreed to bring her sister Erminia
to Miami to work for them. Elvira relates that they both became permanent
residents of the United States within a week of their arrival and that they acquired American citizenship a few years later. Their new status gave them access to more social benefits and granted them the same legal rights as other
Americans. It also increased their ability to bring relatives from Peru to the
United States through family reunification, a right that turned out to be crucial for the transition from phase two to phase three in the evolution of
Elvira's transnational network.

In 1958 Elvira's cousin Dolores, who was also born and raised in Chumbi,
obtained a tourist visa to visit the United States and traveled to Miami (see
figure 4.1). A few years later she managed to bring her husband through family reunification, and subsequently they both left for Chicago, where they currently live. In 1960 Miranda, another sister of Elvira's, came to Miami
through Dolores, who also helped her find an American employer. She soon
obtained permanent residence and later American citizenship. In the same

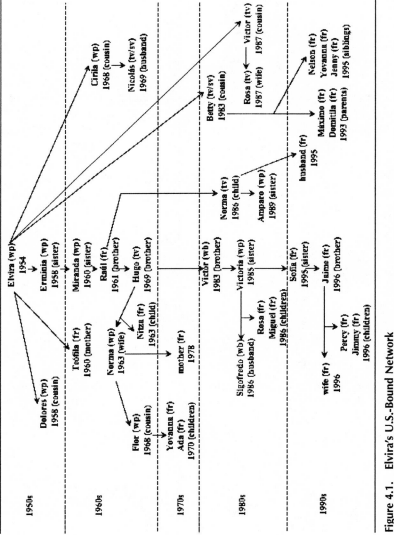

Figure 4.1. Elvira's U.S.-Bound Network

Key: (wp): work permit; (fr): family reunification; (tv): tourist visa; (wb): "wetback"; (sv): student visa

year, Elvira's mother, Teófila, came too, the first of her relatives to immigrate to the United States through family reunification. Her mother, who also comes from Chumbi, had only been in Lima a couple of times before emigrating to the United States, which explained her poor Spanish. During her almost forty years in the United States, however, this initially monolingual Quechua speaker has not only learned Spanish but also considerably improved her communication skills in English. Teófila recalls, "When I arrived I thought everybody in Miami talked English. Of course, I only spoke Quechua at that time but then I learned Spanish, and today I can speak with almost everybody here. I have even learned English, I mean to go and do the shopping and that kind of thing."

In 1963 two more of Elvira's female relatives arrived in Miami. The first was Norma, the sister-in-law of Erminia (Elvira's sister), who found work as a domestic worker for an American family in Miami with the help of her relatives. Norma kept this job until she became a resident two years later. This allowed her to travel to Peru and to visit Chumbi, where she married Hugo, a fellow villager. The second to come was Nitza, the daughter of Hugo's first marriage, who was brought to the United States at the age of five as the adopted child of Erminia through family reunification. Nitza was the first of Elvira's migrant network to attend school in the United States. Today she is an American citizen studying psychology at one of Miami's universities.

In 1968 Cerila, a distant relative of Elvira's from Chumbi, and Flor, a female cousin of Norma's, followed. They both obtained permits to work as domestic workers for American families in Miami a few weeks after their arrival. Cerila later married a Peruvian in Miami and had two daughters, Iovana and Ada, who were both born in the United States and are therefore American citizens. In 1969, Nicolás, Cerila's husband, entered the United States on a tourist visa. When this expired, he applied for a student visa that lasted for a couple of years. Although such a visa only gives the migrant the right to reside, not to work, Nicolás worked as a dishwasher to make a living while the visa lasted. The last villager to arrive in 1960s was Hugo, Erminia's husband, who also came to the United States in 1969.

Hugo's migration history is interesting because his arrival marks the transition of Elvira's network from phases three to phase four. Not only was Hugo one of the first men in Elvira's family to emigrate,[5] but he also arrived at a moment when Peruvians were changing livelihood strategies in the United States. Up to the middle of the 1960s, the national-origin quota system tended to favor Latin Americans over Europeans and Asians. Hence, Elvira and the relatives who followed her experienced little difficulty in obtaining work permits and became legal residents within a few months of their arrival. Today several of them are American citizens. However, when the 1965 Immigration

Act introduced a new visa system for family reunification and work skills, it abolished the old quota system, which for years had protected Latin Americans working as domestic workers and gardeners from competition from other immigrant groups. The new act also made it more difficult for Peruvians in the United States to find employers willing to hire newcomers and to help them apply for work and residence permits. Consequently, the networks were forced to change livelihood strategies and invent new ways to bring relatives from Peru. One was to apply for family reunification; another was to invite their relatives to the United States on a temporary visa (tourism, student, business, entertainment, etc.). A final option was simply to cross the U.S.-Mexican border illegally.

Rather than wait for his sister and wife to apply for family reunification, Hugo opted for the second solution and entered the United States on a tourist visa, which he later exchanged for a student visa. However, without permanent residence or a work permit his legal status in the United States was much more precarious than those of his sister and his wife, and his options in finding work were also severely hampered. In contrast to his female relatives, who found jobs as domestic workers almost immediately after their arrival, Hugo was forced to carve out his own niche in Miami's rapidly growing labor market for undocumented male immigrants. He says, "For my female relatives things were much easier. They were almost sure to find work as domestics as soon as they arrived. When I arrived we were only a few men among the Peruvians. And where were we to find jobs? I had to look for job all by myself. And you know, when you're illegal everything is more difficult." Victor tells how he made friends with another Latin American immigrant, who helped him find work as a dishwasher in a restaurant in Key Biscayne. After a couple of years with temporary jobs, Hugo applied for a work permit, which he obtained in 1972. He then joined the furniture factory, where he still works as an unskilled worker.

In the 1970s and early 1980s a few more villagers from Chumbi made it to the United States. Nicolás came on a tourist visa. He then enrolled in a two-year language program and was granted a student visa. After becoming a resident, he brought his Peruvian wife through the family reunification program. In 1978 Norma's and Hugo's application to be reunited with their mother from Chumbi bore fruit. Initially she came to visit her children on a temporary visa, but when Norma became a U.S. citizen in 1980, their mother was granted residence. In 1983 Bety, a distant cousin of Elvira's, obtained a tourist visa and traveled to the United States. After three months she exchanged this for a student visa, which prolonged her right to stay but did not allow her to work. As a result she was forced to work illegally as a domestic servant. However, three years later she married an American and in 1991 became a U.S. citizen. A few years later she brought both her parents, also from Chumbi, and then her three siblings, Nelson, Yovana, and Jheny, to the United States.

In the 1970s Elvira's Andean network changed gender composition and entered phase four. Not only did a growing number of men from Chumbi join the village's predominantly female transnational community in Miami, but, as it became more and more common for Peruvians and other Latin Americans to be denied tourist visas to the United States at the American Embassy in Lima, Elvira's migration chain started to use the U.S.-Mexican border. Although these newcomers entered the country illegally, many of them, including Elvira's uncles and aunts,[6] obtained legal residence with the help of other migrants by claiming family reunification.

Other villagers who were not prepared to wait for their relatives to summon them or who were denied tourist visas joined the fast growing number of Latin American migrants entering the United States illegally through Mexico. Thus during the 1970s and the early 1980s this somehow more troublesome migration route brought another group of villagers, males as well as females, to Miami. In 1983 Hugo's brother Victor applied for a tourist visa to visit his family in Miami, but as he was turned down he ventured first to fly to Mexico and then to continue overland illegally to the United States. Today he is a legal resident and lives in Miami. Two years later Victoria, Erminia's half sister, also joined Chumbi's community in Miami through this route. Her husband Sigofredo, another Chumbi villager, who crossed the Mexican border on foot, followed her in 1986.[7] Yet another villager, Victor, came to Miami in 1987 after working for several years in Venezuela. His wife Rosa joined him the same year.

In the late 1980s and early 1990s, immigration policy in the United States tightened and border control became more efficient. Moreover, as Mexico started to require tourist visas for Peruvians, the trip from Peru to the United States became not only more hazardous, but also more expensive. Informal agencies now began to emerge in Lima offering Peruvians organized trips to the United States by flying to a Central American country and then illegally over land to California, whence the travelers continue the journey to Miami on their own. The cost of such a perilous experience can easily amount to about US$8,000. In addition, the 1996 Act has made it more difficult for undocumented migrants (whether these are "wetbacks" or visa overstayers) to obtain residence and work permits in the United States.

Despite these obstacles, Chumbi's migration chain continues to produce new immigrant candidates. Over the past forty years, Elvira's migrant network has grown so large that it now covers several generations and wide categories of kin groups, which increases the options in claiming family reunification with relatives abroad. In other words, time is on the side of Elvira's network, which in the late 1980s reverted from the fourth migration phase of illegal border crossing to the third phase, which is now pulling newcomers exclusively through the family reunification program. The latest to arrive is Jaime, one of Hugo's brothers, who came to Miami in 1996 together with his wife and two children after waiting twelve years to be reunited with his mother and siblings.

SOFÍA'S U.S.-BOUND NETWORK: THE MEDIUM-TERM PERSPECTIVE, 1

Sofía was only a young woman when she traveled to the United States in 1969 together with the family she working for in Lima. Like Elvira, her American employers brought her to Miami. And, like Elvira, she later ended up spearheading a decades-long transnational migration chain. Moreover, like Elvira's migration chain, Sofía's network developed as an extension of an already established rural-urban migration network bringing highland peasants from Pichos, Sofía's native community in Peru's central highlands, to Lima.

The first relative to follow Sofía was her brother David, who came to the United States in 1980 (see figure 4.2). David left his native village of Pichos at the age of seventeen to study art in Lima with the support of his relatives there. However, he never finished his studies and after three years he decided to join Sofía in Miami. He traveled to the United States on a tourist visa, which he overstayed, then started to work illegally as a tomato picker in Homestead in southern Florida. He says, "I was lucky to get into the United States as tourist. I didn't have to cross the border like so many others. But later I suffered a lot as illegal worker. They exploit and abuse you all the time." He continued working illegally as a dishwasher in different restaurants in Miami until the 1986 Immigration Act granted him and thousands of other illegal immigrants who had entered the country before the 1982 amnesty legal resident status.[8] Today David is married to a woman from Puerto Rico, with whom he has two daughters.

In 1981 María, a cousin of Sofía's, came to Miami. Like David, she entered the United States on a tourist visa that she later overstayed. With the help of Sofía she found a job as a domestic worker, which she kept until she married. As her husband, a man from Central America, already had residence in the United States, María automatically became a legal resident too. Later Arturo, a brother of María's, also traveled to the United States on a tourist visa and later became unauthorized. Like David, he was granted residence under the Immigration Act in 1986. In 1982 Sofía's brother Armando also entered on a tourist visa. Some years later he married the Puerto Rican sister of David's wife, thus also becoming a legal resident.

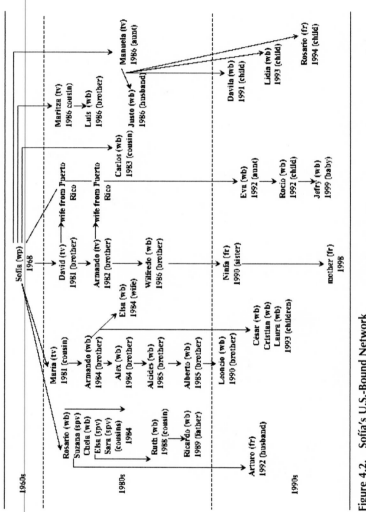

Figure 4.2.   Sofia's U.S.-Bound Network

Key: (wp): work permit; (fr): family reunification; (tv): tourist visa; (spv): special visa; (wb): "wetback"

From 1983 Sofía's migrant network changed strategy and gathered speed. Unlike Elvira's network, which reverted from phase four to phase three in the aftermath of the 1986 Act, Sofía's network jumped straight from phase two to phase four. As Sofía was still the only member of Pichos' Miami community who had become a U.S. citizen, and as less than a handful of her fellow villagers had obtained legal residence in the United States by 1986, her network was not in a position to use the family reunification program as a pulling mechanism on the same scale as Elvira's network. Moreover, as it became increasingly difficult in the 1980s for Peruvians to obtain tourist visas and other types of temporary visas to the United States, Sofía's fellow villagers in Peru were forced to look for other ways to enter the United States. The growing number of villagers making the trip from Peru to the United States by land in the late 1980s was evidence of this change in migration strategies.

Carlos, a cousin of Sofía's, became the first in the network to cross the U.S.-Mexican border illegally. In 1983 he traveled to Mexico by air and entered the country on a tourist visa. In Tijuana he contracted a *coyote*, a nickname for professional agents who assist undocumented immigrants to cross the U.S.-Mexican border. Once across the border, he took a flight from Los Angeles to Miami, where his relatives were waiting for him. In 1984 Armando, a brother of María's, followed Carlos's example and entered the United States accompanied by his wife with the help of a *coyote*. In order to finance the trip, Arturo lent his brother the money, which Armando promised to return once he was established in Miami. Six more villagers followed in 1984 through the *coyote* system. One was Alex, a brother of María, while the other five were female villagers, all distant relatives of Sofía.

In 1985 two more brothers of María's, Alcides and Alberto, made it to Miami through Mexico. They both borrowed the money to travel from Pichos migrants in Miami and flew to Mexico, which they entered as tourists. In Mexico they contracted a *coyote*, who helped them to cross the border to the United States. The following year Sofía's network brought five more villagers to Miami.[9] Alcides says, "We were treated all right by the *coyote* we hired, but I know of others who were abused and blackmailed. You see, the *coyotes* only do it for the money."

From 1987 to 1995 another eighteen villagers came to Miami, all but three as "wetbacks," a nickname for undocumented immigrants who enter the United States from Mexico and often have to walk or swim across rivers to cross the border.[10] As a result, the Pichos migrant community in Miami now numbers more than forty members of Peruvian descent and several American born. Moreover, during the three decades that the network has been active, several new migration chains have been created by Sofía's siblings, cousins, and other remote relatives.

Unlike Elvira, Sofía came to the United States after the 1965 Act, which had critical implications for the gender composition of the migrant network she was about to create, as well as for the migration routes her relatives made use of. Male migrants, then, play a much more active role in Sofía's network than Elvira's; likewise, rather than entering the United States as tourists or through family reunification, most Pichos migrants have joined the thousands of other Latin American immigrants who cross the U.S.-Mexican border as "wetbacks." Thus because Sofía's network lacked the time to establish a community of kin and fellow villagers in the United States to pull newcomers by claiming the right to family reunification, it was forced to jump straight from phase two to phase four.

OFELIA'S TRANSATLANTIC NETWORK:
THE MEDIUM-TERM PERSPECTIVE, 2

One year after Elvira took off for the United States, another young woman from a village neighboring Chumbi left Peru. Ofelia was born and raised in Rivacayo, but before coming of age she went to Lima, where a group of migrants from her village had formed a community. She soon found work with an American family as a domestic servant, and when they returned to their hometown of Miami in 1955, Ofelia was asked to join them. She says, "In those days there were not many Hispanics in Miami and only a few Peruvians. Most of us were young women. And we were all working as domestics at that time." Her decision to say "yes" triggered the formation of a decades-long transnational migrant network and marked the transition from phase one to phase two in Rivacayo's migration history.

Once established in Miami, Ofelia started to look for American families interested in hiring her fellow villagers in Rivacayo as domestics. Although her attempts to find new employers in Miami initially failed, Ofelia managed to help her niece Lucy find a job as a domestic worker for an American family in Lima in 1957. When the family returned to their native city of Miami, Lucy was offered the same choice that her aunt had been given a few years earlier. She decided to go with them to Miami and left Peru in 1958 (see figure 4.3). After a couple of years in Miami she met Máximo, her future husband, who had been in the United States since 1960.[11] Today Lucy lives in Miami and has one daughter born in the United States, who is therefore an American citizen.

In 1960 Lucy's efforts to find an employer in Miami for one of her female relatives finally bore fruit. This brought her sister Benedicta to the United States. Later Benedicta brought her Peruvian fiancé, whom she then married. Today the couple lives in Connecticut with their three children, all born in the

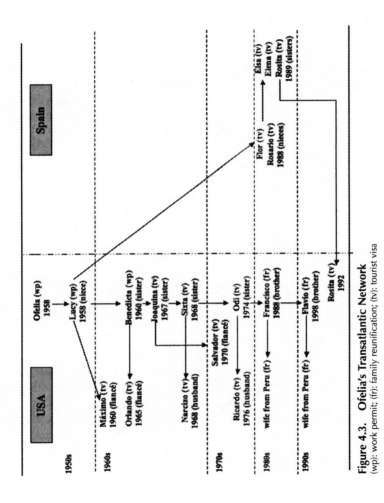

Figure 4.3. Ofelia's Transatlantic Network

(wp): work permit; (fr): family reunification; (tv): tourist visa

United States. A third sister, Joaquina, came in 1967, followed a year later by Lucy's sister Sixta.[12] Both found work as domestic servants for American families. Four years later Sixta met Narcizo, also of Peruvian origin, whom she married.[13] Today they both live in Miami.

Yet another sister of Lucy, Odi, made it the United States a few years later using a different route. After leaving her native village of Rivacayo at the age of ten, she went to stay with Lucy and Benedicta in Lima. Here she finished school and found a job as a domestic worker in the house of a middle-class Peruvian family. In 1968 Odi, now twenty, was asked by a friend to come with her to Venezuela. The friend had been working as a maid in Lima for a Peruvian-Venezuelan couple who were returning to Venezuela and wanted to take two Peruvian domestic workers with them. Odi accepted the offer and spent the following six years in Venezuela working first as a domestic servant, and later as an assistant in a shop selling cloth. During her stay in Venezuela, Odi frequently received information from her sisters in the United States, who encouraged her to come and visit them. Thus in 1974 she traveled to the United States, first to Los Angeles to visit some other relatives of hers, and later to Miami, where she overstayed her tourist visa and became unauthorized. After a couple of years she got a job as a domestic worker for an American family in Miami, who helped her obtain a work permit and legal residence. Today she works in a Burger King restaurant and lives with Paul, her twelve-year-old son, who was born in the United States. Her husband, also a Peruvian, now lives with another woman elsewhere in Miami.

In 1965 Lucy and her sisters received news of their sister Aniceta's death in Rivacayo, while giving birth to twin babies. Two more sisters who, like Aniceta, had stayed put and married local villagers in Rivacayo had died a few years earlier, leaving a total of ten children. As Aniceta's husband had abandoned her several years before her death and as she was the last member of Lucy's sibling group living in Rivacayo, the orphaned nieces and nephews now had to be entrusted to neighbors and distant relatives.

Aniceta's death coincided with the 1965 Immigration Act and prompted Ofelia's migrant network to enter the third phase. For Lucy and her siblings, their main concern now was to bring their nieces and nephews out of Rivacayo, first to Lima and later to the United States through the family reunification program. Lucy says, "In order to use this program we needed to have more family members in the United States. And the best solution is always to have close relatives because they have the highest priority in the family reunification program. So my sisters and I tried to persuade my four brothers who were living in Lima to come. We could easily have obtained legal residence for them at that time. Then they could have help us pull my nieces and nephews out of Peru." However, of the four brothers only Francisco and

Bravio agreed to migrate. As military officers in the Peruvian army, the other two, Angel and Flavio, were well off in Peru and had no wish to leave the country.[14] Francisco traveled to the United States with his family in 1988, followed ten years later by Bravio.

Lucy's and her sisters' plan to reunite the family in the United States was upset by political developments in Peru in the 1980s. In 1987 Rivacayo was attacked first by the Shining Path, a rebel group that caused terror and violence in Peru during the 1980s and early 1990s, and later by the Peruvian military. Many villagers, including the five nieces still living in Rivacayo, were forced to take refuge in Lima. Here the five women stayed with Angel and Bravio temporarily while exploring the possibilities of emigration. As the 1986 Act had tightened the criteria for family reunification in the United States and as illegal border crossing had become a dangerous undertaking, the prospects looked poor. Hence, the five women decided to turn their eyes toward other parts of the world.

In 1988 two of Lucy's nieces were offered help to find work as domestic servants in Madrid by a Peruvian friend living there. The two women decided to leave that same year. In 1989 the other three sisters joined them, forming part of what now was becoming a European branch of Rivacayo's transnational community. This search for new migration routes was prompted not merely by the increasing difficulties of entering the United States illegally in the late 1980s and early 1990s, but also by the growing need for domestic labor in Spain's major cities and the immigration policy of the Spanish government. In other words, Spain emerged as an alternative option for thousands of impoverished and disillusioned Peruvians at a time when Peru's economic and political future looked bleaker than ever and the United States was tightening its borders.

Yet Spain did not entirely replace the United States as the favorite destination of Ofelia's migrant network. In 1998 Flavio migrated to Miami together with his wife, also from Rivacayo, and their daughter through family reunification. Moreover, one of Lucy's five nieces in Madrid, who was finding it difficult to get along with the Spanish family she was working for, went to the United States in 1992 to stay with Benedicta in Connecticut. The niece had previously applied for a tourist visa to enter the United States but had been denied. However, the regulations for undocumented immigrants being implemented by the Spanish government in 1991 granted her legal residence in Spain. One year later she was granted an entry visa into the United States.

Like Elvira and Sofía, Ofelia has spearheaded a migration chain that now is more than forty years old. Moreover, all three networks have made periodic use of the same migration strategies and routes. Yet because they were initiated at different times and have expanded under different legal constraints in the United States and Spain, the three networks have passed through the five migration phases in very different ways. Likewise, because the social relations that give shape to them vary, the possibilities of using loopholes in shifting immigration policies and hence the choice of migration strategy differ. Unlike the networks of Sofía and Ofelia, Elvira's is primarily based on kinship or marriage ties (thus resembling Epstein's "effective" networks, which are constituted by close-knit relations as discussed above). Although it passed to phase four in the mid-1980s at a time when some of Chumbi's villagers were entering the United States as "wetbacks," it reverted to phase three in the 1990s once Elvira and her relatives had established an extensive network of kinship ties and were again in a position to use the family reunification program as a pulling mechanism.

Sofía came to the United States in her turn in the 1960s. In contrast to Elvira's network, established fourteen years earlier, Sofía and her relatives were still struggling to build up an extensive kinship network when the criteria for family reunification were tightened in 1986. Thus her network (resembling Epstein's "extended" networks, which are constituted by loose-knit social relations) was forced to jump straight from phase two to phase four and make sole use of the "wetback" strategy. Almost as old as Elvira's network, Ofelia's did not gather speed until the late 1980s, when Peruvian emigration was growing fast and the "wetback" strategy of phase four had become more hazardous. Hence the sudden jump of Ofelia's network from phase three to phase five, in which female migrants once again act as the vanguard of Peruvian transnational migration, now by crossing the Atlantic. Because of this development, Ofelia's network is today scattered over several continents and linked up to other migration chains.

VANESA'S SPANISH NETWORK:
THE SHORT-TERM PERSPECTIVE

Since Vanesa went to school in the city of Trujillo on the northern coast of Peru, she had been dreaming of going to the United States. She had been informed by some of her former classmates that they had relatives in Los Angeles and Washington willing to pull newcomers. Yet when Vanesa finally made up her mind to leave Peru in 1991, the prospects of going to the United States looked gloomy. The American Embassy in Lima turned down her application for a tourist visa, and she was told that the border crossing from Mexico to the United States had become a dangerous and expensive adventure. She therefore decided to try her luck in Spain, where a couple of her distant cousins were living.

Once she had saved up enough money for the flight ticket, Vanesa left Peru on May 15, 1991, and entered Spain, landing in Madrid on a tourist visa. Initially she had planned to settle in Madrid with her relatives. However, as she did not feel welcome, Vanesa continued to Barcelona within a few weeks of arrival, where, according to fellow migrants, salaries were higher than in the rest of Spain. She explains that "They didn't treat me well. I thought they would help me find work and offer me somewhere to live. But in those days people were concerned with their own problems." Three months after her arrival, Vanesa overstayed her tourist visa and joined the growing community of illegal immigrants in Barcelona. She found a job as a domestic worker in the home of a Catalan family and rented a room with a female relative of Telmo, her boyfriend back in Trujillo.

Unwittingly, Vanesa had chosen just the right time to enter Spain. Not only did she come one year before most European countries lifted the visa exemption for Peruvians, but Vanesa arrived three days before May 18, 1991, the deadline fixed by the Spanish government in the 1991 regulatory process for undocumented immigrants to enter Spain in order to be granted residence. She says, "Can you imagine! First I came to Madrid and there was nobody to help me. I even thought of going back to Peru. And then it turned out that I had arrived just a couple days before the amnesty ended. When I came to Spain, I never imagined that I was going to be that lucky. It solved all my problems. Think of all those who came after. Some of them are still struggling with the paperwork." In effect, Vanesa became a legal resident in Spain in less than one year. In 1992 Telmo followed her. Like Vanesa, he had originally planned to go to the United States, where his father lives. Yet as his parents are divorced and his father is now living with another woman, Telmo found the option of going to Spain more attractive. Moreover, he already had an aunt and several cousins living in the country. Today Telmo works in a factory making what he considers a reasonable salary, while Vanesa has three part-time jobs as a cleaner for retired Catalan women. They live in a rented flat together with Marc, their two-year-old child, who was born in Spain and is thus a Spanish citizen.

Although Spanish immigration control was tightened during the 1990s, Vanesa has succeeded in pulling several of her relatives through the *cupo* system, that is, the annual work permits that the Spanish government grants to different immigrant groups. In 1995 Vanesa and Telmo managed to pull Julia, one of Vanesa's sisters. Julia first flew to Germany on a tourist visa, and then continued to Spain by land, assisted by a Peruvian agent engaged to bring her to Barcelona. With the help of Vanesa, Julia found a retired Catalan woman who was looking for domestic help and willing to apply for the *cupo* required to hire a foreign worker. Julia then returned to Peru and waited until she received notice from the Spanish Embassy in Lima to pick up her documents. Subsequently, she left for Spain for a second time now as a legal alien with permission to work as domestic servant and a permit that is renewed annually as long as she continues to work for the same employer.

In 1995 Telmo and Vanesa pulled Nely, a cousin of Vanesa's, to Spain. Nely had been planning to emigrate for several years. In 1991 she paid a man in Trujillo, her hometown in Peru, US$1,000 for a passport and visa to Japan. Her new identity would have been that of a Peruvian of Japanese descent with the right to apply for a temporary work permit in Japan. However, Nely never received the passport but was cheated by the man, who used the money to pay his own travel costs to Japan. She then turned her eyes toward the United States, where some distant relatives had promised to help her find an employer. As that attempt also failed, Nely eventually decided to go to Spain. Like Julia, she used the German route and traveled to Spain by land. Once she had found an employer, she returned to Peru and waited for her *cupo*. Today, she is working as a domestic servant in Barcelona. Nely says, "Before I left Peru I had no wish to go to Spain. I wanted to go to Japan, where you make more money. I also wanted to go to the United States. That's how life is. Now I'm in Spain."

At the time of writing, Telmo was trying to persuade his Catalan employer to file the papers required to hire yet another of Vanesa's sisters in Peru, who was waiting to come to Spain to work. If Telmo's employer agreed, the sister was likely to be granted one of the desired *cupos* in 1999. Vanesa's transnational network continues to grow, even though Europe's borders are being closed. However, Telmo is sometimes concerned that the social commitment that he and Vanesa feel to pull more and more newcomers out of Peru will prevent them from establishing a new life in Barcelona. He says, "I want to save money to buy my own flat one day. Where we live now, the house is full of relatives arriving from Peru. And I'm always afraid that my employer feels that I'm exploiting him too much. Everybody wants a *cupo*. Of course, it solves all your paper problems. But I can't ask my employer to get *cupos* for all of Vanesa's family."

The recent exodus of Peruvians to countries like Spain, Italy, Japan, Argentina, and Chile differs from previous Peruvian emigration flows. As Peru's economic and political situation deteriorated during the late 1980s and early 1990s, an increasing number of impoverished urban working- and middle-class Peruvians with little or no previous migration experience joined the country's growing emigration. Unlike Andean migrants, who built up their transnational migrant network as extensions of former rural-urban migration chains and experienced little difficulty in finding work as domestic servants in their new social settings, many of the migrants who left Peru in the late

1980s and early 1990s had to create entirely new networks and adjust to unfamiliar working conditions. Moreover, changing immigration policies forced many of these emigrants to look for alternative destinations. In contrast to the United States, the traditional destination for Peruvian emigration, Peruvians in Europe (like those in Argentina and Chile) had not established strong communities at that time. Whereas Elvira's chains made use of the family reunification and Sofía's of the "wetback" strategy, these more recent branches of Peruvian emigration have been forced to develop new means and tactics to get established.

ALBERTO'S TRANSPACIFIC NETWORK: THE RETURN MIGRANT PERSPECTIVE

Alberto, seventy-six, lives in Ashicaga, northwest of Tokyo. He and his two sisters were born and raised in Huancayo in Peru's central highlands by Japanese immigrants. Hence they are classified as *nisei*. Alberto's father came from the Shioka prefecture in Japan, where he was raised together with his five siblings. In 1909 he left on the fourth boat to transport Japanese contract workers to Peru in the first decade of the twentieth century. After he had toiled for four years in the sugar plantations south of Lima and thus completed his labor contract, he returned to Japan to be united with his future wife. The marriage, which had been arranged by the young couple's parents, was a so-called photo marriage, which only allowed Alberto's father and his future bride to be introduced to each other through an exchange of photos. The same year the newly married couple traveled to Peru. In the 1930s a brother of Alberto's father also emigrated to Peru with his Japanese wife. They settled in Huancayo, where they had two children. Alberto's uncle later became a rich businessman importing and selling electrical goods to local companies and consumers.

World War II caused a deep split in Alberto's family, which became divided and isolated from each other on three continents. Before hostilities broke out, Alberto's uncle sent his wife back to Japan together with their two children so that they could study there. The uncle himself, however, remained in Peru to take care of his business, which turned out to be a fatal decision. In 1942 he was detained by the Peruvian police and deported to the United States. Not only did he lose all his property, but he was forced to spend three years in a camp for Japanese prisoners in Texas. After the war he stayed in the United States and settled in Los Angeles, where he married first a German and later a Mexican. His two Peruvian-born children visited him in the United States after the war but then returned to Japan, where they currently live.

Several of Alberto's closest relatives were also living in Japan when hostilities broke out. One of his uncles fought and died as a Japanese soldier in the war. Alberto recounts, "The first thing I did when I came to Japan was to visit my uncle's grave. I felt that I should pay my respects to him. Although I was born in Peru, we were part of the same family." Alberto's oldest sister was also sent to Japan to study before World War II, which prevented her from maintaining contact with that branch of the family who were living in Peru. After the war the woman married and had children in Japan. Alberto says, "We lost contact with my oldest sister. The war prevented us from communicating. Today she has forgotten everything about Peru." His second sister stayed in Peru, where she married a *nisei* and had two children.

Alberto's wife is *nisei* too. Her parents both came from Kúyshú in Japan. The father emigrated in 1912 on the seventh boat to bring Japanese contract workers to Peru. He returned to Japan to contract a marriage with Alberto's mother-in-law, to whom he had been introduced by photo. The couple then traveled to Peru together and settled in Huancayo, where they set up a business and had five children. In 1952 one of Alberto's brothers-in-law emigrated to the United States, where he settled and had a family. Today he lives in Chicago. Two of his sisters-in-law remained in Peru, where they still live, while a third emigrated to Japan in the 1990s.

In 1992, two years after Japan allowed the descendants of its emigrant population to find temporary work in the country, Alberto and his wife also emigrated to Japan. Unlike most other Peruvian *nikkeijin*, who have migrated to Japan in the past decade, they both speak Japanese and have had little difficulty in adapting to Japanese life. Alberto explains, "We were both raised before the war. At that time all Japanese sent their children to Japanese schools and thought of themselves as Japanese. So I feel as much Japanese as Peruvian." He and his wife try to help other Peruvians in Ashicaga. They act as translators when other immigrants communicate with the local Japanese authorities and help when someone is hospitalized. He says, "I think Peruvians in Japan should try to adapt to the Japanese way of life. We can't expect the Japanese to receive us well if we don't make an effort ourselves." When asked whether he ever thinks of returning to Peru, he replies, "No, I feel fine in Japan."

CASILDA'S ARGENTINE-ITALIAN NETWORK: THE ABORTED PERSPECTIVE

Casilda was born in Huancayo in 1974 in Peru's central highlands, where she spent her childhood and youth with her parents and four siblings, three sisters and a brother. Her father works as a driver and a car mechanic, while her mother runs a booth in one of Huancayo's local markets, where she sells vegetables and herbs. Until 1992 Casilda's brother Raúl received economic support from the family to study engineering at the university in Huancayo, while the four sisters assisted their mother in the market, hoping to set up their own business one day. In fact Rosita had already saved enough money to invest in her own merchandise and had established herself as an independent retail dealer. However, the dramatic effects of the *fujichock* in 1990 and the following years of economic recession in Peru forced the family to look for new ways to make a living and consider the possibility of leaving Huancayo.

In 1992 Rosita planned to migrate to the United States together with Raúl. Because the family had no close relatives outside Peru at that time, the two siblings could not draw on any existing networks or relationships of trust to ask for help and assistance to migrate. In other words, no pulling mechanism was available. Consequently, they decided to travel to the United States by land, crossing the border as "wetbacks" and trying to find work and somewhere to live on their own. Raúl says, "We had always heard of the United States and we thought it was easier to get there than to go to Europe. When you don't know how to migrate or where to go you can always travel on land. Of course we had no idea how to survive in the United States. But that would have been the same in other places as well." In order to finance the trip, Rosita sold all the merchandise she had stocked in her newly acquired booth at the market in Huancayo and used the savings to pay US$5,000 to a local emigration agent in Peru, who promised to make all the necessary travel arrangements in return. Raúl, on the other hand, was still studying and had therefore few means with which to contribute to the trip. To the family's regret, however, the two siblings never reached the United States. They were detained by the police in Panama and returned to Peru, thus losing all the money that Rosita had invested in the trip.

Despite the failure to emigrate Rosita was still determined to find work outside Peru, but rather than trying her luck in the United States she now considered the possibilities of going to Europe. Two of her cousins, who were working as domestic servants in Milan, had written to Rosita and her siblings encouraging them to come to Italy. However, by mid-1992 the European Union had imposed new visa requirements on several Latin American countries and had tightened its border controls, which raised the cost of traveling to southern Europe for Peruvians. As a result, when Rosita decided to emigrate for a second time in late 1992 she could not afford the trip to Italy and was compelled to search for other, nearer destinations. Hence, she decided to try her luck in Argentina. Her plan was to spend a few years in Argentina and save enough money to go to Italy later, a migration strategy pursued by thousands of other Peruvian emigrants who left the country in the early 1990s in response to the neoliberal policies of the Fujimori government.

Rosita made the trip to Argentina through Chile by bus, which only took three days and cost a few hundred dollars, without trouble except for some harassment from the Argentinean border police, whom she had to bribe to enter the country on a tourist visa. With the help of two cousins who had arrived a little earlier, Rosita rapidly found a job as a domestic servant for an Argentinean family in Buenos Aires, after three months overstaying her tourist visa and thus becoming an unauthorized immigrant. Although her employment allowed her to apply to the Argentinean authorities for a temporary work permit and thus obtain status as a legal immigrant, Rosita refrained from doing so. She explains, "Why go through all the hassle of doing a lot of paperwork and paying several hundred dollars to apply for a residence permit when I only wanted to spend a year or two in the country?" In 1993 she returned to Peru to coax her younger sisters, Casilda and Amanda, who still were living with their parents in Huancayo, to join her in Buenos Aires. The following year she traveled to Argentina for a second time, this time accompanied by Casilda, who found employment as a domestic servant shortly after her arrival. In 1994 Amanda followed her two sisters, who helped her find a job as a domestic servant for an Argentinean family.

The three sisters spent the following three years in Argentina working as domestic servants, partly remitting the money they had earned to their parents in Peru, and partly saving it to pursue their plan of migrating to Italy. In 1997 Rosita finally decided to travel to Europe. She returned to Peru, where she paid a local travel agent to arrange the trip to Italy for her. She then traveled to Germany, which she entered on a tourist visa, and continued to Milan. With the help of cousins living there, she found a job as a domestic servant for an Italian family, making almost double the salary she had earned in Argentina. In 1998 she benefited from the amnesty granted by the Italian government to all undocumented immigrants in the country, and a year later she received a permanent residence permit. By the same year she had saved enough money to invite Raúl to join her, and in 1999 he traveled to Europe entering Italy as an undocumented immigrant. Raúl spent several months looking for work while living on the support he had received from Rosita. Eventually he got a job in a mechanics' workshop, but after two months he quit because the Italian owner refused to pay his salary. When I met Raúl in Milan in 1999, he said, "I was living on Rosita's salary but finally I got a job. I was so happy to work as a mechanic, but my employer was not a good man. I kept asking for my salary, but he always came up with an excuse for not paying me. Finally I realized that he was cheating me. That's what happens when you're illegal. You can't do anything. So I told him what I thought of him and left." After more than half a year he found a job as a driver for a group of Peruvians who have set up a transport business in Milan.

Rosita's plan to unite all her siblings in Italy has never materialized. By 1999 Amanda had saved enough money to join her sister in Milan and returned to Peru to make the travel arrangements. However, in Huancayo she fell in love with another Peruvian emigrant living in Argentina, who like Amanda was visiting his family in Peru. The couple decided to marry shortly afterward, and because her husband wanted to go back to Argentina, Amanda decided to travel with him.[15] The same year Casilda met an Argentinean in Buenos Aires, whom she plans to marry. Hence both sisters have now decided to stay in Argentina. In Buenos Aires Casilda told me, "Rosita wasn't happy to hear that Amanda and I have changed our plans and that we are staying in Argentina. But what can we do? I'm pregnant now and want to raise a family here." The four siblings all send remittances back to their parents, who live together with Juana, their oldest sister, and her child in Peru. When I met Juana in 2000 in Huancayo, she said, "I may go to Italy together with my mother. We still have to save more money."

THE DEVELOPMENT OF PERUVIAN NETWORKS IN PHASES

Many of the migration networks that have brought thousands of Peruvians to the United States over the past four decades were initiated by women from rural backgrounds who were either brought or invited by American families to come and work for them as domestics. Thus women (Elvira, Sofía, and Ofelia) spearheaded all three networks in the United States that have been examined here. Moreover, women often act as pullers of husbands, sons, brothers, fathers, and other male relatives, searching for employers and finding jobs for them as gardeners, waiters, dishwashers, construction workers, and so forth. In the United States this pattern remained dominant up to the mid-1960s, when the 1965 Immigration Act replaced the national-origin quota system (which made it easier for Peruvians and other Latin Americans to enter the job market) with the more liberal family reunification regulation. Initially, this program served as a useful tool for legal immigrants to *jalar* relatives from Peru. However, since the later acts of 1986, 1990, and 1996 tightened the regulations by changing the categories of family preferences and the time span for applying for reunification, many Peruvians began to look for other legal as well as illegal ways of entering the United States. One is to enter the country on a tourist visa and either overstay it or try to replace it with a student visa. Another way is to join the thousands of other Latin American "wetbacks" crossing the U.S.-Mexican border illegally.

In the past ten years a similar pattern can be observed in Spain, Italy, Argentina, and Chile, where Peruvian women such as Vanesa, the nieces of Lucy, and Casilda and her sisters, and in recent years men too, are engaged by middle- and upper-class families to take care of elderly relatives. Indeed, in southern Europe the recruitment of foreign labor to do domestic work has become so widespread that the governments of these countries issue a number of special work permits every year for Peruvians and other Latin Americans to take care of elderly people, whereas the governments of Argentina and Chile pursue a policy of "benign neglect," which creates many legal difficulties for migrant workers from neighboring countries in finding work, although their presence is unofficially tolerated to satisfy the need for cheap labor in the domestic service industry. Yet what few employers and even fewer government officials in southern Europe and the southern cone countries have anticipated is that within a few years these domestic workers become the spearhead of an extensive migration flow from the Third to the First Worlds or from countries in the South that are relatively less developed to other countries in the South that are relatively more developed.

A similar pattern of migration, though somewhat different in terms of gender, class, and ethnic relations, emerged between Peru and Japan in the same period. This population flow was triggered by the immigration law introduced by the Japanese government in 1990, which allowed the descendants of Japanese emigrants to find work in Japan temporarily in order to meet the growing need for factory workers in Japanese industry. Unlike Peruvian immigration to southern Europe and South America's southern cone countries, which are dominated by women from Peru's impoverished shantytowns, the majority of "guest workers" toiling on Japan's factory floors are working- and middle-class men from Peru's *nikkeijin* community. Moreover, in contrast to many female domestic workers in Spain, Italy, Argentina, and Chile, who either enter the receiving countries illegally or later become unauthorized immigrants, the majority of Peruvians in Japan are legal migrant workers.

Peruvian networks in the United States, Spain, Italy, Argentina, Chile, and Japan are constantly changing in organizational form and geographical course in order to adapt to shifting immigration policies in First World countries. Over the past fifty years, they have developed through the six phases briefly described above. The material presented in this chapter now allows us to discuss these at more length:

1. Traditionally, Andean men working as temporary workers on highland haciendas and in sugar and cotton plantations on the coast have played a dominant role in Peru's internal migrant networks. As rural-urban migration increased in the 1940s and 1950s, however, women from the country's

Andean communities began to participate in the exodus toward Peru's major cities in search of jobs as domestic workers for middle- and upper-class families. In effect, an extensive network of migrant relations today links Peru's rural hinterland to the country's urban centers (Paerregaard 1997; Lund 1994). Most of these networks have developed through the *jalar* mechanism. *Jalar* has wide implications for those who already have been pulled, because they are morally obliged to help other newcomers establish themselves in the new urban setting. As Elvira's and Sofía's networks show, many of the migrant communities formed by Peruvians in the past fifty years have developed through this pulling mechanism and as extensions of Peru's rural-urban networks across national borders.

2. Emigration in the 1950s and 1960s was primarily directed toward Miami and a few other cities in the United States. Women like Elvira, Sofía, and Ofelia, who already had employment in the domestic service industry in Lima and other cities, spearheaded the extension of migrant networks beyond national borders. Some of these women were brought by their American or Peruvian upper-class employers, while others were pulled by female relatives or fellow villagers employed as maids in the United States. Women were therefore the pioneers in this phase. Not only did they initiate the first migrant networks outside Peru's borders and enter the labor market in the United States, they also adapted the pulling mechanism to emigration practice and thus introduced an important tool to speed up the migrant flow from Peru to the United States in the next, third phase. While the art of *jalar* in rural-urban migration is limited to offering food and shelter to newcomers, the pulling of new migrants across national borders often implies huge economic expense and can easily become risky. To *jalar* relatives from Peru to the United States or Spain means lending money for traveling and/or becoming established in the new country, costs that can amount to as much as US$8,000. Furthermore, *jalar* often involves helping the newcomer to find work and obtain new identity papers, sometimes at the risk of jeopardizing one's own legal situation.

3. The growing participation of men in the reunification phase was partly triggered by Peru's rural-urban migration, which gathered momentum in the 1960s and 1970s, and the country's economic crisis, which reached its peak in the late 1980s. Yet, as Peruvians' primary source of income continued to be domestic work, and as U.S. immigration policy mainly granted family reunification for reasons of economic dependence, women's leading role in Peruvian networks remained unchanged. Hence, in this phase new migrants continued to be pulled by female relatives who were already in the United States through the family reunification program. Elvira's history clearly illustrates this. In other words, migration

networks, livelihood strategies, and gender relations were still intricately tied together in this phase.

4. Most of the newcomers in this period crossed the U.S.-Mexican border on land and joined the growing number of undocumented Latin Americans in the United States, as happened with Sofía's relatives. Because male migrants relied less on the support of female relatives already in the United States in this phase, the dominant position of women in Peruvian networks was now challenged. Their pioneer days were over. Moreover, as a growing number of male migrants succeeded in finding jobs in the service sector, the construction industry, and agriculture, women were no longer the only breadwinners in the networks. However, unlike many of their female relatives working as domestic servants, who had legal residence, male "wetbacks" arriving in this phase often spent years as undocumented immigrants struggling to obtain identity papers in the United States.

5. In the late 1980s and early 1990s, Peru was dogged by hyperinflation and political violence, which created consternation not only among the country's rural and urban poor, but also for the middle classes. This development led to Peruvian emigration reaching record heights at a time when U.S.-Mexican border control was becoming tighter. As a result, Peruvians began to look for new horizons, as illustrated by Sofía's network. One alternative migration destination that emerged in this period was Spain.[16] While immigrants were witnessing a tightening of U.S. immigration policy in this phase, southern European countries experienced increasing demand for cheap labor, particularly in agriculture, the service sector, and the domestic service industry. In effect, young women such as Lucy's nieces and Vanesa once again spearheaded Peruvian emigration by initiating new networks and carving out new niches in the national labor markets of Spain and Italy, this time as carers of elderly Spaniards and Italians. Thus Peruvian transatlantic networks in the 1990s were constituted by the same gender relations and propelled by the same livelihood strategies that prompted migration toward the United States in phases two, three, and four. At the same time Japan opened up its borders to Peru's *nikkeijin* community, who found work in Japanese industry in large numbers into the 1990s, as demonstrated by Alberto's family network. This also allowed a small group of Peruvians of non-Japanese descent to emigrate to Japan and find work as undocumented immigrants. Because of Japan's economic crisis in the late 1990s, the national industry was increasingly demanding female labor, which is paid less than male labor, thus permitting a growing number of Peruvian women to find work in Japan. Despite this development, the Japanese exodus continues to be a predominately male migration network.

6. As Casilda's network shows, migrations toward other Latin American countries in the middle and late 1990s developed partly because Peruvian emigrants found it increasingly difficult to enter the United States, southern Europe, and Japan, and partly because Argentina and Chile were offering a cheap and convenient alternative to the already established migration destinations. However, as is also evident from Casilda's case study, migration to Argentina and to some extent also Chile tends to be regarded as a temporary opportunity, exploited in order to save enough money to be able to travel to southern Europe at a later stage. A similar pattern can be observed among Peruvians in Japan, who often dream of migrating to the United States, where they have relatives, once they have saved enough capital to invest in an independent business.

MIGRANT NETWORKS AND POWER STRUCTURES

Researchers into contemporary global migration systems have recently proposed the term "transnationalism from below" in exploring the development of transnational networks by Third World migrants (Smith and Guarnizo 1998). They argue that transnationalism from "below" represents a global movement of Third World migrants, who establish economic and political links across nation states and thus cause a process of national deterritorialization (Basch 1994, Glick-Schiller, and Blanc-Szanton). Although the concept of transnationalism from below is useful in understanding the organizational complexity of female Peruvian networks, the transnational approach runs the danger of ignoring already ongoing migration processes sparked by rural-urban movements in migrants' home countries. As the material presented in this chapter suggests, transnational migration often develops as an extension of internal migration processes. Moreover, my data also indicate that the analytical separation of forces from "below" from those from "above" tends, first, to ignore the intricate relationships between migrant networks and the power structures that try to exploit and control them (for instance, as in the relationships between domestic workers and the middle- and upper-class families that hire them), and second, neglect the fact that migrants often contribute to the reproduction of these structural constraints through their own agency (like many of the networks initiated by domestic workers). This observation has also been made by Mahler, who suggests that "transnational migrants sometimes participate simultaneously in transnational activities that challenge as well as contribute to hegemonic processes," that is, transnationalism from above (1998: 72).

The difficulty in separating agency from structure in transnationalism is clearly evident in Peruvians' dealings with immigration authorities, travel agents, people-traffickers, employers, moneylenders, lawyers, and others. One female migrant, who migrated from Peru to New York in 1939 and moved to Miami in 1959 when the Hispanic community in south Florida was still very small, told me that the only Peruvians she met were a little group of Andean female domestic workers who had been brought there by their employers, who were also Peruvians. She also related that it was common practice for employers to keep the maids' passports, to prevent them from changing jobs, applying for permanent residence permits, or creating a life of their own in the United States. Though this practice is unusual among employers of Peruvians in Miami today, it highlights the extreme vulnerability of female migrants in the early phases of transnational migration. Similarly, many female migrants have little or no knowledge about their legal rights in the United States or are afraid that claiming such rights may upset their employers and thus jeopardize their job situations and ability to stay in the country. Indeed, the fact that some domestic servants work for many years without ever being given a labor contract makes them easy objects of economic exploitation. Elvira told me that several of her previous employers in Miami refused to pay their share of health insurance. Similarly, one of Sofía's female relatives told me that, after fifteen years of domestic service for an American family, she was fired without any notice or compensation being offered.

Most migrants who entered the United States as "wetbacks" claim that they were subject to some form of abuse while traveling illegally. Andrea, an Andean woman I interviewed in Miami, told me that when she entered the United States in 1989, it was actually her second trip. Her first attempt to migrate failed because the *coyote* she had paid to bring her to the U.S. border cheated her. Consequently, she was caught and returned to Peru. Andrea bitterly recalls how she had to borrow the money for the second trip from an agency in Lima that offers loans at exceptionally high rates of interest to Peruvians who want to migrate. Yet Andrea adds that she considers herself among the lucky ones, since nothing worse happened to her. Many "wetbacks" are robbed, raped, or simply disappear on their way through Central America and Mexico. Peruvians in Spain have had similar experiences. I have already described the frustrating experience of Nely, Vanesa's cousin in Barcelona, who first tried to migrate to Japan but was cheated. A later attempt to go to the United States also failed, and she eventually ended up in Spain. Like Vanesa's other cousin, Julia, Nely first flew to Germany, where a Peruvian people-trafficker picked her up and brought her to Spain. Both women remember the price they paid to this fellow countryman as being exorbitant.

Migrants' accounts of their often bitter experiences with power relations that they do not control suggest that we should be careful not to study these two forms of globalization, transnationalism from below and from above, as independent processes. Although migrant networks are an important means of pulling new members and thus forging transnational migration chains from the Third to the First Worlds, they are constantly being forced to reorganize, invent new strategies, and find new routes to adapt to shifting immigration policies. As Wilpert shows in her study of Turkish immigration to Germany (1992), the relationship between networks and power institutions is often extremely subtle. Moreover, we should not ignore the fact that the forces from "above" are often reproduced through the migrant's own agency. As Tilly points out, "networks brought into being by immigration serve to create and perpetuate inequality" (1990: 92). Thus, in order to pay back her debt in Lima, Andrea made use of the *jalar* mechanism and borrowed money from an aunt in Miami. In return, Andrea had to take a low-paid job as a domestic worker for a friend of her aunt's, a Cuban woman. It was only when the aunt died in 1992 and there was no one to collect the debt that Andrea could change her job and apply for residence and work permits (see chapter 7).

STRATEGIES AND TACTICS

I suggest that the study of transnational migration should take into consideration migrants' previous migration experiences and existing rural-urban networks. When crossing national borders and moving toward more remote and global destinations, these networks play a crucial role as an organizational tool in their struggle to overcome visa requirements and cover the financial costs involved in migration. I also argue that forces from "above" have crucial significance for their attempts to extend networks beyond national borders and create new livelihoods abroad. As demonstrated here, Peruvian women are frequently pulled abroad by the middle- or upper-class families for whom they work as domestic servants. Moreover, many of the networks initiated by these women have been stimulated by the demand for female domestic workers in the receiving societies. Thus the United States has long pursued a so-called back door policy that turns a blind eye to local employers' use of undocumented immigrants (Martin 1992: 85–86). Similarly, it was the need for cheap labor to take care of elderly Spaniards and Catalans that opened up the Spanish labor market for Peruvian female migrants in the early 1990s and caused the Spanish government to draw up a new policy permitting the entry annually of a limited number of legal migrants from Third World countries. Hence, migrant networks are often initiated in response to the demands for cheap labor in the First World; likewise, by operating as a *jalar* mechanism for newcomers, they contribute to the reproduction of the same mechanisms of exclusion that seek to contain their movements and exploit their labor power.

However, the ambiguity in the immigration and labor market policies of First World countries also provides migrant networks with room to maneuver in their search for loopholes in existing immigration policies and to exploit new niches in the labor market and thus develop their own migration and livelihood strategies. The processes through which the six networks developed across the six phases discussed in this chapter, in particular the passage from the fourth to the fifth phase, that is from the "wetback" to the transatlantic and transpacific phase, demonstrate this. Thus over time the struggle between networks and immigration policies often takes the form of a "cat and mouse" game that brings to the fore the power struggle between strategy and tactic described by de Certeau (1988: xix).[17] He contends that "the space of tactic is the space of the other. Thus it must play on and with a terrain imposed on it and organized by the law of a foreign power" (de Certeau 1988: 37) and adds that "the weak must continually turn to their own ends forces alien to them" (de Certeau 1988: xix). Rather than reducing migrant networks to mere "tactical weapons of the weak," which "turn to their own ends forces alien to them," as implied in de Certeau's notions of tactics and strategies, I suggest that they represent a migration practice that not only operates within the terrain of a single nation-state, but also exploits differences in the immigration policies and demands for cheap labor of different First World countries, thus contesting the geographical and political spaces controlled by the dominant power structures. The cat may be bigger and more powerful than the mouse, but the mouse often escapes the cate precisely because it is smaller—and smarter.

NOTES

1. People from Ayacucho, to which Chumbi, Elvira's home village, belongs, are so numerous that they have formed their own home region association. In Paterson, New Jersey, migrants from the village of Cocha, Ayacucho, have formed their own local home region association, while migrants in Miami have created an association that organizes Peruvians from the department of Ayacucho (Avila 2003).

2. There are, however, exceptions to this pattern. While women have spearheaded Peruvian migration to such places as Spain, Italy, Argentina, and Florida, Peruvian men have acted as pioneers in the formation of migrant networks in Paterson, New Jersey, and Japan. Men have also played a key role in the formation of Peruvian migrant communities in California.

3. Recently, migrant networks have been the topic of renewed interest by migration scholars studying globalization and transnationalism. Rouse, who studies Mexican migrants in the United States, prefers to use the term "circuit" in preference to "network," "because it more effectively evokes the *circulation* of people, money, goods, and in-

formation, the pseudo-institutional nature of the arrangement (over purely individual ties) and the qualified importance of place (over purely social linkages)" (1991: 20). In a similar vein, Kearney (who also studies Mexican migration into the United States) argues that, "transnational networks contrast with the usual meaning of social networks in network theory, which emphasizes links between persons as opposed to the idea that people move—migrate" (1996: 124). He concludes that, "the social morphology of networks is like an amoeba, a creature with complex internal differentiation but without distinct cells and organs, that correspond to the social components of corporate communities" (Kearney 1996: 125).

4. Gurak and Caces also state that migrant networks "need not be highly institutionalized but can be a set of relationships that revolve around some organizing principle" (1992: 152).

5. The first male member of Elvira's migrant network was Raúl, her brother, who arrived in 1961 through family reunification. At the time of his migration, Raúl had two children out of wedlock, Norma and Amparo, whom he left behind together with their mother. Elvira recalls that, despite several attempts, Raúl never succeeded to *jalar* his two daughters before he died in 1980.

6. This group also included the two daughters of Raúl, who failed to make it to the United States before their father died. In 1986 Norma traveled to Miami to visit her aunts on a tourist visa, while Amparo acquired temporary residence in 1989, after Erminia had found an American family looking for a domestic worker. While Amparo soon became a permanent resident, Norma spent several years illegally in the United States after her tourist visa expired. With the help of a lawyer, however, she got a green card in the early 1990s, which allowed her to *jalar* her husband, also from Chumbi, through family reunification.

7. Victoria and Cirifredo both became residents after a couple of years, which allowed them to *jalar* their two children, Rosa and Miguel.

8. David claims that he was born out of wedlock and that his father never acknowledged paternity of him. Hence he does not feel like a real member of Sofía's family, and rather than making use of his sister's offer to *jalar* him through the family reunification program, he wished to make it to the United States on his own.

9. The first to migrate was Maritza, a remote cousin of Sofía's, who traveled on a tourist visa. She soon found a job as a domestic worker and began to save money to *jalar* more relatives from Peru. Wilfredo and Luís, on the other hand, crossed the U.S.-Mexican border with *coyote* assistance. While Wilfredo, a brother of Sofía's, borrowed money to cover the travel expenses from Rosario, Luís received support from his sister Maritza. In 1986 an aunt of Sofía's, Manuela, also left for the United States on a tourist visa. Simultaneously, her husband Justo, who was turned down when he applied for a tourist visa, entered the United States through Mexico. Later Manuela returned to Lima, while Justo, who is now a U.S. citizen, lives in Miami, where he makes a living cleaning tables in a mall. Justo explains that he is looking forward to returning to Lima when he retires in a few years' time.

10. The three who made the trip directly by air were the parents of María and one of Manuela's and Justo's three children, who all came through the family reunification program. Among the newcomers in this period were the last two children of

Manuela and Justo, the parents and remaining brothers of Sara, another sister of Sofía's, the last of María's brothers, an aunt of Sofía's together with her daughter and newborn baby, and the husbands of Suzana and Sara and Armando's three children, who came in 1984.

11. Máximo, who comes from Huaral on the Peruvian coast and is a Peruvian of Japanese descent, already had a brother living in Washington, D.C. The brother, an engineer, was brought to the United States in 1948 by the American company he was working for in Peru.

12. Like Benedicta, Joaquina pulled her Peruvian fiancé to the United States. The couple later married and settled in Washington, D.C., where their two boys were born. Both children are U.S. citizens and were doing their military service in Germany at the time of writing.

13. Narcizo first migrated to Venezuela, where he spent several years working in a factory. He later traveled to the United States on a tourist visa, which he overstayed. Narcizo relates that he was still an undocumented immigrant when he met Sixta. The marriage allowed him to apply for a residence visa in the United States, which he obtained the following year. The couple live in Miami and have no children.

14. During the same period, Francisco, Flavio, Angel, and Bravio brought fourteen of the nineteen children of the three sisters who had died in Rivacayo to Lima, where they attended school. Eventually Benedicta, now an American citizen, managed to pull one of the nieces to Washington, D.C., in 1988. The niece was joined by Francisco, who came to Miami together with his wife and their three children in 1991. They were all granted green cards through the family reunification program.

15. To my surprise, however, when I revisited Milan in 2006 I met Amanda again. In 2002 she had moved from Argentina to Italy with her husband.

16. As already pointed out, Japan also emerged as an attractive alternative to the traditional U.S. migration route in this period. However, as Japan only granted work permits to foreigners of Japanese descent, the transpacific route is limited to an exclusive group of Peruvians.

17. De Certeau argues that while tactics are the outcome of actions that lack a place, strategies represent the relations of power that emerge when an institution that possesses power is isolated from the surrounding world and thus controls a particular space that forms the basis of its operation (1988: 34).

Chapter Five

Tying the Untied

In the previous chapter, I explored the networks that Peruvians create to pull newcomers to the receiving countries. I also investigated the dialectic relationship between these networks and changing immigration policies in the First World. In this and the following chapter I scrutinize the flows of interchange and communication that evolve between migrants and migrant institutions in the United States, southern Europe, Japan, and Argentina and their country and regions of origin, and examine ethnographically the processes of negotiation and contestation but also identification that these forms of interaction generate. Whereas chapter 6 focuses on the global spread of Peruvian religious icons, the present chapter discusses, on the one hand, how migrants construct ties with Peru, and on the other, how migrants in one place create bonds, economically, politically, and socially, with migrants elsewhere.

In this chapter, I argue that hegemony is inextricably bound up with contestation in transnational engagement and that relations of resistance and domination are often intertwined in migrants' networks and institutional practices. Indeed, these sometimes contribute to the reproduction of the relations of exclusion that prevent from exercising their rights in Peru (where they take the form of an inclusive exclusion) and deny them the same legal rights as the native population in the receiving countries (where they take the form of an exclusive inclusion) through their movements and activities. Rather than conceptually distinguishing transnationalism from above from transnationalism from below as common in the study of processes of contemporary migration, I therefore propose that we study ethnographically how relations of dominance and resistance are embedded and articulated in migrants' daily lives. To do this I draw on the concept of the network (Menjívar 2000), which I find particular useful in exploring the entanglement of relations of reciprocity and

115

exploitation in migrants' struggles to achieve physical and social mobility. More specifically, I suggest that we distinguish between two sets of networks:

1. *transnational links*, by which I refer to bilateral relations of the exchange of things and ideas between migrants in specific locations outside Peru and their relatives or home communities in Peruvian locations.
2. *diasporic bonds*, which are the multi-stranded ties that migrants in different cities and countries establish across social and political boundaries and that foster new relations of identity and feelings of belonging.

   In the rest of this chapter, I explore how Peruvians develop the two sets of networks and discuss the power relations in which they are embedded. By scrutinizing ethnographically how migrants engage in particular events, movements, situations, and institutions, I hope to bring to the fore the processes of domination and exploitation, but also of negotiation and contestation, that shape their networks. More specifically, I present five case studies that in different ways illustrate the tensions as well as potentials of migrants' networks and institutions, as well as eliciting the shifting contexts and circumstances in their lives that define their relationships to other migrants and position within the networks on which they rely. The case studies are organized in subchapters defined by the type of activity and kind of network that migrants engage in and several of them take the form of extended case studies in the Manchester School's meaning of the term, which has helped me to bring to the fore the mechanisms of inclusion and exclusion that unite as well as divide migrants in the United States, Spain, Japan, and Argentina.[1] In the first study I examine the social and political conflicts caused by the labor migration of Peruvian shepherds in the western United States. The second study scrutinizes the economic and political implications of the moral obligation that urge migrants to collect aid for their fellow countrymen in Peru and organize public campaigns to improve their image as an immigrant community in the host society. The social and ethnic divides that migrants reproduce when creating institutions outside Peru is the object of investigation in the third study. Unlike the two first studies, which both seek to demonstrate how political conflicts and charitable activities evolve within transnational networks, this case explores the importance of diasporic bonds for migrant institutional activities. The fourth case study discusses the transnational ties as well as diasporic bonds that migrants draw on to develop trade relationships with both the country of origin and migrant communities in other parts of the world. Finally, the fifth case study examines how individual migrants use narrow but long-term transnational links to create new social identities and to contest the meanings of existing power relations in Peruvian society.

REVOLTING AND SUBMITTING

Since the late 1960s more than 3,000 Peruvians from the villages of Peru's central highlands have migrated on H-2A visas to work as sheep shepherds for American ranchers in the western United States on three-year contracts facilitated by an organization called Western Ranch Association (WRA). Many of them return to work on a second, third, and some even up to eight contracts thus working for many years in remote areas of the United States far away from their families in Peru (Paerregaard 2005b). Although the salaries are low compared to what American citizens earn, the shepherds think that the contracts make up an attractive opportunity to maintain their families in the home communities and save money to invest when they eventually return to Peru. In recent years this migration practice has been the bone of contention in a political conflict that broke out within the Peruvian community in California, where some of the shepherds work, and that later spread to Peru, where the public media and members of the Peruvian Congress engaged in a heated debate concerning the human rights of the country's emigrant population. The heart of the conflict was the exploitation and ill treatment of Peruvian shepherds by the North American ranch owners, a key person in the scandal being an ex-herder named Victor.

In 1991 Victor traveled on a three-year contract to herd sheep on a ranch in California. Unlike many of his fellow migrants he passed most of the contract on the ranch thus avoiding the hard life in the desert and the mountains. However, his experience with his Basque employer was very traumatic and changed his views about labor migration to the United States. On the ranch Victor had the opportunity to observe how employers exploit shepherds' search for loyalty and trust to make them accept working and living conditions that would normally be considered dangerous and degrading. He even saw cases of ranchers and foremen committing outrages against shepherds. When I met Victor in 1998 in Bakersfield he told me that these experiences made him realize that the shepherds must take responsibility for their own lives and limit their dependence on U.S. migration as a source of income. Hence, instead of returning to Peru when his first contract expired in 1994, Victor overstayed his H-2A visa and settled down in Bakersfield, not far from the ranch where he had been working. Here he came across a number of shepherds who were waiting for the WRA to transfer them to new ranch owners. While some came from other ranches, others were newcomers who had just arrived from Peru. He also met several shepherds who had been hospitalized because of accidents at work or diseases they had caught while working. Whereas some were on their way back to the ranches, others were about to be returned to Peru. Moreover, Victor discovered that he was not the only migrant who had decided to drop out of the labor migration chain. Indeed, in the early 1990s Bakersfield had become the center for the growing number of Peruvian shepherds in California who overstay their H-2A visa and settle in the United States as unauthorized immigrants. They now make up a community of more than a hundred Peruvians, who come together every Sunday to play soccer and drink beer. Some of them, including Victor, have married local women of Hispanic background and become legal residents. Others have applied for political asylum or spent years as unauthorized immigrants looking for work in the service sector or as factory workers.

In response to the shepherds' many neglected needs, Victor decided to create an organization to defend the rights of his countrymen in the United States. Together with thirteen other shepherds and former shepherds living in Bakersfield, he formed a trade union for shepherds called Unión de Pastores Ovejeros in 1995. The union was set up to defend the rights of the shepherds and to disseminate information about their situation in the United States and Peru, and it is affiliated with the United Farm Workers of America or AFL-CIO. Although the shepherds launched their struggle with few economic means and little experience, they have been able to put their conditions on the agenda of the leaders of the Peruvian immigrant community in Los Angeles and of politicians in Peru. They have also had success in supporting shepherds who make complaints to the WRA for not complying with the obligations of the work contract. Several former shepherds who were injured because of accidents on the ranch or fell ill in the desert or in the mountains have sued the organization with the assistance of the union. Thus one shepherd, who damaged an arm while managing a vehicle without the required authorization, filed a lawsuit against the insurance company because it refused to pay his medical bills. The man, who fully recovered from the accident, won the suit and received more than US$50,000 in compensation. To the regret of Victor and other leaders of the union, however, he never acknowledged the support they offered him. Today the man owns a gardening company in Bakersfield, using cheap Peruvian and Mexican labor.

The union came to public attention in Los Angeles in the year it was formed because a Peruvian newspaper, Perú en los 90, started publishing a series of articles about the shepherds' situation. The news caused an intense discussion within the Peruvian community in California about solidarity among fellow migrants and the moral and legal rights of immigrants in the United States. The scandal increased further when Perú en los 90 reported that the Peruvian consul in Los Angeles had previously ignored the shepherds' complaints. The consul was later dismissed. The news also reached Peru, where one of the country's major dailies, *La República*, and a weekly magazine in Lima, *Caretas*, reported cases of missing and badly treated Peruvian shepherds in the United States. In addition, a television channel in Lima, Canal 4, produced a documentary on the use of Peruvian labor on sheep ranches in California. The reporters interviewed a Basque ranch owner and exposed the sanitary conditions in which his Peruvian employees were living. The documentary sparked yet another scandal among politicians in Lima, where the president of Congress, Martha Chávez, referred to the shepherds' situation in a heated debate about human rights in Peru. Similar reports on Spanish-language television channels in the United States caused moral indignation among Hispanic minority groups, and in 1996 the Peruvian ambassador paid a personal visit together with officials from the U.S. labor department to several ranches using Peruvian labor.

The debate over the economic exploitation and human rights abuses of Peruvian shepherds in the United States created by the shepherds' union in Bakersfield, and Victor's accusations against the WRA, reflects the economic and social complexity of global migration networks. Once the Peruvian community in Los Angeles, the media in Peru and the United States, and politicians in Lima became involved in the controversy, the shepherds' situation became the concern of economic, ethical, and political interests of very different kinds. Whereas the Peruvian consul in Los Angeles was replaced, the editor of *Perú en los 90* won an award for the paper's coverage of the conflict. Meanwhile, Martha Chávez accused the American government of double standards because, on the one hand, it criticized the human rights politics of the Fujimori government, while on the other turning a blind eye to American ranchers' abuses of Peruvian shepherds. Conversely, the political opposition in Peru traced the situation back to the failure of the Peruvian government to solve the country's economic problems.

In this myriad of global and local perspectives, Victor was not the only former shepherd to articulate the interests of the shepherds in public. When Teodocio returned from the United States in 1989, he made friends with the Peruvian engineer in charge of recruiting shepherds in Lima, occasionally offering him his advice and support in the selection of new candidates. As the WRA and the engineer came under increasing attack in the late 1990s, Teodocio and a group of former shepherds in Huancayo became worried that the Peruvian government would eventually close down the entire migration program and thus encourage American ranchers to recruit shepherds in other countries. They therefore formed the Asociación de ex-trabajadores de la Western Ranch Association (Association of ex-workers of the WRA) to speak in defense of the WRA and the engineer. These former shepherds claim that shepherding in the United States represents a unique opportunity for young men in Peru who are seeking alternative sources of income, and that it is in the shepherds' own interest for the migration program to continue. In 1997 Teodocio was invited to present his views to the committee for human rights set up by the Peruvian Congress. He also participated in a meeting in Lima, at which Victor and representatives of the Peruvian government were invited to exchange views.

The outcome of the dispute was an informal agreement between the WRA and the Peruvian government to respect the shepherds' rights. To Victor's regret but to Teodocio's satisfaction, the program was allowed to continue with few changes. Within a short time public and political interest in the shepherds' situation faded, while the number of shepherds traveling to the United States continued to increase. Although Victor had been successful in calling the public's attention to the situation, he failed to mobilize the support of shepherds in the United States or Peru; by the same token, although many agree that the working and living conditions on the ranches are deplorable, they also share Teodocio's concern that the controversy was jeopardizing their future ability to work on labor contracts in the United States, save up some capital, and create an alternative source of income. The dispute, then, not only exposed the predicaments inherent in Victor's strategy of organizing the shepherds and fighting the WRA and sheepherding industry in the United States through the public media and with the help of Peruvian politicians, but also demonstrated the complexity of the economic, social, and political interests involved in global migration.

Peruvian labor migration to California and other states was initiated by the WRA and American ranchers looking for cheap labor at a time of land reform and social change in Peru. For almost a quarter of a century, the WRA's migration program and the shepherds' networks remained detached from other Peruvian migration networks and immigrant communities in urban metropolis such as Los Angeles and San Francisco. However, when shepherds' working and living conditions became the center of attention for the Peruvian community in California, the public media in Lima, and the Fujimori government, the shepherds' labor migration was suddenly linked to larger processes of globalization and localization in the United States and Peru. Although this linkage initially caused a heated controversy about the economic and human rights of low-paid Third World workers, U.S. labor migration in this context has changed little and continues to be controlled by the WRA and a small group of family and household networks in Peru. Yet what may have crucial bearings for this form of migration in the future is the growing number of shepherds who either quit the work contract or overstay their H-2A visa, and thus become unauthorized migrants and over time join the already existing Peruvian communities in the United States (see chapter 8). As the dropout rate increases, the ranch owners, the WRA, and U.S. immigration officials may simply decide to do what many shepherds fear most: close the program and start importing labor from other countries.

PROVIDING AND INTERFERING

To most migrants, periodical remittances to their close kin is a critical way of demonstrating their continuous commitment to those they left behind and thus a claim to be part of the household and family back home (Altamirano 2006; Hondagneu-Sotelo 2001; Alicea 1997; Tamagno 2003a; Levitt 2001). In fact, remittance agencies crop up wherever Peruvians travel and settle, offering an important resource for entrepreneurs within the migrant communities to create new livelihoods. Many Peruvians also feel obliged to contribute to the material wealth of their fellow countrymen in times of scarcity and crisis, which results in organized attempts to make collections of financial and material help to the Peruvian government or to public or private institutions in Peru.

In 1993 an institution called the Congreso Peruano Americano (CPA) was formed by a group of Peruvians in Paterson, New Jersey, to express their support for former president Fujimori and their approval of his famous *autogolpe*, which had led to the closing of the Peruvian Congress the year before.[2] The first event organized by the institution was a campaign to aid the victims of the earthquake that hit Ica, south of Lima, in 1993. On a single day the CPA collected more than US$25,000, which was handed over to Peru's Civil Defense through the Peruvian consulate in Paterson.[3] However, when the consulate asked the CPA to help collect money for the Peruvian army during the brief war between Peru and Ecuador in 1995, the leaders of the organization declined to cooperate.[4] Instead they suggested an alternative plan to raise a subscription to help the families of the soldiers who had fought in the war and to support the local villagers in the war zone.[5] The CPA subsequently developed into an independent institution, whose aim is to encourage Peruvians in Paterson to participate in local and state government. It also counsels individual migrants who need legal help and organizes an annual event at the end of the school semester to reward the children of Peruvian immigrants who have graduated from colleges in different parts of New Jersey.[6]

In February 1998 el Niño hit Peru and caused huge loss of life and great material damage. The country's main road, which connects Peru's northern and the southern coasts, was blocked, leaving thousands of people whose homes and fields had been flooded outside the reach of emergency assistance. The el Niño disaster also jeopardized the government's policy to spark economic growth and created uncertainty as to whether the recent recovery in the country's economy would last or once again lead to recession. The news about el Niño and the pictures of its devastating effect rapidly reached Peru's emigrant population around the world and stirred many migrants. Individual migrants reacted spontaneously by encouraging friends and neighbors to join them in their efforts to help their fellow countrymen in Peru, and within a short time Peruvian migrant associations throughout the United States were following their example.

In Miami a number of Peruvian migrant associations organized a collection of clothes, food, medicines, tools, and money, which was later sent to Peru by Aeroperú (at that time the country's national carrier) and several private Peruvian freight companies. The collection was announced in local Peruvian newspapers that circulate in Miami and on flyers posted in the city's many Peruvian restaurants and shops. Representatives not just of different Peruvian associations but also from the Peruvian consulate in Miami were present at an event that took place between February 14 and 15, 1998, on Plaza Perú in Kendall, western Miami, to which several celebrities were invited, among others a famous female Peruvian model who offered her signature to those participating in the event. According to one local Peruvian newspaper, more than twenty tons of clothes and other items were collected over the two days the event lasted. Other newspapers called the event a success because it brought together in a common cause a broad variety of Peruvian associations and institutions in Miami which otherwise act on their own and pursue different agendas.[7] Similarly, many participants in the event expressed their satisfaction with the fact that Peruvians in Miami had managed to arrange a collection of such dimensions in collaboration with the Peruvian consulate.

Migrants in other parts of the United States also expressed a desire to send aid to the victims of el Niño disaster, and on March 22, 1998, the AIPEUC,[8] an umbrella organization embracing all Peruvian associations in the United States and Canada, arranged a so-called *telemaratón* (telemarathon), a nationwide collection organized locally by AIPEUC chapters in North America (Los Angeles, San Francisco, Miami, New York, Chicago, and Montreal).[9] In Los Angeles the president of the local chapter of AIPEUC, which represents one of the largest Peruvian communities in the United States, invited a variety of Peruvian artists, musicians, and dancing groups to entertain them in a rented banqueting hall in Hollywood. In addition to the mandatory entrance fee of twenty dollars, the participants were encouraged to make voluntary contributions. The majority discreetly dropped a ten- or twenty-dollar bill in the boxes which the organizers used to collect money, but a few participants were invited up on the stage to hand over their contribution in public. These were all successful businessmen and professionals and known members of the Peruvian community in Los Angeles, who donated up to a thousand dollars. Simultaneously, other collections were arranged by independent Peruvian associations in the Los Angeles area, such as the Arequipa Club in Orange County. In order to stimulate competition between Peruvian communities across North America, the leaders of the AIPEUC constantly

A. The Peruvian consul in Miami with representatives from Peruvian organizations in this city hoisting the American and Peruvian flags at what used to be called Plaza de Peru in Miami's Kendell district. Cover photo by the author.

B. Peruvians participating in a Corta Monte party in Miami. The Corta Monte is an Andean custom in which the participants compete to cut a tree planted by the winner of the previous year.

C. Peruvians celebrating the Lord of the Miracles in downtown Buenos Aires, Argentina.

D. The author with the image of El Cristo Chinito in Kakegawa, Japan.

E. Peruvian gathering in Los Angeles to collect funding for the victims of the Niño disaster that hit Peru in 1998.

F. Peruvians gathered on a Sunday in a public park in Milano, Italy.

G. Peruvian artist Nicario Jimenez showing one of his retablas in Miami. The retabla is an illustration of the subway of New York City.

kept the organizers and participants of the many subscriptions updated of the results in other parts of the country, thus creating a sense of simultaneity and shared commitment among Peruvians in North America. The outcome of the many contributions was later communicated to Peruvians in different parts of the United States and Canada through local newspapers.[10]

Migrants' sense of co-responsibility is not merely directed toward their fellow countrymen, but also to Peruvians living outside Peru. Periodically, this concern triggers debates and campaigns within migrant communities to demonstrate solidarity with Peruvians who are suffering from social injustice and discrimination in the host society or who have otherwise fallen victims of misfortune. In Miami in January 1998 a group of Peruvians formed a committee to support fellow countrymen who were struggling to regularize their illegal status in the United States.[11] The founders of this committee were the editor of one of Miami's Peruvian newspapers (El Chasqui) and the leader of an organization called the Peruvian American Coalition, which, inspired by the success of the Cuban community in Florida, urged Peruvians in the United States to use their right to vote to elect a fellow countryman to Congress.[12] The committee's political message was that legal immigrants have a moral obligation to help immigrants without documents because illegality is a universal condition that may affect the life of all immigrants. By the same token, some of the organizers who used local immigrant newspapers in Spanish to communicate their message claimed that this sense of solidarity should transcend national identities and include immigrants from all Latin American countries.[13] So far, however, these attempts to create horizontal ties across social classes and national groups and to induce the formation of a national identity among Peruvian immigrants in different parts of North America have stimulated only a limited response.

In other parts of the world, similar movements have been formed to create a collective consciousness of a separate demographic unit and to mobilize Peruvian migrants for political purposes. In Argentina a movement called Movimiento de Peruanos en el Exterior (Movement of Peruvians Abroad) was established in 1999 in collaboration with other emigrant communities in the United States and Canada with the aim of promoting a migrant at the elections to the Peruvian Congress in 2001.[14] The movement's political message was that because migrants contribute to Peru's economy through the remittances they send to their relatives back home, the Peruvian government has a moral obligation to support their struggle against the discrimination and marginalization they suffer as immigrants in their new countries of residence.[15] The implication of this position is that emigrants think of themselves as a socially and politically homogenous group, regardless of where they live or who they are. Other Peruvian organizations in Argentina are also concerned with the welfare of their fellow countrymen, though for very different reasons. In the 1950s and 1960s, hundreds of young Peruvian males went to Argentina to study. Many returned to Peru, but others stayed and either married Argentinean women or brought their wives from Peru and settled in Argentina. Some of these women, who today are well established in and integrated into Argentinean society, have formed an institution called the Asociación de Damas Peruanas, whose aim is to do charity work to help newly arrived Peruvians.

Unlike the United States and Argentina, Japan has only recently opened its borders to immigration. Thus the Peruvians who started to arrive on a large scale in 1990 are still struggling to create migrant institutions and form an organized immigrant community. Moreover, because Japan's immigration policy only grants residence and work permits to Latin Americans of Japanese descent, the Peruvian community has for a number of years been divided into two groups, according to migrants' ethnic origin: on the one hand, Peruvians of Japanese descent who enjoy the legal right to work in Japan for periods of one to three years; on the other, Peruvians of non-Japanese descent, who either are married to Japanese Peruvians or are living in Japan on fake identity papers or as unauthorized immigrants (Takenaka 1999). Because Peruvians have been slow to form their own institutions, the Peruvian consulate in Tokyo has played a central role in mobilizing them in Japan. In 1999 the Peruvian consulate in Tokyo, in cooperation with several migrant leaders, launched a campaign called the Campaña de Seguridad Ciudadana y Convivencia to improve the image that many Japanese have of Peruvians and other Latin American immigrants as potential criminals.[16] The target group of the campaign, which was publicized in Spanish-language newspapers, was the Peruvian community in general, which the Consulate urged to respect Japanese law and stay away from crime. However, rather than uniting Peruvians by claiming a right to be heard in the host society (as in the United States) or gaining influence in Peruvian politics (as in Argentina) and thus furthering (unauthorized as well as legal) migrants' integration into Japan and improving their image in Japanese society, the campaign tended to divide the Peruvian community by turning one group of migrants, those without legal status, against another, those with it.

DIVIDING AND UNITING

The social order that emerges from Peruvian emigration reproduces the power relations and cultural and ethnic identities that divide Peruvian society into economic and social classes (Walker 1988). This is evident from the many voluntary organizations and associations that Peruvians create in their new countries of residence. Some of these institutions arrange soccer tournaments, dances and music shows, and other social and cultural events, and are open to all Peruvians. In places such as Paterson, male migrants have formed not one but two soccer leagues, one called the Premier League and a second for senior migrants called the Peruvian Veteran League, which is exclusive to the participation of Peruvian teams.[17] In Los Angeles Peruvians have also formed numerous soccer teams, but because they live scattered all over the city, migrants participate in many different leagues in which teams from different Hispanic communities compete.[18] In places such as Madrid, Peruvians meet every Sunday to play against Bolivians, Ecuadorians, Colombians, and other South Americans at La Chopera in the Parque de Retiro, which in recent years has become a popular rendezvous for Third World immigrants, while in Barcelona Peruvians play in different parts of the city against not only other Latin Americans but also Moroccan immigrants. In Buenos Aires an organization called ADPEBA (Asociación Deportiva Peruana en Buenos Aires) arranges weekly tournaments for Peruvian (and other immigrant) soccer teams on piece of land called Club Penalti, while in Japan Peruvians participate in soccer leagues on the river banks on the outskirts of the cities where they live (e.g., Mooka north of Tokyo), together with immigrants not merely from Brazil but also Bangladesh and other Asian countries.

Although soccer is the most popular leisure activity by far, other sorts of cultural events also attract the attention of Peruvian migrants. In Pasadena, Los Angeles, a small group of migrants has created an institution called the Centro Cultural Peruano, which organizes folklore presentations of Peruvian costumes and dances. In 1985 migrants from the Andean highlands living in Miami created a club called El Sol, which arranges folklore presentations of traditional Inca rituals, such as the Inti Raymi fiesta in Cuzco. According to Raúl, one of the club's founders, the organizers had no previous knowledge of the rituals and either had to produce all the costumes themselves or import them from Peru. He explains that "El Sol was the first Peruvian institution in Miami for people like us. There were other institutions for people with money, you know, Club Florida and Club Miami. The first year we were members of the AIPEUC, but it was too expensive and we didn't get anything out of it." Apart from cultural activities, the institution offers help to newly arrived migrants and raises money to support people in need in Peru. Raúl says, "The money we raise we send to the street children in Lima or the victims of the civil war in Peru. This year we sent money to the school in the village of some of our members."

Migrants from Peru's urban middle classes also create institutions seeking to revitalize Andean and mestizo cultural traditions. In 1991 Peruvians in Miami formed an organization called the Centro Peruano de Cultura y Historia, which puts on exhibitions and promotes Peruvian art and culture. Raúl, the head of the organization, comes from Lima, where he was educated at one of the city's best-known private schools. He left Peru at the age of twenty in 1971 together with his family in response to the economic and political reforms introduced by the Velasco government. After a couple of years in New York, he went to Spain and then to Argentina to study journalism. He says, "Wherever I go I struggle to promote Peruvian culture. In Argentina I was one of the founders of the first brotherhood of the Lord of the Miracles. I feel very proud of being Peruvian. Think of the Incas and what they did. Here in Miami we arrange exhibitions and show photos and videos from Peru together with the consulate and other institutions." Another organization, called Imagen Peruana, arranges shows in which migrants perform Peruvian dances and wear traditional Peruvian costumes. Similar organizations are found in Spain and Argentina.

Other migrant institutions recruit their members according to either regional origin or class and are therefore more exclusive. Regional associations mainly attract migrants who identify themselves in ethnic terms, this being closely linked to the fact that in Peruvian politics and popular discourse geographical identity is conflated with indigenous culture. They can be divided into two kinds: associations based on migrants' attachment to their native villages, or those linked to their home province or department. Although both kinds of organization are based on regional origin and mainly recruit their members from the Andean highlands, they differ in the ways in which they are organized. Village-based associations are above all committed to migrants' places of origin, and they often engage in intense relations of economic and social exchange with their fellow villagers in Peru. Organizations based on migrants' attachment to their home departments or provinces, on the other hand, tend to attract a more heterogeneous group of migrants with urban as well as rural backgrounds and rarely develop stable ties with migrants' places of origin.[19]

In Miami a broad selection of regional associations exist to organize migrants from the different parts of the Andean highland. Some recruit migrants who come from the same village or district, others migrants from the same province, and yet others those from the same department.[20] While the activities of the two latter forms of organization are mainly aimed at preserving Peruvian cultural traditions, the former often serve as a critical tool for migrants to create intimate and enduring relationships with their villages of origin. Thus migrants from a village called Pichus, close to the city of Jauja in Peru's central highlands, habitually collect funds in support of the elected authorities of their home community to construct schools and other public buildings. They also travel to Peru to participate in the annual celebrations in honor of the village's patron saint. Similarly, Peruvians from the village of Chumbi in Ayacucho living in Miami have created two associations. One is called La Asociación de Voto Virgen del Carmen, which is responsible for the annual celebration of the village's patron saint in Miami. Another, called Comité de Damas de Chumbi, collects money for their home village and helps organize the fiesta in honor of the Virgen del Carmen. In other U.S. cities regional associations are less prominent. In Orange County, Los Angeles, migrants originating from the department of Arequipa have created an institution called Club Arequipa International, which arranges cultural events and sells Peruvian food every Saturday in a rented building. Other associations based on regional commitment to the department of Junín and Ancash also exist. The latter organizes folklore demonstrations, sells Andean food, and produces pamphlets that promote the culture of Ancash (*la cultura ancashina*). Finally, in Paterson a group of fifteen migrants from the village of Cocha in the department of Ayacucho have formed a village association with the aim of helping their fellow villagers in Peru in their struggle to achieve recognition as a district from the local provincial authorities (Avila 2003).

In southern Europe, Argentina, Chile, and Japan, migrants have mainly formed regional associations based on their villages and districts of origin. In recent years, migrants from the Andean highlands living in Barcelona have made attempts to create non-governmental organizations (NGOs) to seek funding from the local Catalan authorities and different private institutions in order to support the development of their home villages and communities. In 2001 Peruvians from the community of Sarhua in Ayacucho formed an NGO and raised money to invite a group of schoolchildren from their home village to visit Barcelona. The same year a group of migrants from the district of Mendoza in the Amazonas department raised money from public and private funds in Barcelona to support an agricultural project in their home community to improve the environment of the area. However, both attempts failed because of a lack of support from the leaders of the migrants' home communities in Peru.

Peruvian associations in Japan are exceptional in so far as these recruit their members mainly according to ethnic affiliation, regional commitment being of minor importance for the organization of migrants. The most influential institution, called El Convenio de Cooperación Kyodai (brother/sister in Japanese), is a transpacific organization with offices in both Tokyo and Lima, which recruits its members from the Peruvian *nikkeijin* community in Japan.[21] Up to 1999, when the Japanese police raided its main office in Tokyo and forbade unauthorized money transfers outside the country, Kyodai was the principal means for Peruvians in Japan to remit money to relatives in Peru. The organization offers other communication services between Peruvians in Japan and Peru, runs a shop that sells Peruvian products, and publishes a monthly magazine in Spanish.

Other Peruvian associations also exist in Japan, but these rarely last very long because migrants are constantly moving from place to place to find work. In some places, however, Peruvians have managed to create stable associations. Thus in Aichicaga, a city northwest of Tokyo that is home to approximately four hundred Peruvians migrants, an institution has been set up called Asociación Perú Aichicaga. Up to the mid-1990s the Peruvian community in this city was much larger, but when the local Sony plant closed down because of Japan's ailing economy and financial crisis, many migrant workers were laid off and forced to seek work elsewhere. Despite these difficulties, a core of migrants remained who continue to assist the activities of the association.

By contrast, institutions that are class based normally recruit their members from Peru's urban middle or upper classes of mostly mestizo or European descent from Lima and other major cities in Peru. These institutions are of different kinds, but are usually private clubs, professional organizations, chambers of commerce, or charity organizations. They exist in places with more established Peruvian communities, such as New York, Miami, Los Angeles, Barcelona, Buenos Aires, and Santiago, which have been destinations for Peruvian emigration for almost half a decade. Thus during the 1950s and 1960s hundreds of young men from Peru's middle- and upper-class families traveled to Spain and Argentina to study medicine, law, agriculture, and so forth at universities in the two countries. Many later decided to stay and married local women, obtained good jobs as lawyers, medical doctors, or veterinary surgeons, and became part of Spanish and Argentinean society. However, most of them maintained their Peruvian identity by forming associations. During the late 1980s and early 1990s Spain and Argentina received a new wave of Peruvians, headed by a large number of working-class migrants from Peru's urban shantytowns who were emigrating at a time of economic and political crisis. Today many of these newly arrived migrants live on the margins of the host society, forming an emergent proletariat of immigrant workers in Spain and Argentina. Hence their migration and livelihood experiences are radically different from those of their predecessors, which periodically cause strife within Peru's immigrant communities in these countries. Thus migrants who came in the 1950s and 1960s are referred to as *profesionales* (professionals) and as *sobrados* (arrogant). Conversely, many old-timers deplore the recent immigration because it has altered the former more favorable image of Peruvians in Spain and Argentina.

In Barcelona migrants formed the first Peruvian association, called Centro Peruano, as early as 1963.[22] The institution is still directed by migrants who arrived in the late 1950s and early 1960s to study medicine or law, as is reflected in its activities. One of its principal goals is to support migrants who have studied in Peru in their struggle to persuade the Catalan authorities to recognize their professional qualifications. However, because it is the only established migrant association in Barcelona, the Centro Peruano became an important rendezvous for Peruvians who arrived in the 1990s to exchange experiences, seek help, and express their national identity. Accordingly, the institution now supports the Peruvian soccer team, which participates in the Catalonian soccer league for immigrants, arranges cultural excursions in Barcelona for newly arrived Peruvians, and helps them make friends with the local population. It also organizes cultural activities on Peru's national holiday (July 28) and Mother's Day, and arranges special events for Catalan businessmen to encourage them to invest money in Peru.

The division of Peru's migrant population into economic and social classes has important implications for migrants' ability to establish diasporic identities. Thus, as already shown, migrants from Peru's rural areas and urban shantytowns tend to organize themselves in regional and ethnic associations, which serve as vehicles to sustain ties with their places of origin and to engage in transnational relations of exchange with their relatives in Peru. However, they rarely develop links to migrant communities in other parts of the world, and, even if they do so, these bonds are usually secondary to the relationships that link them to the homeland.[23] Migrants from Peru's better-off classes, on the other hand, are more likely to create relationships with other migrant groups because their social and professional status in Peru eases their problems in obtaining residence and work permits in the host countries and because they suffer from social and cultural prejudice less than other Peruvians. Their privileged position enhances their mobility, permitting them to establish migrant institutions based on class and profession, and to create networks with Peruvians of their own class in other parts of the world.

One of the oldest migrant institutions in North America is PAMS (the Peruvian American Medical Society), formed by Peruvian medical doctors who migrated to the United States to work during the Vietnam War.[24] Today this association has around 1,500 members and is organized nationally, its main office being in Chicago, but with a number of local chapters in the major cities in the United States.[25] Peruvians who studied at Spanish and Argentinean universities in the 1950s and 1960s and later established families in Spain and Argentina have created similar institutions. In Spain migrants formed an organization called the Convención Nacional de Médicos Hispano-Peruanos, which includes approximately eight hundred Peruvian doctors and has seven chapters in Spain's major cities. In Argentina, on the other hand, Peruvian doctors are organized in the Asociación Peruano-Argentina de Médicos, which is also divided into local chapters. The main chapter in Buenos Aires represents two to three hundred Peruvian doctors. Apart from the annual meetings that these institutions organize nationally for their members, a global gathering for all Peruvian doctors living outside Peru has been arranged on a number of occasions.

Similar types of professional organization are found in Paterson, New Jersey, where a group of primarily female migrants who were trained and who worked as schoolteachers in Peru before emigrating have formed an institution called the Peruvian Teachers' Association. The head of the association is a fifty-year-old woman who worked as a schoolteacher in Peru until she emigrated to the United States at the age of twenty-seven in 1977. In her first years as an immigrant she made her living as a factory worker in Paterson, but after five years she managed to get her Peruvian qualification as schoolteacher recognized by the local authorities, and in 1985 she formed the Peruvian Teachers' Association, which has thirty-five members. According to her, there currently are more than a hundred Peruvians in the United States who have followed her example, have succeeded in having their professional qualifications as schoolteachers recognized, and are currently working in North American schools.

In Miami a group of migrants have formed an organization called the Association of Professional Peruvians to offer help and advice to Peruvians in south Florida who are applying to the American authorities to have their professional qualifications from Peru recognized. The association was formed in 1993 and is led by an economist who graduated from a university in Lima and migrated to Miami in 1990. After a couple of years working for a former classmate who had formed his own company in Miami, the man had saved enough money to establish his own business importing and exporting goods from and to Peru. Today he owns a company that transports goods in the Miami area. He says, "There are many Peruvians in the United States who have professional qualifications from Peru, but only a few are allowed to exercise their professions. Our organization tries to help these people have their qualifications recognized." He proudly refers to a young Peruvian male who studied for two years at a military school in Lima and who succeeded in converting these studies into a BA degree at a college in Florida with the support of the Association of Professional Peruvians. The association also offers seminars and other activities for Peruvians, and supports an initiative by other migrant organizations in Miami to create a fund to award an annual prize called the TUMI to migrants or the children of migrants who graduate from colleges and universities or who otherwise attract attention because of their achievements.

In several North American cities, an exclusive group of male Peruvians have formed associations for ex-students from Leoncio Prado, Peru's most respected military school located in Lima.[26] These associations function as the institutional anchors of a global network of ex-students of Leoncio Prado, who today include architects, engineers, doctors, bank directors, and businessmen, and who live in the United States, Mexico, Panama, Venezuela, and different parts of Europe. They also act to help ex-*leonciopradinos* who want to emigrate to find jobs and become adjusted to their new environment. Because of the support they receive from the network, many ex-*leonciopradinos* feel as much at home in their new countries of residence as in Peru. As one such ex-student explains: "We are very well organized because we are all professionals with good jobs. We use the Internet and communicate by e-mail. We help each other whenever there is a need. They help me find a job, and later I help somebody else." This exclusive sector of Peru's emigrant population has genuinely created a stable network of diasporic connections that allows migrants to feel Peruvian without having to maintain active ties with their homeland.

REMITTING AND PROFITING

Studies of international migration reveal that migrants draw on social relations based on kinship, neighborhood, friendship, trust, cooperation, or ethnicity, not only to pull newcomers (Massey et al. 1987), but also to provide for those who have remained behind and to create transnational communities (Levitt 2001: 197). On the basis of my findings, I will add that whereas such networks and communities reduce the cost of migration by providing new migrants with important information about how and where to travel, and offering them economic and emotional support once they arrive in the host society, they also limit migrants' agency by encouraging them to migrate to the same places and to take the same jobs as those who arrived before them. For most Peruvians, this means working as unskilled labor in agriculture or the manufacturing and service industries (Julca 2001). Moreover, because migrant communities are highly stratified and differentiated and gloss over relations of inequality and power, migrants' opportunities to convert relations of trust and cooperation into social capital are far from equal (Menjívar 2000; Mahler 1995: 202–13; Paerregaard 2002).

However, for many Peruvians, migrant networks based on reciprocity represent the only means of overcoming social and economic disadvantages, achieving social mobility in the host society, and obtaining any influence over social and political processes in the homeland (Lanolt, Autler and Baires 1999). Migrants who decide to pursue such an avenue often prefer to invest in remittance agencies, restaurants, or shops that primarily service Peruvians. Thus in the United States several migrants have established restaurant chains in not just one but several cities.[27] Others start a business by selling air tickets or offering legal counseling. Not surprisingly, the most prosperous sector of Peru's emigrant population are the owners of the remittance agencies in the United States, Canada, Spain, Italy, and Argentina, some of whom have created their own transnational networks to transfer money. Among these are Jet Peru, which operates in the United States, Spain, Italy, Argentina, and Chile and has local offices in a number of cities in Peru, and Argenper, which is owned by a Peruvian group of siblings and is based in Buenos Aires. In the last ten years this agency has expanded its activities and established offices not merely in other parts of Argentina, but also in other Latin American countries, as well as in North America.[28]

With the exception of a few large transnational corporations such as Inca Cola and Cuzqueña, which produce and sell Peruvian soft drinks and beer in North and South America, Europe, and Japan, most Peruvian trade connections are based on informal networks and restricted to small circuits of individual migrants. One such network is centered on Los Angeles, where two brothers run a wholesale business importing Peruvian products and selling them to restaurants and shops in California.[29] In 1998 these brothers, who were both born and raised in Peru but are descended from Chinese emigrants, traveled to Japan to establish a trade link with local Peruvian businessmen. Their plan was to re-export some of the products they import from Peru to Japan and to exploit the emerging market that is the Peruvian community in that country. To the brothers this business contact represents an extension of an already existing migration link between Peru, Japan and California that was established by Japanese labor migrants in 1898 and reactivated by Japanese Peruvians who return-migrated to Japan in the early 1990s and then re-migrated to California. The junction in this transpacific migration and trade triangle is Los Angeles, which provides the most direct air link between Peru and Japan. In Japan, on the other hand, several Peruvian shop owners started to import Peruvian products in the mid-1990s using trade connections created by the Brazilian community, which is much bigger and more established than the Peruvian one. However, to these businessmen a more direct link to Peru through the Peruvian community in Los Angeles offers a far more attractive option than trading through the Brazilian business community.

In Spain, Peruvians have been less successful in establishing transnational trade links. Although a number of Peruvians have opened ethnic shops and restaurants in Madrid and Barcelona, only a few have established business contacts outside the country. One of the pioneers in Barcelona's Peruvian community arrived in Spain in 1987 together with his wife. They settled in Barcelona, where they opened a restaurant in the Olympic Port. During the week the restaurant looks like any other Spanish bar, but on weekends the owners serve Peruvian food. Unlike the Peruvian brothers in Los Angeles, who are trying to expand their ethnic trade links across the Pacific, the couple has invested the money they make on the restaurant in a shopping center in their home city of Huancayo. However, rather than return to Peru, they intend to move to North America, where the woman has close relatives, and to establish a business there.

Although migrant entrepreneurs find it extremely difficult to establish a business in Japan, some Peruvians have succeeded in doing so. One of the requirements is proficiency in Japanese, in order to be able to communicate with local authorities, financial agencies, and customers. Another is to have a residence and work permit, which is required to rent or buy a place and be granted permission to open a shop or undertake other forms of commerce. Familiarity with Japanese codes of conduct and business management is, of course, also an advantage. Marco, thirty-five, is a prosperous businessman who originates from the city of Huacho north of Lima. Both he and his wife are *sansei*, that is, third-generation Japanese. In 1989 they migrated to Japan with the first wave of *nikkeijin*, who went to the land of their parents or grandparents in search of a better future. After several jobs as a factory worker, Marco decided to try his luck as an independent businessman and opened a shop in Isesaki, northwest of Tokyo. Trained as a butcher by his father, Marco started to sell meat to Peruvians in the neighborhood. He also sells imported Peruvian products, such as Inca Cola, Cuzqueña beer, and canned species and herbs and beans, which are not available in Japan. Later he began to rent videotapes of recordings of Peruvian television programs.

The videotapes are the product of a transnational business network organized by Marco and his two brothers. One lives in Lima, where he records more than 50 percent of all programs broadcast by television channels available in Peru. Three times a week, a messenger travels from Lima via Los Angeles to Tokyo, where Marco's second brother receives the master tapes of the video recordings. He rents a small workshop fifteen minutes by car from Narita airport, where he has installed more than two hundred video copying machines. As the transpacific flights usually arrive in the afternoons, the brother in Narita has approximately fifteen hours to copy the master tapes brought by the messenger from Lima. The following morning Marco drives from Isesaki to Narita, a trip that takes him three hours, and collects the more than five hundred tapes that his brother has copied from the master tapes. Around midday he returns to Isesaki, where he offers the tapes for rent in his shop. The charge is 1,000 Yen for eight tapes to be returned after a couple of days. In the late afternoon he fills up a van he has installed as a mobile shop with Peruvian products and, of course, videotapes and drives around Isesaki, Takasaki, the closest larger city, and from time to time Nagano, several hours' drive away, to offer his products to the local Peruvian migrant community.

Marco's business is based on relationships of mutual trust and ethnic solidarity created when he tours the Gunma and Nagano departments in his mobile shop, delivering Peruvian products. The list of telephone numbers and addresses of hundreds of migrant families that he has assembled over the years, allowing him to tell his clients where and when they should wait for him on these trips, speaks for itself. Although Inca Cola, *salsa de culandro* or *huacatay*, *ají-no-moto*, *salchicha tipo Huacho*, and a personal service in Spanish provide Marco with a regular income, the most profitable part of his business is the video recordings of the most recent television programs in Lima, including the news (*Noticiaras*), sports events (*Goles en acción*), Latin American soap operas (*Los ricos también lloran*), Peruvian talk shows (*Laura en América*), and movies and cartoon films in Spanish translation that give Peruvians in Japan a sense of proximity to Peru, despite the distance in time and space.

In fact, Peruvians living in the Isesaki, Takasaki, and Nagano areas are not alone in seeking distractions from their frustrations as factory workers in a society that only reluctantly accepts their presence by consuming products and watching video recordings from their country of origin. According to Marco, at least four other Peruvians are reported to have created similar transnational business networks.[30] He also claims that his business concept was invented by Japanese Brazilians who started to record soap operas from Brazilian TV channels in the early 1990s in response to demand by Brazilian immigrants in Japan for entertainment in Portuguese. In order to satisfy a similar demand for TV programs in Spanish by Japan's Spanish-speaking immigrant population, the Peruvians imitated the Brazilians.

IMAGINING AND IDENTIFYING

The emergence of a market for Andean music and folk art in the western world has been accompanied by a growing interest in Peruvian emigrant communities in identifying customs and practices that appropriately express what migrants find typical or representative of Peruvian culture and history. This is particularly evident in Miami, where the presence of Andean migrants is more visible than other places in the world.[31] The following case study illustrates how these identity processes are negotiated and contested among Peruvian migrants.

Nicario Jiménez was born in Alqaminka, a Quechua-speaking peasant community in the department of Ayacucho, in 1957. He was raised in a group of seven siblings. In 1968 he moved to Huamanga, the capital of the department of Ayacucho, together with his family, the first move in a long chain of migration that eventually brought him to Lima and finally to the United States. In Huamanga he finished elementary school and began to receive training as a folk artisan in accordance with the family's tradition. As both his father and grandfather were *retablistas*, Nicario learned to make *retablos* or rectangular wooden boxes with two painted doors, which contain small figures representing people and animals engaged in social and ritual activities, such as agricultural work, cattle-herding, trade, and exchange, and religious celebrations of mostly Christian events.

In the early 1980s the political violence in Ayacucho forced Nicario to migrate to Lima, where he first stayed with an aunt in Miraflores, an affluent residential district, and then moved with his family to Año Nuevo in Comas, a huge shantytown in the northern part of the city. Nicario recalls that he found Miraflores unfriendly but enjoyed living in Comas because the surrounding hills reminded him of the mountains of his village of Alqaminka. After a couple of years he moved first to Zárate and then to Barranco, a district located on the coast at Lima, which traditionally attracts many artists, writers and poets. In 1986 Nicario was invited by a North American historian to lecture about his work as a folk artisan at one of Miami's universities. In the years that followed he continued traveling to United States to participate in academic events. However, he also started to show his works, which he produced at his workshop in Barranco, at local art exhibitions in Florida, and when he was granted a temporary residence visa in 1997 he decided to move permanently to Miami together with one of his daughters.

While lecturing in Miami, Nicario changed his notion of what it means to be a *retablista*. He learned that the distinction between folk art and true art is very fuzzy and that his *retablos* are valued not only because he manufactures them according to an Andean folk art tradition, but also because of his own individual ingenuity and creativity. In other words, he discovered that the *retablos* he makes are not just a reproduction of an inherent tradition (folk art), but a unique creation, the value of which only can be determined by its individual quality, namely art. This reconceptualization of his own identity as an artisan encouraged Nicario to engage in what he considers a personal struggle to win recognition as an artist, not only within the Peruvian community in Miami, but also at the official art exhibitions throughout the United States. In 1997 he established a workshop in a rented flat in Miami, which served as his main base for producing *retablos*. He later moved the workshop to Naples in west Florida, where he currently lives with his daughter. Periodically he travels all over the United States to display his works at art festivals, which over the years has won him numerous prizes and opened the doors to the North American market. Yet Nicario does not feel that his works have won the recognition they deserve. When I interviewed him in Miami in 1998, he said "They always try to place me in a special section of folk art and they gave me all those prizes. But I wanted them to recognize my work as real art. So I ask them to place it in the section for art. Sometimes they let me do it.

See, they think I'm a folk artisan because I'm Peruvian and make *retablos*. But I want them to understand that I'm an artist."

Nicario's struggle to win recognition as an artist is reflected in his search for new motifs of the *retablos* he creates. Originally the *retablos* were called Missa Mastay or Cajón de San Marcos, and provided religious protections of the cattle belonging to the hacienda owners in Ayacucho. Later use of the Cajón de San Marcos became a local tradition among the Indian population in Ayacucho, who redesigned the box and separated the figures on two floors, upper and lower, one symbolizing the world of the hacienda owner and the other those suffering from his tyranny, that is the Indians (Urbano and Macera 1992: 59–62). Today the *retablos* have become the object of commercialization, and contemporary artisans mainly sell their products at Peru's tourist markets. In this modern version, the *retablo* is a colorful and vivid illustration of the social and ritual activities related to the agricultural calendar of Peru's peasant population. Indeed, to many urban Peruvians, as well as Peru's growing tourist industry, the *retablo* has become a romantic and nostalgic emblem of the Andean world. However, instead of using the dual opposition traditionally employed in the *retablo* to reproduce conventional interpretations of the Andean world as being divided into an upper part inhabited by either the European and *mestizo* power elite or the religious forces that control human life and a lower part populated by Peru's marginal Indian population, Nicario portrays the relationship between the dominating and the dominated in situations of social injustice and discrimination in the contemporary world. Among the most spectacular motifs of his *retablos* are Miami airport divided into an upper world of legal travelers and an lower world inhabited by undocumented immigrants, who are detained by airport officials; Tijuana pictured divided into an upper world occupied by helicopters policing the U.S.-Mexican border and a lower world belonging to the undocumented immigrants trying to enter the United States; New York City divided into an upper section inhabited by people either walking or driving on the streets and a lower section populated by the commuters who use the city's subway; and Peru's bloody civil war, pictured as a dual opposition between the victims of violence, that is the civil population, and the aggressors, that is the country's military and rebel groups.

To Nicario, however, the artistic value of his *retablos* consists in their quality and originality rather than their motifs and symbolic meanings. A good *retablo* can depict North America's modern urban world and Peru's political history as well as the rural life of the Andes. He conceives the *retablo* as a genre of art that is constantly changing and that can be adopted to new environments, and he believes that its transformation from a sacred object used for ritual purposes into first a commercial folk product symbolizing Andean culture and now an individual art project revives rather than jeopardizes the folk art history of Ayacucho. Similarly, he thinks that the folklore tradition of his family endorses his attempts to win recognition as an artist. Whereas his grandfather was a local producer of the Cajón de San Marcos, his father mainly manufactured modern *retablos*. And just as his father trained him as a *retablista*, Nicario has instructed his son and daughter in the production of *retablos* as a folk art. To Nicario, then, the struggle to be acknowledged as an artist embodies the artistic spirit of his father and grandfather, a vision to which he gave testimony in an exhibition he arranged displaying the works of his family's four generations of *retablistas*.

As a recognized *retablista* who symbolizes what to many represents an authentic Andean folk art, Nicario is periodically invited to display his work at cultural events arranged by Peruvian migrant organizations in Miami. However, his *retablos* often create confusion about not only what folk art means, but also Andean culture and identity. In 1997 he participated in an exhibition hosted by a Peruvian organization in Key Biscayne, an island on the outskirts of Miami mostly populated by upper-class North Americans and wealthy Latin American immigrants but he felt disappointed by the response of the visitors. He recalls, "Many of those who came to see my work were Peruvians, but they asked me if I was from Guatemala. And when I said that I come from Peru, they seemed surprised and asked, 'Which part of Peru?' You know, many Peruvians in Key Biscayne come from Miraflores and San Isidro. They don't know anything about Andean culture. But they think they know better than I what Andean folklore is." Nicario was also asked to participate in an exhibition of Peruvian culture at the Peruvian consulate in Miami arranged by an organization called the Centro Peruano de Cultura y Historia. However, the organizers first refused to accept the works that Nicario wanted to display because they were different from what they expected of the conventional Andean *retablo*. He recalls that one of the organizers exclaimed, "How can you do that, Nicario? That's not a *retablo*. *Retablos* show nice things about people in Peru. Not these kinds of things." To Nicario, upper-class Peruvians have no knowledge of the culture and history of their own country, particularly where its indigenous population are concerned, and he feels frustrated that Peruvians from Lima who ignored Peru's indigenous cultures before they migrated now claim to know what *retablos* should look like and even correct him for not creating proper Andean folklore.[32] He says, "I make art, not folklore. Who are they to tell me what to do?"

Nicario moves within a transnational network that allows him to renegotiate his role as a folk artisan in Peru and to redefine the meaning of folklore and art. In Lima his wife and son continue to exhibit his *retablos* as folk art at a gallery in Barranco that also serves as a vehicle to promote the works of other Andean artisans. Nicario himself, however, invests most of his time exhibiting *retablos* at art festivals in North America, thus winning recognition as an artist. At the same time, he acknowledges the cultural roots of his *retablos* and the continuity between the traditional Cajón de San Marcos and his own creations by displaying his works together with the works of his grandfather, father, and children. These fluid and apparently contradictory identities as traditionalist, rural folklore artisans, and modern artists emerge from a migratory process through which Nicario links Alqaminka to Lima and Miami and a transnational network that connects him to artists and academics in the United States, folk artisans in Lima, and fellow villagers in Ayacucho.

FROM TRANSNATIONAL LINKS TO DIASPORIC BONDS (AND BACK AGAIN)

The events, activities, and relations examined in the case studies in this chapter can be distinguished according to the extent to which they draw on and exploit the two set of networks I defined above. The political conflict caused by the shepherds' labor migration to the United States, and the accusations that Victor's union and Perú en los 90 made against the ranchers and the Peruvian consulate in Los Angeles, represent examples of what I have called transnational links, that is, a network of relations that tie migrants to Peru through bilateral links. To begin with the shepherds' own networks, these are based on a set of narrow kin ties that connect specific families in villages in Peru's central highlands to individual ranch owners in the United States. Furthermore, the conflict over the shepherds' working conditions developed as an exchange of information and ideas between representatives of the shepherds themselves based in Bakersfield and Huancayo, leading members of the Peruvian community in southern California, representatives of the WRA in Sacramento and Lima, the national press in Peru, and members of the Congress and the government in Lima. The outcome was a bilateral flow of communication between Peruvians in California and Peru that, for a short time, reached the headlines of the Peruvian press and the agenda of Peruvian politicians, but had few repercussions on Peruvian emigration in general.

On the one hand, the reports about and pictures of the inhuman working conditions of Peruvian shepherds in the United States attracted considerable attention in Lima and Huancayo as well as in Los Angeles; similarly, the dismissal of the Peruvian consul in Los Angeles because of his neglect of the shepherds' conditions was sensational news, given that the country's diplomatic representatives are normally considered immune to complaints from Peru's emigrant population. In a similar vein, the subsequent accusations of human rights abuses against the North American authorities were regarded by many as a welcome opportunity to create a public debate in Peru, not only of the causes of the current exodus, but also of the nature and quality of life of Peruvian migrants, and the legal and moral obligations of the Peruvian government to protect and defend the rights of the country's emigrant population. In contrast to the predominant conception of emigration as an avenue to a better and more prosperous life, then, the media's coverage of the conflict offered a picture of migrant life as extremely harsh, with few if any expectations of ever achieving social mobility. Yet once the dust of the scandal had settled and other issues reached the media headlines and the politicians' agenda, public attention for the shepherds' case evaporated, and concern for Peru's emigrant population lost ground to other urgent matters. This, I would argue, is to a large extent due to the nature of transnational links that on the one hand facilitate intense flows of communication between migrants in specific places and particular institutions and groups of people in their country of origin, while on the other hand rarely developing multi-stranded networks that encompass migrants in more than two locations and therefore contribute little to the formation of a diasporic consciousness.

Migrants' sense of co-responsibility and national solidarity induces many Peruvians to take part in collective efforts to collect aid for their fellow countrymen when the latter are suffering from natural disasters, wars, and political crises. Such forms of emergency aid often imply close cooperation between migrant associations, the Peruvian government, and different state institutions and NGOs in Peru, and they tend to enhance existing ties and encourage the creation of new transnational links with their country of origin. As with the flow of information and ideas stirred up by the conflict over the shepherds' working conditions described above, emergency aid and expressions of solidarity are mainly directed through bilateral networks that connect migrants directly with their country of origin, and that are activated from time to time due to sudden emergencies, as happened when el Niño hit Peru in 1998, the Ica earthquake occurred in 1993, and the war between Peru and Ecuador broke out in 1995. And as happened after the press and the politicians lost interest in the shepherds' conditions, the momentary feelings of solidarity with the victims of natural disasters and political crises fade away as fast as they emerge once other matters for concern take over. Transnational links, in other words, constitute an effective means for the state and private institutions in Peru to mobilize support from its emigrant population; likewise, they serve as an important vehicle for migrants to express their national solidarity and confirm their loyalty to their country of origin. However, apart from AIPEUC's *telemaratón* on behalf of the victims of el Niño in 1998, most of the charity work described above has drawn on bilateral relations between migrants in specific locations in the United States and Peru.

In contrast to the collection of emergency aid to their fellow countrymen in Peru, movements to support fellow immigrants or improve migrants' own images in the receiving countries tend to make use of multi-stranded rather than bilateral networks. Thus both the Peruvian newspapers in Miami, which launched a campaign to mobilize moral support for undocumented immigrants, and the Peruvian consulate and leaders of migrant institutions in Japan, which made a public appeal to their fellow countrymen to stay away from crime and integrate into Japanese society, conveyed their messages through the web of bonds that connect migrant communities in different parts of the host society and that bring together Peruvians from different social strata and ethnic groupings. Such movements force migrants to raise the questions, What are the shared values and symbols of our diasporic identity? What is it that makes us feel that we belong to the same national minority, despite conflicting class interests and ethnic identities? In short, they urge Peruvians living outside Peru to look each other in the eyes and ask, Does the mere fact that we all emigrated from the same country imply that we are the same? Clearly, the campaign on behalf of fellow migrants who lack proper ID documentation was more successful in inciting such a sense of imagined community than the appeal to obey the law in Japan. Whereas the former prompted a large group of legal immigrants to question the legal classification of immigrants in both undocumented and documented cases and thus to identify with the problems from which many of their fellow migrants traveling without proper ID papers suffer, the latter increased an already existing division within the Peruvian community, namely between *nikkeijin* immigrants recognized by Japanese immigration law as temporary legal labor migrants, and non-*nikkei* Peruvians, who are tolerated as the spouses of *nikkeijin* or Japanese citizens, but are otherwise regarded as unwanted aliens.

The Movimiento de Peruanos en el Exterior, which was formed in Argentina in 2000 to capture migrant votes for the presidential elections in Peru in 2001, represents a unique initiative to mobilize migrants as a constituency with legitimate rights to be represented in the Peruvian Congress and serviced by the Peruvian state. The organization is particular interesting because it shows how a migrant movement may draw on both transnational links and diasporic bonds, thus creating an awareness among its followers that they constitute a separate population while at the same time claiming a Peruvian identity. In other words, it demonstrates how existing bilateral links to their country of origin can be used as new multi-stranded ties with migrants in other parts of the world and thus plant the seeds of a possible diasporic consciousness. The attempt represents a so far exceptional example of how to unite migrants of different social and ethnic backgrounds. Although it failed to mobilize migrants on a large scale either inside or outside Argentina or to win a migrant a seat in the Peruvian Congress, the brother of the movement's leader, Alejandro Toledo, was actually elected the country's president in 2001. Once in office, on several occasions he addressed migrants in the United States and other places as "the diaspora of Peru," thus appropriating the political vocabulary of the Movimiento (personal communication with Ulla Dalum Berg). This rhetoric contains a strong moral appeal to migrants' sense of co-responsibility and is intended to encourage them to send more remittances to their relatives at home and to invest their savings in Peru. Whether Toledo's use of the term "diaspora" will promote the creation of a diasporic identity is still an open question.

The use of concepts such as community, nation, and diaspora in political rhetoric is always problematic, because it glosses over relations of inequality and power hierarchies. Thus, Peru's more than two million emigrants encompass a broad variety of economic, social, and cultural groups. This is reflected in the organizations and institutions they create, which can be distinguished according to their purpose and the networks they draw on. Some organizations arrange leisure activities and cultural events. However, because their members are primarily recruited from the local migrant population, their ties with other migrant communities are weak. On the one hand, associations that recruit their members on the basis of ethnic or regional commitment often establish transnational links with their region of origin, thus enabling them to develop extra-local networks. Yet other institutions are based on class and organize migrants according to their professions or educational background. Rather than creating bilateral ties back to Peru, these often establish multi-stranded networks across regional and national boundaries. In fact, the only migrants who have developed enduring diasporic bonds are affiliates of the professional migrant associations, such as the medical associations in United States, Spain, and Argentina, and the more confined and exclusive networks of former students of Peru's elite schools and military colleges. Although these networks exclude a large sector of migrants and show little interest in developing their bilateral links with their fellow educational or professional institutions in Peru (with the exception of PAMS) or the Peruvian state and therefore lack strong transnational links, their multi-stranded global ties represent a significant contribution to the formation of a diasporic identity.

Because mass Peruvian emigration is a relatively recent phenomenon, trade and business networks are still weak and sporadic. Economic transactions and exchange relations are primarily focused on Peru and consist mainly of migrants' individual remittances to relatives and fellow villagers in their regions of origin. Such monetary transfers make a substantial contribution to Peru's economic growth and play a critical role in the country's regional and local development. They also offer an important opportunity for entrepreneurs to create remittance agencies and profit from migrants' relationships of trust and reciprocity. Hence, most ethnic businesses make use of transnational ties between specific migrant communities and cities in Peru, such as Lima, Trujillo, or Huancayo. A few remittance agencies, such as Jet Peru and Agenper, offer services between several migrant destinations and cities in Peru. Interestingly, the candidate Movimiento de Peruanos en el Exterior launched in the 2001 election campaign for the Peruvian Congress was the owner of Agenper, suggesting that multi-stranded trade and business networks may indeed prove to be a critical vehicle for the formation of a possible political diasporic identity.

Another important source of income for migrant entrepreneurs specializing in ethnic business is Peruvian food and beverage products, which in recent years have encountered new markets in the countries of destination for Peru's growing emigration. Particularly the producers of soft drinks such as Inca Cola and beer brands such as Cuzqueña have experienced a boom in the demand for their products, which has allowed them not merely to increase existing bilateral and transnational export links with cities and countries with major Peruvian emigrant communities, but also to create new multi-stranded diasporic bonds to re-export their products to new markets in different parts of the world. Thus Inca Cola uses a bottling plant in New York from which to re-export its products to Japan and Europe. To entrepreneurs like Marco in Japan, global distribution networks such as those developed by Inca Cola or the two Chinese Peruvian brothers in Los Angeles described earlier offer promising opportunities to develop a diasporic market for Peruvian products and to exploit established immigrant communities in order to create an ethnic business. However, as Marco's video renting business indicates, the economic profits that these multi-stranded networks generate are still small compared to those of more direct bilateral transnational links.

The recent emergence of a global market for Andean music and handicrafts has not merely generated a new source of income for a growing number of Peruvian migrants, it has also prompted many migrants to rethink their own cultural heritage. In the wake of this demand for indigenous cultural products, two apparently conflicting processes are taking place within Peru's emigrant population. On the one hand, middle- and upper-class migrants are taking a renewed interest in Andean music and folk art, which they regard as emblematic of Peruvian history and identity; on the other hand, migrants from Peru's highlands and Peruvian artists who live outside the country are creating new livelihoods by commercializing handicrafts from their regions of origin in Peru and transforming traditional Andean folklore into modern art.

Thus Nicario, a traditional folk artist from Ayacucho, has engaged in a multi-sited experiment that allows him to act as a folk artisan in Lima as well as a modern artist in the United States and thus to recast the *retablo* artisan tradition into a new and more self-conscious genre of art. However, his works also cause conflict among migrants because they contest dominant notions of Andean culture and identity, and thus question middle- and upper-class migrants' use of indigenous culture in representing themselves as Peruvians. In other words, migrants' search for symbols with which to redefine their national identity has provided new ammunition for traditional tensions between social classes and ethnic groups in Peru.

DISPUTED UNITY

In chapter 4 I demonstrated that migrant networks play a critical role in contemporary Peruvian emigration. These networks are based on family relations, ethnic affiliation, and regional origin and serve as an efficient means to pull newcomers to the receiving countries, find work, and maintain contact with relatives in migrants' home regions. In this chapter I have discussed how Peruvian migrants create relations beyond the social, ethnic, and regional boundaries that define the networks I examined in chapter 4. The conclusion of this scrutiny is that the transnational ties and diasporic bonds that emerge from such relations are extremely fragile and often ridden by conflict and strife, which hampers migrants' efforts to generate an awareness of constituting a diasporic population. Indeed, in their effort to identify social or cultural commonalities that may unite them and provide them with a sense of national identity Peruvians who live outside Peru recurrently reproduce the mechanisms of inclusion and exclusion that divide Peruvians who live in Peru. Thus, migrants originating from Peru's rural highland form long transnational ties to pull family members and fellow villagers; similarly, migrants belonging to the country's urban upper class create strong diasporic bonds to support close friends and professional colleagues. Between these two opposed groups migrants from Peru's urban middle class and working class struggle to form their own networks to pull family members and overcome the barriers that exclude them from obtaining legal rights and find work in the receiving countries. From time to time other migrants from all these groups come together to create a common sense of Peruvianness but often these efforts end up dividing rather than uniting them. In the following chapter I describe how migrants try to overcome such divisions by forming religious brotherhoods and organizing Catholic processions in the cities where they live.

NOTES

1. Mitchell defines the extended case study as follows: "Whereas the analysis of a social situation is limited to a single situation or at most to a restricted set of events located in the same situation, an extended case study, by contrast, typically covers the same actors over a series of different situations. This implies that an extended case analysis recounts events over a relatively long period of time, typically over several years." (1984: 238). See also Rogers and Vertovec (1995).

2. A similar initiative was taken the same year by another group of Peruvians in Paterson who tried to form a political movement in favor of former president Alan García and against Fujimori.

3. The Peruvian consulate in Paterson was set up in 1985 in response to a request from the local migrant community.

4. Emigrant Peruvians also showed a concern for the their home country during the brief war which Peru fought against Ecuador in 1995 over the border that separates the two countries. However, rather than uniting migrants, as happened in 1998 when Peruvians raised subscriptions to aid the victims of the el Niño disaster, the dispute with Ecuador tended to divide Peruvians into two groups: those supporting President Fujimori in his martial rhetoric against neighboring Ecuador, and those in favor of a pan-American rather than a national identity, who argued for a peaceful solution to the conflict.

5. In 1997, when one of Peru's rebel groups held a large group of visitors hostage in the Japanese Embassy in Lima, Peruvians organized public demonstrations in Paterson and New York (in front of the UN building) to express their support to the victims of the actions. Similar events were organized in Miami.

6. The Congreso Peruano Americano originally received help from the local Puerto Rican community, which has a strong tradition of forming migrant political organizations. Because the Congreso prefers to remain an independent institution, it is not member of the AIPEUC, an umbrella institution for all Peruvian associations in North America.

7. *Peru News* 2, February 1998.

8. Asociación de instituciones peruanas en los Estados Unidos y Canadá.

9. *La Crónica* 5 (42), Jan. 1998, Chasqui 3 (98), Feb. 1998; Peru News 2, March 1998.

10. *Peru News* 2, March 1998.

11. *Chasqui* 3 (98), Feb. 1998.

12. A similar movement called La Plataforma Socio-Política Peruana Americana (Peruvian American Socio-Political Platform) was created in California in 1998 (Perú de los 90 9 (2), Feb. 1998).

13. *Ultima Hora* 1 (5), April 1998; *El Panamericano* 5 (72), April 1998; *Actualidad* 6 (82), April 1998; *L.A. Peruvian Times* 7 (13), March 1998.

14. *El Heraldo del Perú* (Buenos Aires) 3, Oct. 2000; *Gaceta del Perú* (Buenos Aires) 217, Oct. 2000.

15. One of the leaders of the movement is a brother of the current president of Peru, Alejandro Toledo. The person promoted by the movement as a candidate for

Peru's congress was the owner of the largest Peruvian remittance agency in Argentina (Argenper).

16. *International Press* (Tokyo) Aug., 1999.

17. The Peruvian Veteran League was formed in 1991 and has twelve teams. These are either named after the most renowned soccer clubs in Peru or in accordance with the geographical origin of the players. They are Chacarilla, Callao, Chosica, Alianza, Yayirca, Melgar, Cañete, Surquillo, and Cristal. Although the league is organized on the basis of national origin, it also allows non-Peruvian teams and players to participate.

18. The earliest Peruvian soccer teams in Los Angeles were formed in 1961 (the Inca) and 1962 (the Sport Boys). Today Peruvians are represented in the Liga Olímpica with six teams, the Sunset Soccer League, the Liga de Santana and the Liga del Valle San Fernando with three teams, and the Liga de Redonda Beach with two teams. Peruvian weeklies and soccer magazines report these events and the results of the games on a regular basis.

19. Other kinds of institutions also exist. Thus in Spain Peruvians have created gender-based organizations to mobilize women working in the domestic industry (Escribá 1999).

20. This division of regional associations is reflected in migrant institutions that have evolved through rural-urban migration in Peru (Paerregaard 1997: 65–70).

21. Peruvian *nikkei* associations exist in other parts of the world, such as North America (e.g., in Los Angeles), but these are not connected to the Peruvian Japanese communities in either Peru or Japan.

22. No similar institution exists in Madrid, where the Peruvian Embassy has traditionally played an important role in organizing the migrant community. In the 1990s Peruvians formed an institution called ARI (Asociación de refugiados y inmigrantes) that primarily aims to support migrants to obtain political asylum or stay and work permit in Spain.

23. Considering that the majority of Peruvians who have emigrated in the past twenty to thirty years belong to an emergent working class of immigrants in the First World, this observation underscores Schnapper's point that "proletarian populations are undoubtedly less likely to maintain themselves as a diaspora" (1999: 33).

24. PAMS also has a few Peruvian dentists on its lists.

25. Some members of PAMS deplore that the fact the institution is recruiting so few new members, which is attributed to the growing difficulties which Peruvian doctors who have studied in Peru and who later emigrate encounter when trying to revalidate their academic degrees in the United States. In effect, PAMS is increasingly becoming an institution for middle-aged or senior doctors, which over the years will fade away.

26. In Los Angeles two such institutions exist: the Asociación de ex-Cadetes de Colegios Militares del Perú, and the Asociación Leonciopradina Internacional.

27. The best-known Peruvian restaurant chain is Inca Pollo, with eight restaurants in Los Angeles and one in Miami. Five Peruvian weeklies also provide the Peruvian community in Miami with information in Spanish about the situation in both Peru and the United States, while approximately twenty-five Peruvian restaurants and shops offer migrants the smell and taste of food from their country of origin or home region.

A number of Peruvian agencies providing such services as money transfer, travel arrangements to Peru and immigration consultancies are also available.

28. *Perú al Día* (Santiago, Chile) 15, Sept. 2002.

29. A few other, smaller companies, such as Andes Food, have emerged in response to the growing demand for Peruvian products among migrants in the United States, southern Europe, Argentina, and Japan. They specialize in food products such as chili, and Andean species, herbs, and root crops.

30. I personally visited two other Peruvians engaged in the same video recording business as Marco. One is the owner of a Peruvian restaurant called Pollo Rico located in Harumi on the western outskirts of Tokyo, while the other owns a Peruvian restaurant in Mooka. Apparently, these businessmen have agreed to divide the migrant community north and northwest of Tokyo, thus assuring each of them a share of the market for Peruvian products and videotapes.

31. This is reflected in the broad spectrum of regional institutions, including associations for migrants from Cajamarca, Ancash, Huancayo, Ayacucho, and Arequipa, which arrange activities such as *carneval*, *corta monte, festival folklórico*, and *pachamanca*. Although they recruit members on the basis of regional origin, migrants from all over Peru, including Lima, join in these activities.

32. In contrast to other Latin American groups in the United States, who make a clear distinction between what they view as indigenous and mestizo cultures and tend to form separate immigrant communities according to their ethnic and regional identities in the country of origin (Kearney 1996; Popkin 1999), Andean folklore has become an issue of contestation and conflict between Peruvians from the urban middle class and the rural working class in their efforts to forge immigrant identities and generate new forms of income.

Chapter Six

Global Secrets

Take a walk on Miami's Calle Ocho on October 18, and you'll see a group of Latin Americans shouting "¡Viva el Señor de los Milagros!" and singing religious songs in honor of the image they are carrying. At the same time in Madrid, Milan, and Buenos Aires, and even in Hamamatsu, Japan, you can witness similar events. The participants in these processions are Peruvians who have emigrated to the United States, Spain, Italy, Argentina, and Japan in search of a better life, but who nevertheless feel a need to honor their religious icons in the streets of their new countries of residence. The image they are carrying represents the Lord of the Miracles and is an imitation of the original icon kept in the Nazarenas Church in Lima, the capital of Peru. The procession gathers a multitude of people united by a common hope that the Lord will protect them against disease and accident and give them strength in their daily lives. To the followers of the Lord of the Miracles, faith in the icon means having somebody accompany you like a talisman wherever you go.

Among Peruvians it is commonly assumed that the Lord of the Miracles is an image of Jesus Christ and as having been the object of his revelation. The icon is also believed to be a representation of a mural painted on a wall in Lima by an enslaved African in the seventeenth century that has come to be known as the Cristo Moreno (Colored Christ) because Jesus Christ is portrayed as an Afro-Peruvian.[1] This makes the image a critical symbol of Peru's long history of cultural hybridity and reflects the collective consciousness of the process of *mestizaje* (ethnic mixture) that has shaped the country's history and society. It also turns the legend of the Savior who reveals himself to humans into an important message to millions of Peruvians and other Latin Americans of mixed racial heritage, for whom conventional images of Jesus Christ and other Christian icons are difficult to identify with.[2]

Traditionally, the icon personifies fear of the earthquakes that periodically hit Lima and the rest of Peru and respect for the powers that control these natural forces. However, the symbolic meaning of the Lord of the Miracles has changed over the last twenty to thirty years: from representing protection against natural disasters, the icon has become a symbol of unity and hope against other dangers, such as Peru's current economic and political crisis. The transformation of the Lord of the Miracles into a national emblem has been spurred on by the mass exodus of Peruvians in the past three decades to different parts of the world in search of new livelihoods and better living conditions. Despite geographical dispersal and social heterogeneity, however, immigrants share a common interest in forming *hermandades* (religious brotherhoods) and in participating in annual processions to honor the Lord of the Miracles. Currently, there are more than sixty such brotherhoods in the United States, Canada, Spain, Italy, Japan, Argentina, Chile, Mexico, Bolivia, Colombia, and Venezuela, the countries with major concentrations of Peruvian migrants.

In this chapter I explore those aspects of Peruvian emigration that have led migrants to expatriate religious icons, establish religious brotherhoods and organize processions in their new countries of residence. I examine the changing social and cultural meanings of the images and discuss the conflicts that have arisen within the brotherhoods because of disagreements over how to adapt existing religious practices to the host society and to interpret the socio-religious meaning of the icons. Although Peruvians are devoted to a number of images, I shall concentrate on the Lord of the Miracles, by far the most popular. I shall argue that three dimensions of the belief in this icon have facilitated its global dispersion:

1. The *migratory* dimension. The Lord of the Miracles has its roots in Peru's past as a receiving country of immigrants from Europe, Africa, and Asia who brought their religious traditions and beliefs to the New World. A similar process is taking place today when Peruvians migrate to other parts of the world. As a result, when establishing brotherhoods and honoring the Lord of the Miracles in North and South America, Europe, or Asia, Peruvians are evoking the migratory imaginary that is immanent in the icon.
2. The *syncretic* dimension. The icon is the outcome of a process of creolization and syncretic belief influenced not only by the Christianity introduced by the Spanish conquerors, but also by the faith and religious practices of other immigrant and ethnic groups in Peru. Hence the Lord of the Miracles contains aspects of both mobility/localization and globalization/creolization, which have prompted Peruvian migrants in the twentieth and twenty-first centuries to adapt it to other parts of the world.

3. The *transnational* dimension. The Christian identity of the icon allows Peruvian migrants to draw on the already existing transnational institution of the Catholic Church and to continue their religious practices in the places where they settle (see Casanova 1997). As most Peruvian migrants go to countries that either claim to be Catholic or have large Catholic communities (except Japan, where Christians are a minority), they always find institutions that are willing to house their icons and help them establish brotherhoods and organize processions.

So far research on transnational migration has mostly focused on the economic, political, and social links that tie migrant communities to their places of origin and foster transnational communities and identities. However, recent studies on the relationship between migration and religion suggest that belief systems shape migrants' transnational engagement in significant ways (Avila 2005; Brodwin 2003; Menjívar 1999; Popkin 1999; Pulis 1999; Ruiz Bahía 1999; M. Vásquez 1999; Vertovec 1997; Warner and Wittner 1998; Werbner 2002a) and that they often use religious practices and imaginaries to maintain ties to their place of origin and to negotiate and contest power relations and social conflicts related to the transnational experience (Levitt 2003; Mahler and Hansing 2005; Perera Pintado 2005; Tweed 1997). Indeed, as Rudolph points out, "Religious communities are among the oldest of the transnationals" (Rudolph 1997: 1). In a similar vein, Levitt reminds us that "One way that migrants stay connected to their sending communities is through transnational religious practices" (Levitt 2003: 851) and asserts that "We need to understand what difference it makes for sending and receiving-country communities when migrants express their continued allegiances through religious rather then ethnic or political arenas" (Levitt 2003: 852). In other words, faith and religion must be taken into consideration when studying transnational and diasporic networks.

The aim of this chapter is to pursue this insight and examine Peruvian migration and religious practice as an example of what Werbner calls "chaordic" transnationalism. Such chaorders have no center, but consist of webs of transnational ties and gloss over a paradox "of the one in the many, of the place of non-place, of a global parochialism" (Werbner 2002b: 119). They emerge as networks at the interface between national and transnational institutions such as the Catholic Church, but do not develop their own transnational organizations. Rather, they are propelled by ideascapes or religioscapes (McAlister 1998: 133), whether in the form of regional cults, messianic movements, or other belief systems. My argument is that by bringing out the Lord of the Miracles in the public space of the metropolis of the industrialized world Peruvians achieve two aims. On the one hand, they use the image as a symbolic tool to sacralize public space in the receiving countries and hereby make a moral claim to be recognized as legal subjects with the right to take residence and work in the receiving society. In Agamben's terms the processions reveal the bare life behind migrants' status as tolerated but not recognized foreign subjects and underscore the moral and human aspects of the relation of exclusive inclusion they are subject to in the United States, Spain, Japan, and Argentina. On the other hand, the processions allow migrants to anchor their religioscapes in the host society and localize their religious practice in their new life-worlds. Whereas the Lord of the Miracles thus facilitates migrants' adaptation to the cities and neighborhoods where they live it also makes them visible as a national minority to be distinguished from other immigrant groups in the receiving countries. My point is that this tension between globalizing the meaning of the Lord of the Miracles and using it to make universal claims on behalf of all immigrants and localizing it and using it to claim a particular national identity is inherent in the very nature of regional cults such as the Lord of the Miracles. Because these provide both for particularism and universalism, they allow migrants to simultaneously forge new, hybrid identities that embrace not merely other minority groups, but also the majority population and reify their sense of belonging to Peru while creating new links with the host society.

THE HISTORY OF THE LORD OF THE MIRACLES

Peruvians' belief in the image itself can be traced back to the first Africans who were brought to Peru by the Spaniards in the sixteenth century to work in the plantations on the Peruvian coast (Lockhart 1968: 171–98; Rostworowski 1992: 135–48). The slaves rapidly learned Spanish, converted to Christianity and, inspired by the Spaniards, formed their own religious brotherhoods (Aguirre 2005: 102–13).[3] The newcomers from Africa were also influenced by the indigenous population on the Peruvian coast, who taught them to make mural paintings, which were believed to please the spiritual forces that control the frequent earthquakes in this region. However, instead of painting images of local Andean gods, the Africans made murals of Christ (Rostworowski 1992: 149–60). In 1655 an earthquake hit Lima, creating panic among its citizens and causing extensive physical damage. Yet, according to the legend of the Lord of the Miracles, the wall with the mural of the image painted by the Afro-Peruvian enslave remained intact (see Banchero Castellano 1972), as it did during later and stronger earthquakes in 1687 and 1746, which left large parts of Lima in ruins. This prompted a growing number of mestizos and Spaniards to join the enslaved Africans' deification of the image.[4]

Since the eighteenth century a religious brotherhood has arranged annual processions in honor of the Lord of the Miracles on October 18, during which male devotees organized in teams (*cuadrillos*) carry the icon through the streets of central Lima.[5] Currently, there are twenty such *cuadrillos* in Lima. Female devotees also participate as *sahumadoras* (women carrying the thuribles) and *cantadoras* (women who sing). Together with the *cargadores* (men carrying the icon) they are organized in a brotherhood called Hermandad de Cargadores y Sahumadoras, established in 1878. Other devotees participate as *martilleros* (male devotees ringing a bell to guide the bearers of the image) and *capataces* and *subcapataces* (male devotees directing the *cuadrillos*) (Rostworowski 1992: 181–84).

In 1996 the brotherhood decided to extend the processions to other parts of the city in response to the growing attention that the icon has attracted from among the city's inhabitants during the past three decades. As a result, a crowd of more than one million people participated in the procession when the icon was transported on a truck around Villa María del Triumfo and Villa El Salvador, two huge shantytowns on the southern outskirts of Lima. This is proof of the tremendous popularity that the image has won among Peru's urban poor, including many migrants from the country's Andean hinterland. Obviously, the legend about the enslaved Africans' and later urban mestizos' search for religious strength and social unity to cope with natural disasters appeals strongly to Peruvians, who are either descended from the country's indigenous population or else are of mixed race and who came together in opposition to the Spanish rulers of Peru's colonial society.

GLOBALIZATION AND FRAGMENTATION

Peruvians in Hartford, Connecticut, formed the first religious brotherhood honoring the Lord of Miracles outside Peru in 1972. The painted image that these migrants brought to the United States more than thirty years ago is today kept in The Lady of Sorrow Church in this city. Because of internal disagreements over the management of the brotherhood, the founders of the institution left it. Shortly after migrants in New York City also formed a brotherhood. They brought an image of the saint that today is kept in the Sacred Heart Church in Manhattan.[6] The brotherhood then broke into two, and a second institution was created. Shortly after the split, the followers of the new institution brought another icon from Peru, which is housed in the Church of Saint Benedict (also in Manhattan). Later, migrants in other parts of New York City, such as Queens and Yonkers, in Westchester and Long Island, New York, and in neighboring cities such as North Bergen, Paterson,

Elizabeth and Kearny, New Jersey, established their own brotherhoods. In the late 1970s and early 1980s, Peruvians also formed new institutions in Stamford, Connecticut, Washington, D.C., and Virginia. The latter two, however, each soon split into two independent brotherhoods, each with their own icon.

This adoration of the Lord of the Miracles by Peruvian migrants in New York and other parts of the northeastern United States in the 1970s was only the first of several waves of religious awakening among Peru's emigrant population. During the late 1970s and early 1980s, migrants in the New York City area established a number of similar institutions to honor other Catholic saints or icons. These included brotherhoods honoring San Martín de Porres in Brooklyn, Queens, and Manhattan, New York City; Paterson and Union City, New Jersey; and Hartford, Connecticut. Similarly, brotherhoods honoring Santa Rosa of Lima, the Lord of Muruhuay, and the Virgin of Cocharcas were formed in New York City.[7] In response to the mushrooming of Catholic brotherhoods in the northeastern United States, Peruvians in the New York City area created a national organization, OCHAPERUSA,[8] in 1977 to strengthen and coordinate the activities of the many separate organizations. However, as new brotherhoods continued to crop up in other parts of the United States during the 1980s independently of the organization, it gradually started to lose importance. Today, Peruvians have formed brotherhoods in honor of the Lord of the Miracles in Fort Lauderdale, Broward and Dade County, Tampa, Saratosa, Florida; Chicago; Atlanta; Houston and Austin, Texas; Arizona; Los Angeles, Pasadena, San Diego, and San Francisco, California; Denver and Baltimore; as well as in Toronto, Canada.[9]

In recent years migrant communities in other parts of the world have also created religious brotherhoods in honor of the Lord of the Miracles. In 1988 Peruvians in Buenos Aires established the first brotherhood in Argentina, and in 2000 migrants in Chile formed a brotherhood in the capital, Santiago. Likewise, religious institutions were formed by Peruvians in Spain in the early 1990s. The first was created in Madrid (which then split into two independent brotherhoods), and later another one saw the light of day in Barcelona. In a similar process in Italy, migrants first formed a brotherhood in Rome, then one in Milan, and finally, further ones in Turin and Genoa, the four Italian cities with major concentrations of Peruvians. Finally Peruvians in Japan also started to form brotherhoods, and today approximately eight religious institutions celebrating the Lord of the Miracles exist in the country.

Throughout the world, Peruvians create migrant associations, organize soccer matches, arrange folklore shows, and engage in collecting activities (such as the collection of economic support for their fellow countrymen in Peru after the el Niño disaster in 1998), which evoke memories of their past lives in Peru and produce a notion of shared cultural identity. However, few other activities are considered more symbolic of being Peruvian than arranging processions in honor of the Lord of the Miracles and bringing the icon into the streets of foreign countries. Wherever Peruvians go, the Lord of the Miracles follows them. Or, as one Peruvian in Los Angeles told me, "El Señor always accompanies us. We just have to bring his image with us and take it into the streets wherever we are." Indeed, to many migrants, faith in the Lord is regarded as the essence of being Peruvian. Religion has become the glue of migrants' sense of belonging.

THE CATHOLIC CHURCH AS A MEDIATOR

In order to organize processions and thus honor the Lord of the Miracles, Peruvians first need to acquire an icon representing their religious protector. As most devotees agree that such an image must be an exact copy of the original drawing in the Nazarenas church in Lima, the first step in forming a new brotherhood is to collect money to send someone to Lima to hire a professional artist to make a painting of the Lord on *lienzo* (canvas).[10] Such reproductions can cost several thousand dollars, which represents a considerable expenditure for migrants who mostly work as poorly paid and often undocumented workers. A more feasible option is to start with a photograph of the original image on a *lámina* (lamina) and wait until the brotherhood can afford to pay someone to paint the image on canvas. Other items needed for the procession are a decorated *arco* (arch) that serves as a frame for the icon, and *el anda* (a trestle of wood with four legs) used to support and carry the image. Whereas many brotherhoods start out by producing these articles themselves locally, they usually have replacements made in Peru as soon as they can afford it. Likewise, the *cargadores*, *sahumadoras*, and *cantadoras* must be dressed in the purple-colored *hábitos* (monks' habits) similar to those used in the original procession in Lima.[11] Again, because of the huge cost of acquiring such outfits from Peru, many brotherhoods use locally made habits during their initial processions until they can afford to pay the seamstresses of the Nazarenas church in Lima to produce a set of "true" *hábitos* for their members. Finally, *el estandarte* (the flag), which bears the name of the brotherhood and is carried in front of the icon during the procession, *la campana* (the bell) used to mark the rhythm of the carriers, and different kinds of adornments to decorate the icon are also required.

Once an icon has been provided and a brotherhood has been formed, the devotees start looking for a Catholic church where the image can be kept. Usually a group of migrants forms a committee to approach the local priest and ask him to keep the icon, a petition that, according to Peruvian migrants, is received very differently by the ecclesiastical authorities in Spain, Italy, Argentina, Japan, and the United States. In Buenos Aires, Peruvians reported that they had difficulties in finding a Catholic church that was willing to shelter the first icon they brought from Peru in 1988. Raúl, one of the founding fathers of the original brotherhood in this city, related that when a small group of migrants first asked the priest of La Basílica de Santa Rosa de Ocopa to shelter the image he turned them down, arguing that "We don't need more sacrificed souls in this church."[12] Raúl explained that he and three other migrants then went looking for somewhere else to house the icon. "We followed the flowers of the color purple [traditionally associated with the Lord of the Miracles] in the streets of Buenos Aires until we got to the church of Our Lady of Candlemas, where the local priest welcomed the icon and agreed to house it. You see, I knew all the time that we would find a church for the Lord. We just had to keep on searching." In 1993 the brotherhood brought a new *lienzo* of the icon from Lima, which is kept in the Lady of Piety church in central Buenos Aires as a stationary image, while the original icon is used as a mobile image in the annual processions.

Peruvians in Miami, who formed their first brotherhood in 1986, had a similar experience.[13] Zoila, one of the pioneer immigrants in this city, who came to the United States in 1939, tells how, the year it was formed, the brotherhood appointed her to go to Lima to acquire an icon of the Lord of the Miracles. The cost, including freight charges, was US$4,000. However, the brotherhood experienced great difficulty in finding a church that was willing to provide shelter for the icon when it arrived. They first asked the priest of the Santa Rosa church on Miami Shores but were refused, and it was not until 1992 that the icon was taken in by a Cuban priest in charge of the Corpus Christi church in the central part of Miami. Recently another image has been brought from Lima, and an independent chapel to house it has been constructed with money collected from among the Peruvian and other Hispanic communities in Miami. The icon is worshipped by not only by Peruvians, but also by a large number of migrants from other Latin American countries. In 1994 the brotherhood even brought La Banda Republicana from Peru, which had eighteen musicians.[14] This cost more than US$40,000 and required the Peruvian Consulate in Miami to make a special request to the immigration authorities to grant the musicians entry visas into the United States.

The clergy in other parts of the United States have been more positive about requests from Peruvian brotherhoods to keep their icons. The principal brotherhood honoring the Lord of Miracles in Los Angeles, formed in 1986, keeps its icon in the colonial Placita Olvera Church in the city's old center. Jorge, the current president of the brotherhood, explains, "They let us have our image in the church, and we can also use a hall in the building next to the church for the brotherhood's monthly meetings. The priest doesn't interfere in our activities. But we have to pay the fee each month and also for the masses they hold for us."

In Europe, by contrast, Peruvians have only met a few obstacles in seeking new homes for their religious icons. In Madrid the first image brought to the country by Peruvians in the early 1990s is kept in a small church in the Ascao district. A second brotherhood keeps its icon in the Majadahonda church outside Madrid, but organizes the annual processions in the center of the city. Similarly, migrants in Barcelona brought an icon of the Lord of the Miracles from Lima in 1991. Although the ecclesiastical authorities were initially reluctant to house it they eventually agreed, and today it is kept in the city's cathedral.

In many Italian cities the Catholic Church plays an important role in social work, particularly by helping the growing number of Third World immigrants to find lodging and work. In 1992, at a time when Peruvian immigration in Italy was at its peak, a group of migrants brought an icon of the Lord of the Miracles from Peru to Milan. They asked the nuns of the San Martín church to house it. The request was approved, and for a number of years the image was kept in the monastery attached to the church. In 1996 a brotherhood was eventually formed, and the icon was moved to the Copérnico church in the center of Milan, where it currently is kept.

In Japan, where Christianity is regarded as a foreign religion, most Catholic priests are of either southern European or Latin American origin. As foreigners in a society that regards itself as culturally homogenous, they tend to be understanding of the needs of other ethnic or religious minorities, including requests by Peruvians that the shelter their icons of the Lord of the Miracles. In Yamato, southwest of Tokyo, a local priest of Japanese Argentine origin has not only agreed to shelter the icon brought to Japan by a local group of Peruvian immigrants, but continues to play an active role in the annual processions in the neighborhood. Similarly, the French priest in the Catholic church of Kakegawa openly supports the local brotherhood in honoring the Lord of the Miracles, while a priest of Japanese Peruvian origin in Kyoto personally put in a word for the local Peruvian community when they requested that the ecclesiastical authorities house their icon in a local Catholic church.

NEGOTIATING WITH LOCAL AUTHORITIES

Once a church or chapel has been found to house the image, the devotees start making preparations to take it into the streets. While the Catholic church in Japan has welcomed Peruvian religious images, the local Japanese authorities are extremely reluctant to grant permission for processions.[15] So far only one of the eight existing brotherhoods has been successful in taking the Lord of the Miracles into the streets of Japanese cities. In 1996 the Argentine Japanese priest in Yamato helped the local brotherhood obtain the required authorizations from the municipality and the police to organize a procession in public. Although permission was granted, the brotherhood was only allowed to carry their icon on the pavement on one side of the street ten blocks from the church to a nearby chapel. The event was anticipated with written notifications to all the neighbors, and the brotherhood had to hire the emergency services, including ambulance assistance, to follow the procession. Permission was also granted in the following years, though with much difficulty.

In other parts of Japan, similar petitions by brotherhoods have been rejected because the authorities are worried that the processions may cause disorder and disrupt the traffic. Hence, migrants have been forced to invent other ways of introducing the Lord of the Miracles to the public. In 1996 migrants formed a brotherhood in Hamamatsu. When their petition for a street procession was turned down by the local authorities, they decided to celebrate the icon on the riverbank outside the city, which was traditionally used for sports and leisure activities. Similarly in Mooka, also north of Tokyo, one of the first cities in Japan to accept Peruvian labor migrants in the early 1990s, the local brotherhood has celebrated their annual processions in honor of the Lord of the Miracles on a nearby riverbank for a number of years. By contrast, in Kakegawa the annual procession is held in the yard of the Catholic school, which lies next to the church. Because the families of the children in the school are either Japanese Catholics or immigrants of Japanese descent from Brazil and Peru, the school board readily approved the request from the organizers of the procession. Likewise, migrants in Tsukuba, north of Tokyo, who formed their brotherhood in 1992, have had to organize their annual processions in the yard of the Catholic church where the icon is kept.

To encourage social integration and intercultural communication, the authorities in several municipalities in Japan with major concentrations of immigrants have in recent years invited these communities to exhibit cultural art and perform folklore shows at the local *matsuri* festivals. These are events that are celebrated in Japanese cities throughout the year to honor local gods and to display local religious shrines, which attract visitors from other parts of the country. In response to this invitation, migrants in Kakegawa have demonstrated what they regard as typical Peruvian culinary traditions at the city's *matsuri* for a number of years. In neighboring Hamamatsu, on the other hand, Peruvians use the occasion to honor the Lord of the Miracles. For the migrants in this city, who previously organized religious processions on the river bank, the invitation to participate in the *matsuri* festival was an important step in their struggle to take the Lord of the Miracles to the streets of Japan and thus claim visibility as an organized and articulated immigrant minority. Richard, the leader of a union that organizes Peruvian and Brazilian factory workers in the Hamamatsu area, asserts, "Participation in the *matsuri* has improved our image here. Japanese have many prejudices against Latin Americans. They believe we do all the robbing and cannot be trusted. Sometimes it's true. But now they can see not all of us are like that."

Unlike Japan, the United States has been a multicultural society for a long time. The presence of ethnic minorities in public life is particularly evident in the major cities, which receive the bulk of the country's immigrants. Hence, when Peruvians in New York started to organize processions in honor of the Lord of the Miracles in the 1970s, they simply followed an already established practice among immigrant groups of celebrating their religious saints (e.g., St. Patrick's Day) or national holidays (e.g., the Puerto Rican Parade) in the streets of the city (see Kasinitz and Freidenberg-Herbstein 1992; Reimers 1992). Similarly in Miami, where Cuban and other Latin American immigrant communities make up more than half of the population, the annual processions of the Lord of Miracles have become a well-known public event in the city's famous Calle Ocho, with the participation of large numbers of Catholic immigrants of mestizo or indigenous origin who identify with the icon's religious significance and ethnic history. In contrast, Peruvian brotherhoods in Los Angeles have been less successful in uniting their efforts in organizing processions and directing public attention to their religious icons. Jorge says, "I know that there are at least two other brotherhoods of the Lord of the Miracles in Los Angeles, but we do not have any contact with them. We arrange our procession in the center of Los Angeles, while they do it elsewhere. That's fine for me. After all, Los Angeles is so big, and Peruvians live all over the city."

In Spain the local authorities in Barcelona were initially reluctant to allow Peruvians to arrange processions in the central streets of the city. Hence they were obliged to celebrate the Lord of the Miracles in the yard of the Cathedral, where the icon is kept. Although their request was granted later, the brotherhood is only allowed to carry the icon a few blocks around the church. Miguel, one of the migrants who founded the institution, recalls: "I had to do a lot of paper work. I remember that we wrote letters to the municipality, police etc., and had many meetings. It wasn't easy. It took several years before they let us walk even one block around the Cathedral. The Catalans are not used to seeing processions in the center of Barcelona, so we had to explain everything about how we take the Lord into the streets."

Peruvians in Argentina encountered similar problems. In 1990, when the brotherhood first asked the authorities of a school in Buenos Aires called La República Perú for permission to use its yard to pay their annual homage to the icon, they were turned down. Marino, the president of the brotherhood, explains, "We thought the school authorities would receive us well because the Lord is Peruvian and the name of the school is the Peruvian Republic." He continues, "When we showed them the image of the Colored Christ and told them about the African slave who painted it, they were very surprised. They had expected an image of the Inca." According to Marino, the school's concept of Peru was too simplistic. He says, "The school authorities were worried how the parents and children would react when they saw the image of Jesus as an African. Don't forget that Argentines aren't used to Blacks."

The following year the brotherhood was allowed to celebrate the procession in a small square in Buenos Aires. As they still lacked money to acquire an *anda* to carry the icon, they put it on top of a used cardboard box for toys. And as the priest was in a hurry that day, he ordered them to be back in the church within the hour. Marino remarks, "Imagine, the priest treated us like children! We still didn't know how to organize the procession well. We even had to ask the women to help carry the image. But people were happy because we took it into the streets." The following years the brotherhood obtained permission from the police to carry the image through the streets around the church. In 1998, after the icon had been moved to the Lady of Piety church, the procession walked several blocks through the streets of central Buenos Aires. "It was a great success until a new problem emerged: people started to sell food and beer, leaving the garbage on the streets and creating a disturbance. Many neighbors complained, and the priest told us it that couldn't go on this way. So we had to reorganize everything the next year." The following year the procession was celebrated in Congress Square, and in 2000 the Bishop of Buenos Aires agreed to hold a mass in honor of the Lord of the Miracles in the city's Cathedral on the Plaza de Mayo after a six-hour march from the Lady of Piety church. The procession was headed by a van with a huge loudspeaker, from which a priest from Buenos Aires' Mother of Immigrants church not only preached the spiritual message of the Lord of the Miracles and the Bible, but also made claims for civil and political rights on behalf of Argentina's undocumented immigrants. The priest shouted "¡Viva el Señor de los Milagros!" "¡Viva el Señor de los inmigrantes!" "¡Viva El Perú!" and "¡We hope that the Lord helps regularize all immigrants so they get their DNI [national ID document]!" Marino says, "We have gone a long way. Thanks to the Lord, we have improved our image in Argentina."[16] Clearly, the organizers of the procession and the priest supporting the arrangement interpreted the Lord of the Miracles not only as an emblem of Peruvian national identity, but also as a symbol of the social and political marginalization which all undocumented immigrants suffer in Argentina.

Although the local authorities in Spain and Italy have gradually granted Peruvians permission to organize processions, migrants report that the icon's appearance in the streets of Madrid, Barcelona and Milan continues to attract the attention of the local population. In 1997, while participating in the annual celebration of the Lord of the Miracles in Madrid's Ascao district, I witnessed how Peruvians' performance in public space affects Spaniards' perception of the country's new immigrant minorities. The Spanish neighbors carefully observed the procession, which lasted for two hours.[17] While watching the scene I heard one Spaniard asking, "What's going on? Where are they from?" A man next to him responded, "It's some kind of saint. They are probably Andalusians." To the two observers, the Lord of the Miracles was a symbol of an already ongoing flow of cheap migrant labor from Andalusia and other marginal regions of Spain. In other words, Peruvians were perceived as Spaniards, though of a special kind.

SOCIAL CONFLICT AND BROTHERHOODS

Although devotion to the Lord of the Miracles lends Peruvians in North and South America, Europe and Japan a feeling of unity and shared identity, religious brotherhoods often become fraught with conflict and contestation. The brotherhoods in cities such as New York, Chicago, Paterson, and Miami are traditionally directed by migrants from Lima's mestizo middle class, who have a reputation as lifelong devotees of the Lord of the Miracles or of other images in Peru. In Miami pioneering migrant Zoila asserts, "Before we founded our own brotherhood in Miami, I traveled to Lima to participate in the procession there every year. I also have friends who used to be members of the brotherhood in Lima, so I knew a lot about how to do all these things." However, the recent influx of large numbers of migrants from Peru's shantytowns and rural areas who have little or no previous experience as devotees of the Lord of the Miracles has created divisions in many brotherhoods between one group of "professional" followers, who are strongly dedicated to the icon and already know how to arrange processions, and another group of migrants, who join the activities to meet other Peruvian or Hispanic migrants rather than to celebrate the image.

These divisions are evidence not only of divergent ideas of religious belief, but also an emerging class conflict within the migrant communities that reproduces the hegemonic structure of Peruvian society. In 1998, when I was conducting fieldwork in Miami, a new brotherhood had just been formed in West Kendall, a neighborhood on the city's southwestern outskirts with a large concentration of middle-class Limeños. The migrants promoting this new institution belonged to the more prosperous sector of the Peruvian community in Miami who migrated to the United States in the late 1980s and early 1990s in order to escape the economic and political crisis in Peru. Many of them make their living in business and commerce and feel a need to carve out a separate social space within the Peruvian community and thus distance themselves from the majority of less well-off migrants, many of whom live on the margins of the dominant society. These tensions were aggravated when some of the prominent figures in the community complained about the management of the Peruvian consulate, thus adding a political dimension to the existing conflicts.[18] As rumors started to circulate that one of the employees of the consulate wanted to prolong his term in Miami, a group of Peruvians in Kendall responded by creating several new institutions as platforms to promote their point of view and force the consulate to change its personnel.[19] Thus the Lord of the Miracles, and the history of ethnic discrimination and social inequality personified in the legend of the image, had become a pawn in a social and political dispute that went beyond simply religious belief.

In Argentina I observed a similar conflict. The first Peruvian communities in this country were formed in the 1950s by young men who came to the cities of Buenos Aires, La Plata, and Rosario to study, but later decided to stay on. As most of them married local women and found good jobs as lawyers, medical doctors or veterinarians, they rapidly integrated into Argentinean society. However, during the late 1980s and early 1990s Argentina received a new wave of Peruvians headed by a large number of working-class migrants from Peru's urban shantytowns. They arrived at a time of economic and political crisis in both Peru and Argentina and still live on the margins of society, forming an emergent proletariat of illegal workers. Not surprisingly, the migration and livelihood experiences of these more recent migrants differ radically from those of their predecessors, causing conflict within migrant communities in cities such as Buenos Aires and La Plata. In Buenos Aires I often heard migrants from the 1950s and 1960s referred to as *profesionales* (professionals) and described as *sobrados* (arrogant). In reverse, many earlier migrants deplore the recent immigration that has changed the former image of Peruvians in Argentina.

In 1997 a group of *profesionales* in La Plata decided to form a brotherhood in honor of the Lord of the Miracles.[20] Although Peruvians in this city created their first migrant associations as early as the 1960s, they had no previous experience in forming religious institutions. Hence, the founders approached the leaders of the neighboring brotherhood in Buenos Aires to exchange experiences and explore the possibility of future cooperation. However, contact between the two groups of migrants was cut after the first meeting because of mutual mistrust. Elsa, a female member of the brotherhood in Buenos Aires, explained to me, "Just because they are professionals and have been here longer than we have, they come here and want to teach us how to do things.

The only reason they are now wanting to form a brotherhood in La Plata is that they are jealous. Otherwise, why didn't they do it before?" Today, another group of recent migrants in La Plata has formed a second brotherhood honoring La Virgen de la Puerta (the Virgin of the Door), the female patron saint of their home city of Trujillo in northern Peru.[21] An image of the saint has been kept in the city's cathedral since 1999. To Elsa this development shows that the professionals' attempt to create their own brotherhood has failed. She says, "They are professionals but don't know how to organize processions." Then she adds, "Look at The Virgin of the Door! It's only a couple of years old, but it is already bigger than the Lord of the Miracles and pulls more people than the Lord. They even have an image in the Cathedral." When founding brotherhoods, then, Peruvians tend to reproduce the conflicts that divided them economically and regionally in Peru before migrating.

Some brotherhoods receive substantial economic support from local Peruvian communities so that they can have their icon made in Peru and acquire the paraphernalia required for the processions. However, it is not unusual for such contributions to become a bone of contention, with disagreement over use of the money or accusations of stealing and cheating. In some cases this leads to brotherhoods splitting, as occurred in the Miami area, where four existing institutions are today competing to arrange the largest and most spectacular procession in honor of the Lord of Miracles on October 18 (El Peruano News 1996). A comparable situation developed in Spain in 1996, when a group of Peruvians in Madrid broke away from the first brotherhood to be founded in this city and formed a new institution, reportedly because of disagreements over funds. One year later a similar split within the Barcelona brotherhood was only prevented through the intervention of the Peruvian consul.

Although such conflicts usually break out because of disagreements over funds, they also reflect more profound social and ethnic divisions among migrants, as well as controversies between followers over the aims of the brotherhoods and the significance of the processions. Tensions within brotherhoods occur particularly in countries such as Spain, Italy, Japan, and, to some extent, Argentina, where Peruvian immigration is relatively new and has been dominated by migrants from Peru's urban shantytowns and rural areas. These often have little previous experience as devotees of the Lord and tend to use the brotherhoods to establish networks and social contact with other migrants rather than as platforms to bolster Peruvians' traditional faith in religious images. In Buenos Aires, Marino recalled, "I had never been a devotee of the Lord before migrating. But you see, I've always been keen to create new things. I was elected president in 1991, and since then we have started a lot of social activities. We even had the best Peruvian soccer team here in Buenos Aires. That's what I like about it." However, because they lack a group of core followers and experienced devotees, these migrants find it difficult to generate stable and enduring institutions similar to those in Lima or in cities like New York, Chicago, and Miami. Liliana, the current president of the brotherhood in Kakegawa, Japan, says, "A couple of years ago all the people who formed this brotherhood moved to other places because they had lost their jobs. And because none of us were devotees in Peru, we have had to learn everything first: how to organize the brotherhood, how to arrange processions, how to decorate the icon, etc."

THE CHANGING MEANINGS OF THE ICON

In Peru the organizational and ritual practices of the brotherhoods honoring the Lord of the Miracles has grown out of a centuries-long tradition of devotion to the icon and is therefore only slowly undergoing changes. By contrast, outside Peru migrants are forced to adapt to foreign environments and to invent new ways of expressing their religious beliefs, forming brotherhoods, recruiting new devotees, organizing processions, collecting funds, and so on. In this process of adjusting former cultural and religious customs to the new social milieu, many brotherhoods become an arena for the contestation of migrants' different experiences as devotees and different understandings of the symbolic implications of religious icons. To some, participation in the annual procession represents a mere continuation of their previous religious practice in Peru. To others, faith in the Lord of the Miracles has been triggered by the migration process. They join the brotherhoods and participate in the processions because it offers them an identity different from that of other Third World immigrants. For them the image is an important national symbol that represents Peru and is thus an emblem of their sense of belonging.

These variations in religious beliefs and migration experiences are reflected in the different, often divergent meanings that migrants attribute to the Lord of the Miracles. Raúl recalls that when the first brotherhood was formed in Argentina in 1988, he and a group of migrants suggested that they celebrate the processions on one of Argentina's national holidays in order to recruit new followers among native Argentineans and other non-Peruvians. He explains, "We wanted to create an institution that was open to all Catholics. We thought it would be best for Peruvians not to appear as different from the Argentineans. After all, we are all Catholics. That was also why we suggested that we called the brotherhood by its real name, Hermandad del Señor de los Milagros." However, the proposal to change the date of the procession was opposed by one of the brotherhood's co-founders, who accused Raúl and his friends of "Argentinizing" the Lord of the Miracles and betraying their faith in the icon. The same woman also insisted on calling the brotherhood Agrupación Cristo Moreno (the Group of the Colored Christ), in order to emphasize the ethnic and national identity conveyed by the image. Eventually, both the woman and Raúl withdrew from the brotherhood, and in 1991 the leadership was taken over by Marino, its current leader, who transformed it into a migrant institution that organizes social as well as religious activities. Until recently it even had its own soccer team, which won numerous trophies in the soccer league arranged by the Peruvian Sport Club in Buenos Aires. Indeed, the team became so popular among the brotherhood's followers, and so feared among its rivals, that Marino decided to dissolve it: "I had to think of the reputation of the brotherhood. After all, we are devotees of the Lord, not soccer players. Not that I mind. But people started to complain that there was too much drinking and things like that because of the team."

In order to adapt the Lord of the Miracles to the host society, Peruvians in Japan have also made changes in the icon's institutional and ritual practices. In 1997 a group of migrants in the city of Kakegawa decided to reorganize their former soccer club, called Inca Sport—which was on the brink of disintegration because of disagreements over the management of its funds—into a brotherhood. Although the soccer players of Inca Sport had little or no previous religious experience as devotees of the image, they felt a need to create an institution that would allow Peruvians "to come together and preserve their cultural customs," as one of them told me. Another objective of the new organization was to collect money for Peruvians and other Hispanic immigrants in Japan who needed help. Liliana, the current president of the Kakegawa brotherhood, says that so far the institution has paid the airfare for a Brazilian woman who fell ill and had to return home and helped a Peruvian man in Japan who was injured in a car accident and needed a wheelchair. It is also planning to send money to a Colombian woman who developed cancer while in Japan and wishes to return home. She says, "The brotherhood should be a place where all migrants from Latin America can ask for help. We are not well treated here in Japan, so we have to work together." Arguably, the Kakegawa brotherhood (and, as demonstrated in Marino's statement above, to some extent the brotherhood in Buenos Aires) serves not only as a religious institution, but also as a voluntary migrant association that arranges social and cultural activities for its members and assists them in adjusting to the host society (see Kerri 1976; Hirabayashi 1986).

Once the migrants in Kakegawa had founded the brotherhood, they asked a local Japanese artist to paint the image of the Lord of the Miracles, rather than ordering a *lienzo* from Lima. The outcome is an almost exact copy of the original image, except that the artist has painted the Lord of the Miracles with *ojos jalados* (slanting eyes). Although this rather unconventional representation of the image initially caused a commotion among the devotees in Kakegawa, the members of the brotherhood now recognize and celebrate it as their icon. However, Peruvians in other parts of Japan still disapprove of the painting and question its value as a religious image. Victor, one of the leaders of the brotherhood in Tsukuba, told me that he considers it wrong to produce local versions of the icon with the aim of attracting Japanese followers. Yet Liliana claims that she has come to care for this hybrid icon, which is known as *cristo chinito* (Little Chinese Christ). She explains that the founders of the brotherhood no longer live in Kakegawa, and that no one in the brotherhood can now recall why it was decided to have the image made in Japan and not in Peru. However, she rejects Victor's interpretation and asserts that the brotherhood's objective is to make Peruvians recognize that they are living in a new and different society. In order to do this, they need support from religious powers such as the Lord of the Miracles. She says, "I'm fond of the image of *el cristo chinito*. The Japanese who painted it still keeps in touch with the brotherhood. He's crazy about Peru and our Inca past. I don't know why he made the image with slanted eyes. But there are many *nikkei* who may prefer it that way. That's fine with me."

The conflict over the image of the Little Chinese Christ reflects the diversity of cultural meanings embedded in the Lord of the Miracles and the ethnic and social tensions that the image symbolizes. To Liliana and other followers in Kakegawa, the Little Chinese Christ is an adapted version of the original icon. Yet it also transcends the popular connotations of the Christian faith that gave rise to the legend of the Lord of the Miracles. Just as the original image made by the enslaved African in Lima was created as an alternative representation of Jesus, the Little Chinese Christ was painted as a hybrid version of the Lord of the Miracles. While this caused indignation among more orthodox believers, the icon may well appeal to a new potential group of followers within the Peruvian community in Japan. Thus although Peru's *nikkeijin* population generally shows little interest in the Lord of the Miracles, it is not impossible that the religious and national message of the Little Chinese Christ in Kakegawa will, in the future, reach out to this group of migrants, who increasingly feel rejected, ethnically and racially, by the Japanese majority (Sellek 1997; Takenaka 1999).

THE LORD OF THE MIRACLES AS DIASPORIC IMAGINARY

The transformation of the Lord of the Miracles from a protector of the citizens of Lima against earthquakes to an emblem of national unity embodies the process of political crisis and social change that Peru has experienced in the past thirty years. During this period Peruvians have witnessed not only profound changes in the country's traditional class structure and ethnic divisions, but also the formation of an emigrant population spread over a wide range of metropolitan centers across the industrialized world. As a result, the icon has become emblematic not merely of the sufferings inflicted on Peru's dominated classes in colonial times, but also of the dangers and distress that the country's migrants face when traveling as low-paid workers to unknown countries and hostile environments. Thus Peruvians often picture their struggle to introduce the icon to their new places of settlement as a modern odyssey, similar to their own migratory experiences. This representation of the icon's expatriation consists of four phases: a) the transportation of the image from the church of the Nazarenas to the receiving country; b) the search for a new home for the icon and the collection of funds to finance its ritual celebration; c) the formation of brotherhoods; and d) the organization of annual processions to honor the Lord in public spaces in the host society.

Migrants' recounting of the expatriation of the Lord of the Miracles begins with the troubles they experience when bringing the icon to their new setting. Zoila, the pioneer migrant who brought the first image of the Lord of the Miracles to Florida, relates that before leaving Peru she wrapped the icon in cloth and covered it with cardboard so that no one could see what it was. Although the immigration officials at the airport in Miami told her to open her luggage for inspection, they never discovered the image. Zoila explains, "When they asked me what was inside the cardboard, I said it was a family picture that I had brought for some friends. They believed me and let me pass." She adds, "I didn't want to tell the truth because they would never have believed me. Americans are not like Peruvians. They don't believe in images. Moreover, if the immigration authorities find something suspicious about your papers or the things you bring with you, they use it as an excuse to reject you when you try to enter the country. So I had to tell them another story. But the Lord got here, that is the only thing that matters." To this woman and thousands of other Peruvian migrants, who feel obliged to change or hide their Peruvian ID papers when they travel to First World countries, the image represents an identity that was not to be revealed to immigration authorities.

Another aspect that comes to the fore in migrants' narrations of the Lord's expatriation is the search for a home for the icon. Thus Raúl's reconstruction of Peruvians' first attempt to find a church in Buenos Aires to house the icon took the form of a travel account in which the ecclesiastical authorities rejected the Lord in the same way that many immigration officials refuse Third World migrants entry in the First World. The same narrative style was used by Raúl to describe the despair that spurred him and his companions to follow the purple-colored flowers in the streets of Buenos Aires, which eventually led them to the Church of Our Lady Candlemas. In this account of the devotees' search for a new home for the icon, Raúl evokes the same feeling of powerlessness that many undocumented migrants experience when they put their fate in the hands of people-traffickers, immigration officials, and abusive employers. A similar juxtaposition between the Lord's odyssey and migrants' experiences of arbitrary discrimination was implicit in Zoila's account of Peruvians' struggle to find a home for the icon in Miami.

The last dimension of Peruvians' narrations of the expatriation of the Lord of the Miracles that draws our attention is the organization of annual processions in the streets of New York, Miami, Madrid, and other cities. Often these events are presented in a form that is reminiscent of migrants' own struggles to gain recognition as potential co-citizens in their host societies. Liliana relates that she intends to continue pestering the local authorities until they grant the brotherhood permission to organize its annual processions in the streets of Kakegawa. She asserts, "We would not be content with an offer to carry out the procession at Kakegawa's *matsuri*, as they did in Hamamatsu. We believe that the right way to celebrate the Lord is to bring him into the streets." In her view the procession is a way of conquering public space and obtaining recognition in the receiving society. A similar viewpoint was expressed by a Peruvian I interviewed during the procession organized by migrants in Madrid's Ascao district in 1997. He said, "See, they think we are Andalusians because they believe all immigrants are from Andalusia. But once they discover that the Lord of the Miracles is Peruvian, they will know where we are really from. Perhaps they will become devotees of the Lord themselves one day."

In Miami, where a large number of immigrants from other Latin American countries participate in the annual processions in honor of the Lord of the Miracles, many Peruvians think that the icon has become a symbol of not only Peruvian, but also Latino identity. One migrant pointed out to me that, "We Peruvians are only a small minority here in Miami and the United States, but thanks to the Lord of the Miracles we have contributed something important to the struggle for the rights of Latinos." The same pan-Hispanic vision of the icon was implicit in Raúl's proposal to open the brotherhood to all Catholics in Argentina, as well as in Liliana's suggestion that *nikkei* Peruvians in Japan may identify with the Little Chinese Christ. Clearly, to these migrants the icon has become a symbol not merely of Peruvians' attempts to conquer public space in the host societies, but also of their endeavors to gain recognition as an ethnic minority.

UNIVERSALISM AND PARTICULARISM

Peruvians' attempts to extend the symbolic meaning of the Lord of the Miracles to include other immigrant groups (e.g., in Miami and Kakegawa) as well as the native population of the host country (e.g., in Buenos Aires and Madrid) in the celebration of the icon prompts us to ask three questions. First, why do migrants feel compelled, wherever they go, to import the religious practices of their home country, and why do they choose this particular image among the many icons that are worshipped in Peru? Second, why do migrants struggle for the right to carry the icon in procession through some of major cities of modern world? Is it to conquer the urban spaces of their new countries of residence? Third, why do a growing number of migrants regard the icon as emblematic of their national identity, and how is this related to the fact that their ties to Peru and the mythical home and of the icon remain weak? In other words, what does it mean to be Peruvian, and how does the Lord of the Miracles contribute to this identity?

To answer these questions, we need to explore the complex relationship between universalism and particularism that is inherent in religious cults such as the Lord of the Miracles, which assert, simultaneously, membership in a wider Catholic community, and attachment to more personalized religious manifestations rooted in Peru, which are associated with ethnic and cultural meaning. In his analysis of pilgrimage in the Andes, Sallnow contends that regional cults "provide at once for both universalism and particularism, for both the recession and resurgence of social and cultural differentiation" (1987: 10). He explains that regional cults are commonly linked to wider, external social processes, which they are not only shaped by, but also actively influence. He further suggests that the cults "enshrine a persistent, fundamental, spatial-religious tension," which underlies and animates these processes (Sallnow 1987: 10). To explain this endurance and persistence in time, Sallnow points to the internal momentum of regional cults, which "makes them more than mere functional integrators, or structural antitheses, of relations external to them" (Sallnow 1987: 10). Indeed, Sallnow adds, regional cults "can actively redirect and reshape those relations at all levels, from interpersonal to international" (1987: 10).

The global odyssey of the Lord of the Miracles illustrates how the perpetual conflict between its universal appeal to all human beings and its particular regional and ethnic origin allows its followers to use the icon as both a political symbol to claim legal rights on behalf of immigrants, regardless of their origins, and an exclusive symbol of Peruvians' national identity. On the one hand, the image is identified with a particular place in the world, Lima. This tendency toward particularism is especially prevalent among the brotherhoods in the northeastern United States that were founded in the 1970s and 1980s by Peruvians who were devotees before migrating and who have maintained their ties with the brotherhoods in Peru (Ruiz Bahía 1999). Many of these migrants are of mestizo origin, primarily from Lima's middle class, who construct their new identity as immigrants in the United States by emphasizing their national origin. Hence, they regard the Lord of the Miracles as emblematic of Peruvianness, which they associate with Lima's urban lifestyle. On the other hand, by invigorating the historical interpretation of the icon as the protector of the powerless and the ostracized, and by evoking its links with the Catholic Church, migrants also make a more universal reading of the Lord of the Miracles, which allows them to bring other immigrant groups into the cult. This tendency is widespread among the brotherhoods in the southern and western United States and in southern Europe, Argentina, Chile, and Japan, which were formed by migrants from Peru's urban shantytowns and rural areas who left the country in the 1980s and 1990s at a time of economic and political crisis. As many of these migrants had little experience as devotees before migrating and still are struggling to adjust to their new countries of residence, they use the brotherhoods as voluntary migrant associations to create networks with the host society and other immigrants and to claim social and political rights. Their interpretation of the Lord of the Miracles as a symbol of all the sufferings, which not only Peruvians but all human beings go through when emigrating, represents a tendency away from regional and ethnic exclusiveness and toward global inclusiveness.

The transformation of the icon's classical meaning as the guardian of Lima's population against earthquakes to being the protector of the world's immigrant populations against social injustice and ethnic discrimination has important implications for our understanding of the religio-symbolic meanings of regional cults and their role in the formation of diasporic communities. Theoretically, it implies that we conceive of the universalism and particularism embodied in religious images as tendencies that complement rather than pull against each other, and that we think of them as forces that are potentially present in the cult, depending on the historical context and external changes. Both tendencies, then, are immanent in the Lord of the Miracles, which serves both as an inclusive symbol with which to create links to other immigrant groups, the host society, and the wider world, and as an exclusive symbol of Peruvian national identity.

GROUNDING THE LORD OF THE MIRACLES

Apart from the attempt to create a nationwide organization of Peruvian Catholic brotherhoods in the northeastern United States, the global odyssey of the Lord of the Miracles and the formation of brotherhoods in four continents have been propelled by a sea of local and, to a large extent, independent initiatives, rather than being triggered by an initiative in one part of the world and then dispersed to the rest. Most brotherhoods in the United States, Spain, Japan, and Argentina are established by individuals and small groups of migrants who feel a need to introduce "a piece of Peru" (*una parte del Perú*), as one migrant in Japan expressed it, into their new surroundings.

These are, moreover, run independently of religious institutions in Peru. First, although migrants occasionally communicate with the Nazarenas church to ask for help or advice in the initial phase of establishing a new brotherhood, these contacts seldom last long. Marino, the president of the brotherhood in Buenos Aires, explains that he wrote a letter to the Nazarenas church in Lima to ask for its approval to form a brotherhood and organize processions in honor of the Lord of the Miracles in Argentina. In her reply the *priora* (prioress of the church) said that no such permission was needed. To Marino this implies that "We are an independent institution. We don't need the approval of anybody, at least not of any church or brotherhood in Peru. The only things we need from Peru are the icon, the equipment to carry it and the habits we wear in the processions."

Second, most brotherhoods honoring the Lord of the Miracles recognize the church of Nazarenas as the "home" and origin of the image, and therefore bring copies of the original icon and the other articles used for the processions to their new settings. Nevertheless, these ties are limited to the initial phases of forming brotherhoods, and while there are exceptions to this—like the brotherhood in Miami, which invited Peru's Republic Band to play at its annual procession—such activities do not involve a permanent link with other institutions in Peru. Similarly, whereas some brotherhoods participate periodically in the collection of funds for their countrymen in Peru organized by other migrant organizations, as happened in the United States during the el Niño disaster in 1998, or to raise money to relieve the distress of fellow Hispanic return-migrants, as the brotherhood in Kakegawa does, these links are very fragile and irregular and do not imply any kind of ongoing contact with fellow brotherhoods or ecclesiastical institutions in Peru.

Finally, although neighboring brotherhoods in the same city or host country occasionally communicate or establish some form of contact, these links rarely play an important role in the formation of new institutions or in their regular activities. Indeed, devotees often have little or no knowledge of neighboring brotherhoods, and even when some kind of a link is established, relations often turn out to be hostile (as between the brotherhoods of Kakegawa and Tsukuba), and may even lead to fragmentation and open conflict (as between competing brotherhoods in Madrid, Miami, and Paterson, and contesting factions of the brotherhoods in Barcelona and Buenos Aires). Thus, with the exception of the attempt by Peruvians in the northeastern United States to create a national organization comprising all the brotherhoods in North America, the more than sixty existing Peruvian religious institutions in the world that honor the Lord of the Miracles have emerged on the basis of migrants' independent initiatives in the places where they live. My data therefore suggest that transnational ties and diasporic bonds between religious institutions both outside and inside Peru are the exception rather than the rule.

It is also evident from my research that Peruvians who use the brotherhoods as vehicles to strengthen ties with the host society and contest their status create an alternative identity to that of Third World immigrants, rather than as a means to maintain transnational connections with their home country. Their lives as migrants are firmly grounded in the locations where they reside and work; similarly, their identities as Peruvians and as immigrants are forged in response to the receiving societies. Migrants' struggle to bring the icon from Peru to their new setting, find shelter for it in a Catholic church and take it into the streets of New York City, Madrid, or other world metropolises, then, expresses a wish to present themselves publicly in the First World as an organized and self-aware migrant minority with legitimate claims to civil and political rights in the host country, as articulated by the priest heading the procession in Buenos Aires. Hence, rather than focusing on the bilateral relationships that connect migrants to their places of origin, as proposed in recent theories of transnational migration, I suggest that we examine Peruvians' religious practices by paying attention to the social and political environment that shapes their everyday life and the multiple economic, social, and political ties that link them to the host society and other diasporic groups. By taking the Lord of the Miracles into the streets, Peruvians are pointing out their self-identity as a separate national group that should be distinguished from other Latin American immigrants. However, Peruvians also use their religious icons to create new, hybrid identities across ethnic and national boundaries and to establish contact with other minority groups, as well as the majority population. Thus whereas in Miami Peruvians have encouraged other Hispanic groups to participate in the processions, in Catholic countries such as Spain and Argentina they attempt to adapt these to local religious traditions.

The differentiation of the followers of the Lord of the Miracles into social classes and regional and ethnic groups is reflected in the conflicts that occasionally break out between the members of the brotherhoods and that sometimes lead to their splitting. While these conflicts are often triggered by disagreements over the management of funds, the deeper cause of the recurrent splitting of brotherhoods should be sought in the relations of inequality and domination in Peruvian society that migrants reproduce in the diaspora, and which are played out through the class tensions of the receiving society. In places such as New York City and Miami, where the Peruvian community is represented by migrants from almost all of Peru's social classes and ethnic

groups, disputes mostly occur because of social and political tensions between the better off sectors of the Peruvian community and the majority of
migrants who live on the margins of the dominant society. By contrast, in
countries such as Spain, Italy, Japan, and Argentina, which have only recently
begun to attract Peruvian immigration on a large scale, the followers of the
Lord of the Miracles are still struggling to form stable religious institutions.
Here many newcomers join the brotherhoods in order to establish contact
with other migrants, affirm their sense of belonging, and negotiate their identities as Peruvians and immigrants, thus giving rise to disagreements about
the icon's symbolic meaning.

REVEALING THE SECRET

Because they can extend across national boundaries and form branches wherever their followers happen to settle, regional cults such as the Lord of the
Miracles constitute a force capable of mediating between migrants' countries
of origin and the many places they move in and out of. They thus provide a
sense of order in a chaotic world and a feeling of belonging in the global
space. From this perspective, the icon represents a vector pointing from Lima
and Peru into the world, which migrants use to navigate when moving in a social space that they do not control and to identify at once with a specific place
in the world and feel at home anywhere else. In other words, it allows them
to create "chaordic" diasporism, to introduce "a part of Peru" wherever they
go, and thus to claim a particular identity as Peruvians while simultaneously
broadening the symbolic meaning of that identity to include not only other
marginalized and ostracized, non-Peruvian immigrants, but potentially all human beings within the cult.

NOTES

1. Most religious icons adored by Peruvians are images of official Catholic saints
that have been adapted by peasants or urban migrants to their local life-worlds
(Cánepa Koch 1998: 161–234; Marzal 1988: 103–202), natural forces that are attributed divine powers in local Andean belief systems (Allen 1988: 37–66; Isbell 1985:
137–65), or sites in nature (mountains, rocks, etc.) that, in regional legends, were de-
ified by the revelation of God (Molinié 1999: 245–79; Sallnow 1987: 207–42).

2. Rostworoski suggests that a similar identification of pre-Hispanic deities with
Christian spirits and saints has occurred in Bolivia and Mexico, where the Virgin of Co-
pacabana and the Virgin of Guadalupe represent images of colored women and today
are celebrated by the two countries' indigenous and mestizo populations as powerful

symbols of religious as well as regional and national identities (1992: 170–73). She suggests that, as with the Lord of the Miracles, these virgins represent "an accumulation of faith, symbols and roots of a remote American past." (1992: 173).

3. Afro-Peruvians formed their first *hermandad* (religious brotherhood) in 1540 as a branch of a local Spanish religious institution (Rostworowski 1992: 150).

4. Initially the Catholic Church regarded this practice with great mistrust but, according to the legend, when it ordered the mural to be erased in 1671, the painting revealed its godly power once again and resisted efforts to destroy it. In the aftermath of the event, and after another terrible earthquake in 1687, Lima's citizens produced a copy of the mural and took the icon out in a procession through the streets of the city to ask for protection (Rostworowski 1992: 158). Eventually the Lord of the Miracles was recognized by the ecclesiastical authorities in Lima, and the hermitage of Pachacamilla, where the enslaved African had painted the image of Cristo Moreno and where the Lord's miraculous revelation had occurred, was turned into a convent. Later this became the church of the Nazarenas (1992: 151–53).

5. Rostworowski states that the tradition of celebrating the Lord of the Miracles in October goes back to 1746, when a terrible earthquake hit Lima on October 28. Later the date of the celebration was changed to October 18 (1992: 159).

6. While the brotherhood in charge of organizing the procession is based in the Sacred Heart Church, another brotherhood, called La Hermandad de Sahumadores y Cargadores, is affiliated with St. Patrick's Cathedral. The members of this latter brotherhood carry the image and thuribles and scatter incense during the procession.

7. While San Martín de Porres and the Lord of the Miracles are both images of male *mulatos* (mulattos), Santa Rosa de Lima represents a mestizo woman of Limeño origin, who lived in extreme austerity, strongly committed to her faith to God. In contrast to San Martín de Porres, the Lord of the Miracles and Santa Rosa de Lima, which all are Lima-based icons, the Lord of Muruhuay and the Virgin of Cocharcas are images of Andean origin (the former in Tarma in the central highlands, and the latter in Apurímac department; see Weston 1999). As icons associated with regional legends, they primarily attract followers on a geographical rather than a national basis.

8. Organization of Peruvian Catholic Brotherhoods in USA (Organización de Hermandades Católicas Peruanas en USA).

9. Many of these brotherhoods have little or no contact with Peruvian religious institutions in other parts of the United States or Canada. Thus when I interviewed the leaders of brotherhoods in Los Angeles and Miami and asked whether they were associated with the national organization of Peruvian brotherhoods, many replied that they did not know that such an institution existed. Rather than identifying themselves as part of a national or global religious movement, their faith in the Lord of the Miracles reflects a wish to invest alternative meanings in being immigrants in North American societies. This attempt by migrants to localize belief in Peruvian images in their everyday lives is evident in the growing number of brotherhoods in the United States that design their own home pages on the Internet. Despite the global compass of this media, the information and news offered on these home pages are primarily directed toward local communities.

10. On the back of the original icon in the Nazarenas church in Lima is a drawing of the Virgin of the Clouds (La Virgen de las Nubes), a religious image of Ecuadorean origin. According to Rostworowski, the Virgin of the Clouds was incorporated on the back of the image of the Lord of the Miracles in 1747 (1992: 158). Most brotherhoods also have a drawing or photo of this saint made on the back of their icon.

11. Ruiz Bahía provides an interesting piece of information about gender roles in the Catholic brotherhoods of Paterson, New Jersey. Traditionally, Peruvian males play the dominant role in the annual processions as the carriers of the icon, women being responsible for singing and carrying the incense. However, in Paterson the brotherhood of San Martín de Porres has endorsed the creation of a women's *caudrilla,* that is, the team in charge of carrying the wooden frame on which the icon rests during the procession. Moreover, this change in gender relations has generated an echo in Peru, where local brotherhoods of San Martín de Porres recently also introduced female *caudrillas* (Ruiz Bahía 1999: 99–102).

12. "No nesecitamos más sacrificados en esta iglesia."

13. The first brotherhood in Florida was formed in 1982 by migrants in Fort Lauderdale. Later brotherhoods were established in 1986 (Dade county), 1995 (North Miami Beach) and 1997 (Kendall).

14. La Banda Republicana is the brass band of La Guardia Republicana, a special police force in Peru. The band plays a symbolic role in Peruvian national identity because it plays at important events such as July 28, when the president heads the celebration of Peru's day of independence.

15. Once permission has been granted by the local priest to accommodate the Lord of the Miracles in his church, most brotherhoods are allowed to keep control over the funds they collect from their followers and to plan their own activities independently of the church. However, some priests and clergy housing Peruvian icons interfere in the affairs of the brotherhoods, demanding not only that they contribute economically to the church, but also insisting on participation in its work (see Ruiz Bahía 1999: 102–3).

16. While doing fieldwork in Buenos Aires in 2000, I participated in the procession together with more than 10,000 Peruvians on the last Sunday in October. According to some participants, it was by far the largest since the brotherhood was founded in 1988. After the mass, the procession continued to the San Ignacio church, where the local priest received the icon. An event of such magnitude and duration (it began at noon in the Lady of Piety church and ended at 10 p.m. in the San Ignacio church) was only possible because the brotherhood has 250 active members organized in four *cuadrillas* of male carriers (formed in 1992, 1998, and 1999) and one group of female *sahumadoras* and *cantadoras*.

17. The procession was headed by a group of male Peruvians dressed in the traditional purple-colored habits, who carried the icon five blocks around the church where it is kept. The image was decorated with an almost complete set of adornments and sat on top of a wooden frame. A crowd of several hundred Peruvians participated in the procession, which looked much like the original one in Lima. Halfway through each block a member of the brotherhood rang the bell, indicating that it was time for

a break. Accordingly, the bearers stopped and sat the wooden frame and the image down on the ground. After a while he rang the bell again, indicating that it was time to continue the procession. The pause was used by the followers to lift their children up to the image to let them kiss it, which was believed to keep them healthy and bring them luck.

18. In 1998, while I was doing fieldwork in Miami, I was invited to a party to celebrate the brotherhood's first anniversary. The event was organized as a *cena bailable* (dinner with dance) in a rented hall in Miami's West Kendall district, and the participants, who paid US$25 to enter, were mostly middle-class Peruvians. During the party the organizers paid homage to political leaders, businessmen, artists, students, and others from the Peruvian community in Miami who stand out because of their talents and achievements. They also appointed an honorary member of the brotherhood, who was greeted with great applause. The man is a wealthy real estate dealer from Huancayo, a commercial city in Peru's central highlands, who migrated to the United States in 1990 because of economic and political disagreements with local politicians and slum dwellers living on his properties. In 1999 he was elected president of the Convention of Peruvian Institutions in the United States and Canada, an umbrella organization of Peruvian migrant associations in North America.

19. This group of migrants is headed by the man who was appointed an honorary member of the newly established brotherhood in Miami in 1998. The same group also formed a migrant club based on regional ties with Huancayo.

20. A third brotherhood of the Lord of the Miracles is reported to be under process of foundation in Mendoza. One member of the brotherhood in Buenos Aires told me that a Peruvian student who participated in the procession in 1999 returned to his home community in Córdova with the intention of creating a brotherhood in this city.

21. In fact, the Virgen of the Door is not the patron saint of the city of Trujillo but of the province of Otuzco, from where a large number of migrants in Argentina originate. However, as many of these migrants have spent most their lives in Trujillo as rural-urban migrants in Peru, they associate the Virgin of the Door with this city.

Part III

CATEGORIES AND TRAJECTORIES

Chapter Seven

Home, Bittersweet Home

In the previous chapters I have documented the conflicts and divisions that recurrently occur within the communities and organizations that migrant establish in their new countries of settlement. I have also claimed that migrants often credit these tensions to the feelings of mistrust that prevail between Peruvians because of differences in class, geographical origin, and ancestry. In other words, Peruvians in the United States, Spain, Japan, and Argentina continue to classify fellow migrants in terms of the social, regional, and ethnic labels that divided them in Peru before emigrating. In this chapter I pursue this insight by inspecting the social and cultural meaning that migrants attribute to these labels and examining the impact that their discriminatory and excluding import have on migrants' decisions to emigrate and their choice of country of destination. Finally, I examine in what way such labeling fashions migrants' expectations that emigration will improve their lives and shapes their construction of notions of belonging and ideas of a possible return migration in the future.

My argument is that regional and ethnic labels form a hierarchy of categories that gloss over Peruvians' migration history and indicate their families' geographical origin and the social status associated with this origin. In this hierarchy of categories Peruvians descending from European immigrants are opposed to Peruvians belonging to the country's indigenous population. Between these two groups we find Peruvians who are of mixed descent (denoted mestizos) or either descend from rural-urban migrants of indigenous background (called *cholos*), enslaved Africans or contract workers from China and Japan (often referred to as *chinos*).[1] The trust of my argument is that these categories and the migration histories they epitomize have crucial bearings on Peruvians' inclination to emigrate and perhaps later return to Peru. Of course,

177

this should not lead us to assume that regional and ethnic labels can be studied as self-reproducing categories of thought. Quite on the contrary, such terms are a product of Peru's economic and political history and the relations of inclusive exclusion that have sustained and legitimized the country's class structure since the colonial period. In effect, class, regionality, and ancestry and the categories coined to conceptualize economic, geographical, and cultural difference have been mutually constituted in Peruvian history.[2] However, regional and ethnic labels do not go away easily and although economic and political changes in the past fifteen years have transformed the country's class structure cultural prejudices and the discriminatory practices they entail continue to exclude thousands of Peruvians and prevent them from achieving social mobility.

To study exactly how economic status, geographical origin, and family ancestry shape Peruvians' expectations that emigration will yield upward social mobility I examine twelve migration trajectories based on interviews with Peruvians in the United States, Spain, Japan, and Argentina. The trajectories illuminate not only the particular circumstances that prompted each of the twelve Peruvians to emigrate but also the way that these experience the migration process and reconfigure their ideas of home and belonging in response to their new life situation. In this way I hope to bring to the fore how social inequality in Peruvian society spurs migration but also how migration leads to a change in migrants' notion of social and ethnic status. The sample includes five female and seven male migrants who belonged to different social classes and ethnic groups in Peru at the time of emigration and who were between twenty-four and eighty-four years of age at the time of the interview. The chapter is divided into subsections that each includes two migrants who share same social and ethnic background in Peru.

INDIGENOUS PERUVIANS

Livio

Livio, sixty-four, was born in Chacapalca, a little town in Peru's central highlands. In 1951, after finishing school, he moved to Oroya, where he got his first job selling tickets on the city's urban buses. At the age of eighteen he was granted a driver's license, allowing him to assist his father, who made a living as a driver offering a service known as *colectivo* (transport in privately owned cars). A few years later he married a woman from Pichos, a village not far from Chacapalca that has large migrant communities in both Lima and Miami. In the 1960s Livio, his wife, and their three children moved to Moquegua in southern Peru, where he opened a small shop selling groceries to the workers in Southern, an American-owned copper mine. When the company laid off a large number of workers in the early 1980s, Livio and his wife decided to close the shop and move to Lima, where they bought a house and made a living buying and selling merchandise. However, because the business went slack they decided to go to Florida, where one of their daughters had been living for several years together with her husband. Thus in 1985 Livio and his wife entered the United States on a tourist visa, which they later overstayed, becoming unauthorized immigrants. Livio recounts, "I was lucky to get a tourist visa. I got it because of my wife's business. They thought I didn't go because I needed work but because I wanted to do tourism." In Miami their daughter and her husband helped them finding a place to live. A couple of years later Livio's two other daughters followed them and also settled in Miami.

Whereas his wife immediately found a job as domestic servant for an American family in Miami Livio spent several months unemployed. Being an unauthorized immigrant who only spoke Spanish, he did not know where or how to look for work. He recalls, "I just walked around asking anyone who looked like they spoke Spanish where to find work. I felt ashamed that my wife and daughters made money but I didn't." Eventually he got a job as an unskilled construction worker. He says, "One day someone told me where they were looking for construction workers, and when I got there they asked me whether I could start working the following day. I said yes, and the next day I worked for ten hours. I didn't even ask for the salary." Later he got a job in a 7-Eleven shop, but had to quit because there were too many violent assaults. Four years ago he found a job as a table cleaner in a fast-food restaurant in Ventura Mall in northeast Miami.

Although Livio and his family all have been granted American citizenship, Livio has not made up his mind where to live. His wife currently lives in Lima, where she makes a living renting rooms in the house they bought in San Luís when they moved to Lima and a flat in San Borja that they later acquired. Livio and his three children, meanwhile, live in Miami. Two of their daughters are studying at college, while the third works. When I interviewed Livio in 1998 in Ventura Mall he claimed, "I'm content with my life in the United States and I'm grateful to this country." Livio looked at me quickly and added, "Look, you don't have to work as hard as me because you're a professional. If not, you would have to work like me." He continued, "I like living here. But my wife is in Lima, and I may go back to live there too when I retire. I go home every year, although it costs a lot of money. I always bring a lot of presents, which I give to anyone who is in need." Livio concluded, "I have three houses, one in Miami, one in Lima and one in Chacapalca. As an

American citizen I can go anywhere I want once I retire." Livio laments the fact that he belongs to the lower strata in both the United States and Peru, but recognizes his fate and feels satisfied with the life he is following because he is free to move wherever he wants. Indeed, Livio's network is far-reaching: his daughters all live in Florida, his wife in Lima, and he still has close relatives in Chacapalca. For him, home is not one specific place but changes meaning according to his current needs and future plans.

Silvia

I first met Silvia in Lima in 1990. At that time she was twenty-three and was living with her family in a small flat in San Luís, one of Lima's working-class neighborhoods, and working as an assistant in a dental clinic in San Isidro, an upper-class residential district. Born in Sarayka, a remote village in the department of Apurímac, Silvia was raised with Quechua as her mother language and did not learn Spanish until she started school at the age of six. When she was eighteen her father sent her and Andrea, her older sister, to stay with one of their aunts in Lima. In 1986, two years later, when Peru's political violence reached Sarayka, Silvia's parents and younger siblings had to escape, leaving most of their belongings behind in the village. To Silvia's relief, the family was now reunited in the flat of a relative in San Luís. However, because her parents were unemployed and her sisters and brothers were too young to work, Silvia had to maintain the entire family financially together with Andrea. This new role as a breadwinner put in jeopardy her plan to save money to study and make a future career as a dental technician. To make things worse, Silvia's boyfriend, Fredy, was pressing her to formalize their relationship and agree to become his wife. Hence I came to know Silvia at a time when she was making new plans for the future. One of these was to emigrate to the United States, where Andrea, her older sister, had been living since 1989.

In 1992 Silvia left Peru, following the same route as Andrea had done three years earlier, and paying the same amount of money, US$5,000. Unlike her sister, who was caught by the police while crossing the border between Guatemala and Mexico and returned to Guatemala, Silvia was lucky and made the trip without being detained. Yet she recalls the journey as extremely harsh and risky. She says that the toughest part of the trip was crossing the U.S.-Mexican border at night, and recalls, "the *coyote* took us over a river in a group. We all walked in water up to our necks and using bamboo sticks so we could breathe. When we got to the other side, we were all wet and freezing but had to wait until the sun rose." The only luggage they could bring with them was a small back sack with a few clothes and the money they had brought to buy food and pay for lodgings during the trip. Silvia adds sardonically, "That's why they call us wetbacks." In the United States Silvia first went to Los Angeles and then continued straight to Miami, where Andrea was waiting for her.

Silvia comes from one of Peru's poorest regions and most marginal social strata, so for her any dream about a better life begins by moving to the city. To her migration is synonymous with social mobility and an essential part of her struggle to *progresar* (make progress) and create a life of her own. She left her native Quechua-speaking village in the country's Andean highlands because it was the only way to study and improve the conditions of her life. Her first stop was Lima, where a hostile mestizo world forced her to conceal her Andean descent and to speak Spanish instead of Quechua. The next stop was Miami, where she feels more comfortable than in Lima. She says, "I feel more Peruvian now. I never liked Lima. I never felt at home there. In the United States people look at me as a true Peruvian. Here I am more distant from my family and more independent. And people accept me here and respect my desire to make progress." When asked whether she ever thinks of returning, she says, "No, why should I? Of course, I miss my family and Sarayka, but I can always go back to visit them. I feel as much home here as in Lima." Hence, for Silvia emigrating was just another step in a lifelong process of migration that one has to go through in order to make progress. Migration means conquering new worlds and creating new livelihoods.

From Peruvian Indigenous to American Peruvian

To Livio and Silvia migration is a means to achieve social mobility. They both had previous experiences as rural-urban migrants but found the prospects of changing social and ethnic status and creating new lives in Peru too bleak. Hence, they used emigration as a strategy to *progresar*. Although the two migrants have taken unskilled, low paid jobs in the United States, they think they are better off than in Peru. Not only do they make more money in Miami than before emigrating but they also feel that the receiving society recognizes them for what they do and not for whom they are. Moreover, although they both have passed time as unauthorized or undocumented immigrants in the United States Livio and Silvia consider this experience as one among many obstacles in their migration trajectory, which not only include the legal barriers they encounter in the United States but also the cultural prejudices that prevented them from claiming their citizen rights and achieving social mobility in Peru. Finally, rather than imagining home as their village or region of origin they associate it with the recognition they have achieved and the relations of trust and respect they have created in the United States. In effect, neither of the two migrants dream of a soon return to Peru.

JAPANESE PERUVIANS

Antonio

The son of Japanese immigrants in Peru, Antonio identifies as a *nikkeijin*, that is, a descendant of Japanese emigrants. Encouraged by a Japanese contractor, who offered them a loan to finance the trip and helped them find work in Peru's sugar plantations, his parents left Japan in 1934 on the same boat on which former president Fujimori's parents traveled to Peru. During his first years in Peru Antonio's father labored hard to pay off their debts. However, after some years he succeeded to save enough capital to buy a lot of land in Huaral, north of Lima, which at that time had a large colony of Japanese settlers. Here Antonio and his five brothers and sisters were brought up in an environment that was still strongly influenced by the customs and values of their parents' place of origin. Antonio recalls that his oldest brother, who was born before World War II, was the most "Japanese" of the six siblings, the others being more "Peruvian." He also remembers that when the family had visitors, their mother instructed her children carefully in their responsibilities. To her mother Japanese visits had to be "perfect."

World War II radically changed the situation for Peru's Japanese colony. It reminded many *nisei* and *sansei* (second- and third-generation Japanese immigrants) that the ties which their parents and grandparents maintained with Japan and the exclusive identity as an ethnic minority that they claimed before the war was placing their position in Peru in jeopardy, and that their own future lay in the country where they were born. As a result all Japanese schools in Peru were closed after the war, and the postwar generation of *nikkeijin* were given European names and learned to speak proper Spanish. This shift in orientation away from their nation of origin and toward their country of residence is reflected in the fact that since 1945 Japanese immigrants in Peru have married outside their own ethnic group to a much greater extent than *nikkeijin* in other South American countries such as Brazil. Unlike their parents and older siblings, who grew up with the idea that they were real Japanese and therefore were going to return to Japan one day, the generations born after the war increasingly identify themselves as a mixture of Peruvian and Japanese cultures.

Antonio is painfully aware of the impact that World War II had on his life. Not only did the authorities confiscate his father's properties when Japan and Peru suddenly became enemies, but the family was forced to hide on the farm of a Peruvian friend to avoid deportation to prison camps in the United States. After the war his parents became less insistent on maintaining Japanese traditions, which allowed Antonio and his younger siblings to become much more familiar with the Peruvian way of life and to integrate into the surrounding society than their older brother. He relates that they particularly enjoyed the freedom to go to parties in the Peruvian style, which they found spontaneous and open to individual initiative. Eventually they all defied their parent's wishes and entered marriages with non-Japanese Peruvians.

In the 1950s and 1960s Antonio's father went to Japan to visit relatives a number of times. At that time Peru was experiencing a period of economic boom, and Antonio's family's business prospered. Thus his father was received as a hero in Japan. Antonio says, "My father left Japan as a poor man looking for work in Peru. And he came back a rich man. In Peru he gave each of his nephews a gold necklace that was worth a car in Japan in those days." However, the relationship between the two countries was reversed in the following three decades.

After finishing school Antonio found a good job at the office of Nissan's Peruvian branch in Lima. However, as he wished to make a career in the car industry and his father knew of a Japanese *contratista* looking for workers from Peru, Antonio decided to try his luck in Japan, where a new immigration law in 1990 allowed foreign-born *nikkeijin* to work temporarily in the country. In Japan he visited the sons of one of his father's brothers, who invited him to stay with them and take a job in a small company they owned together. However, Antonio declined the offer because he lacked proficiency in Japanese and because he felt estranged from the cousins. He says, "I didn't feel they understood my situation. I only wanted to make money and return to Peru as soon as possible." His Peruvian wife had just passed away and their three children were living in Peru. He continues, "I had a good job in Peru making US$500 a month. I only went to Japan because the *contratista* had promised that I could improve my skills and make good money. In the contract I was promised work similar to what I had in Peru."

To his regret, he ended up as a factory worker in Japan's "bubble" economy together with thousands of other *nikkeijin*, not as a white-collar worker as he had been promised by the *contratista*. The *enganche* practice has changed little since his father migrated to Peru almost seven decades ago. Today, after five different factory jobs in Japan, Antonio has retired at the age of forty-eight. He bitterly adds, "They only want young people today, preferably women." Yet Antonio has no intention of returning home to Peru. His Peruvian wife died several years ago and his three children, who all emigrated from Peru during the 1990s, now live with him in Japan. He declares, "My children do not feel Japanese as I do. They were raised as Peruvians. To them, Japan is not home. They don't understand me when I insist that they are Japanese. Maybe they're right. After all, we don't feel welcome here in Japan."

Inja

Inja is a so-called *issei*, that is, a first-generation Japanese emigrant. He is eighty-four years old and was born in Okinawa, one of Japan's most southerly islands. His parents, who had a total of nine children, were farmers of very little means. In 1925 his oldest brother left for Peru, followed some years later by two more brothers and a sister. In 1935 it was Inja's turn. He left Okinawa on a trip that lasted one and a half months and brought him to Yokohama, Hawaii, San Francisco, and Panama before he disembarked in Callao, Lima's port where his brothers received him. Unlike many Japanese immigrants who came to Peru at the turn of the century as contract workers, Inja arrived as a free man and soon after his arrival he got a job on a Japanese newspaper in Lima. However, when World War II broke out the newspaper was closed down. Hence Inja opened a shop in downtown Lima, which proved to be a profitable business until Peruvians looted it agitated by anti-Japanese sentiments. Inja even came close to being deported to the United States, but was hidden by his neighbors when the police came to pick him up. After the war his brothers returned to Japan to search for their wives and children, who had been sent back before hostilities broke out. Inja and his sister, on the other hand, stayed in Peru.

Inja's business prospered again in the postwar period, and in 1952 he married an *issei* women, also from Okinawa. Together they had three children classified as *nisei*, that is second-generation Japanese emigrants. In 1968 the couple visited Japan and their relatives in Okinawa for the first time since they had left. Inja recalls that when they arrived in Tokyo "my wife was so surprised that she could not say a word." In Okinawa Inja met his siblings who had stayed behind and got to know their children. Two weeks after their return to Peru Inja's wife died, leaving him not only with the three children they had together but her own two and a sixth child that Inja had out of wedlock.

In 1990 Inja's oldest son, who was twenty at that time and had been trained as a police officer and received a diploma in judo in Peru, went to Japan. Inja says, "My son had hoped to work as a watchman, but the only work he could get was in the factories." In 1991 Inja's second son, who had married a *sansei* in Peru, followed, and in 1992 Inja's daughter also migrated to Japan, together with her non-Japanese Peruvian husband. The same year Inja and his sister and her husband also returned to Japan, and today the entire family lives in Isesaki, northeast of Tokyo. Inja finds that Japan has changed a lot since he emigrated. And so has Peru. He says, "When I left, Japan was poor and Peru was much richer. People were very nice in Lima and it was safe to walk in the streets. But now Peru is poorer, and I have had to fight off thieves who wanted to rob me in the street." Yet Inja misses Peru, where he spent more than fifty years of his life and where he would like to return to live for the rest of his days. He says, "Here in Japan we all work in factories and feel estranged. In Peru I feel more at home."

From Peruvian Japanese to Japanese Peruvian

At first glance Antonio's and Inja's migration histories seem very different. Antonio was born in Peru by Japanese immigrants. Inja, on the other hand, is a Japanese citizen who emigrated to Peru as a young man. However, a closer look also reveals commonalities. Although Antonio and Inja were raised in two different parts of the world they both grew up with the idea that they are Japanese. In effect, for many years the two migrants honored Japanese values, dreamed of a future life in Japan, and conceived of themselves as different from the rest of the Peruvian population; likewise, they both contracted marriage with Peruvian women of Japanese descent and taught their children Japanese values. By the same token, in the 1990s when Peru's economy was in decay and Japan's economy was booming they both left for Japan joining the migration wave that brought thousands of Peruvians of Japanese descent to Japan. Much to their regret, however, Antonio and Inja ended up as ostracized immigrants making a living as unskilled factory workers. This experience has prompted the two migrants to revise their idea of home and notion of belonging and today Antonio and Inja both claim that they feel more Peruvian than Japanese.

CHINESE AND AFRO-PERUVIANS

Goyo

Goyo is the grandson of Chinese emigrants who traveled to Peru in the 1920s to work. The family later settled in Nazca, a city on the Peruvian coast south of Lima, where Goyo's father married a local woman and became a successful businessman. Despite the family's economic wealth and social status, however, the father constantly reminded his thirteen children that their family name, Li, and physical appearance would determine their ethnic identity as *chinitos* wherever they went. Goyo recalls that when one of his older brothers asked for the family's consent to enter Peru's military school, their father refused. He said, "No one called Li will ever be accepted in the Peruvian army." Not surprisingly, Goyo and his siblings had mixed feelings about their dual identity as Chinese and Peruvian.

At the age of ten Goyo migrated to Lima to study at one of the city's many universities. A few years later he graduated as an engineer and set up a small print shop. However, because of the economic and political crisis that affected Peru in the late 1980s, Goyo had to close his business and leave the country. He recalls that he decided to emigrate after a bomb placed by one Peru's terrorist groups exploded two blocks from his workshop in Lima. He says, "They could have killed me as well. The workshop they blew up was no different from mine. Next time it could be me." However, Goyo's decision to emigrate was triggered not merely by Peru's political crisis, but also by the problems caused by his marriage to a Peruvian woman. In 1978 Goyo's oldest brother, who was identified as the principal heir in the family's will, had also married a Peruvian woman without his father's consent. As a result the father sent him to Los Angeles, where a business contact of his promised to look after him. When Goyo also defied his parents' wishes and married a woman outside the family's ethnic group, he too was forced to emigrate. Thus in 1989 Goyo traveled to the United States on a tourist visa together with his wife and two children. With the help of a friend of his brother's in Los Angeles, he found a job in a small company that was looking for engineers, and after a while managed to obtain a so-called H-9 visa, which allowed him to stay in the United States and work. Today he owns an import/export company together with his brother.

Ironically, Goyo feels more Peruvian in Los Angeles than in Peru. He says, "Maybe I look Chinese, and that's probably why people here in the United States believe that I'm Asian. But I always say that I'm Hispanic. I don't feel Chinese here but Peruvian or Latino." Goyo's father is now dead but his mother and a number of his siblings still live in Peru. However, Goyo has no plans to return. He says, "The Hispanic community here in Los Angeles is so big, so why should I go back?"

Pedro

Pedro was born in La Victoria, one of Lima's largest and oldest working-class neighborhoods, and raised as one of a family of eight children. His parents were both Afro-Peruvian and came from Peru's African population, which was brought to Peru in the colonial and early republican period to work on the coastal plantations as slaves.[3] As his father made a living as a blue-collar worker and his mother worked as a street vendor, Pedro's and his siblings' opportunities for studying and making a traditional career were few. Hence Pedro, who was known as Pelé among his age mates because of his ability to kick a football, decided to try his luck as a professional soccer player. After a couple of years he succeeded in obtaining a contract in a local soccer club, but when Peru's economic situation deteriorated in the mid-1980s he was forced to find another way of making a living. In 1985 Pedro contracted marriage with a Peruvian woman of African descent and the couple decided to set up their own restaurant in La Victoria. As Pedro's wife is a good cook known for her *tamales* and *criollo* food, the business was quite successful at the beginning. However, as Peru's economic crisis deteriorated in the late 1980s, it became increasingly difficult to keep the business going. Eventually, Pedro decided to emigrate to the United States. That was in 1987.

As Pedro had no relatives or friends outside Peru, he traveled alone and did not know what his final destination was going to be. He recalls that he first went to Mexico by air and then continued to the United States on land together with a small group of Peruvians he met on the way. After crossing the U.S.-Mexican border as undocumented immigrants together, they continued to Los Angeles, where they split up. Pedro says that although he ended up staying in Los Angeles, he had no idea where to go when he arrived. He recalls, "I might as well have ended up in New York or New Jersey. In fact I don't even remember why I ended up in Los Angeles. But this was where I arrived." In Los Angeles Pedro spent several months all by himself before he ran into a fellow Peruvian migrant and established contact with the Hispanic community. Later his family followed.

In Los Angeles Pedro's wife set up a new business selling *tamales* and Peruvian food, finding her customers from within the city's huge Hispanic community. Pedro, meanwhile, established himself as the manager of a local association of Peruvian soccer teams, while also working as a sports reporter for one of the Peruvian newspapers in Los Angeles. Indeed, the couple have been quite successful economically and gained much fame within the Peruvian community. By combining soccer and food, they seem to have touched the cultural essence of what many migrants identify as Peruvian and what they associate with home. As Pedro points out, "When I arrange a soccer match, my wife always comes by selling *tamales*. And people always buy them. That makes them feel like they were in Peru. Later I write about the event in the newspaper using my nickname Pelé." When I asked him whether he has ever thought of returning to Peru one day, Pedro replies, "We're doing fine here. In Peru people always looked at me as Black. Not that it really bothered me, but in the United States I feel more Peruvian."

From Chinese/Afro-Peruvian to Hispanic Peruvian

Goyo and Pedro belonged to different economic and social strata in Peru before they emigrated. Whereas the former comes from a fairly well off provincial middle-class family the latter was born in one of Lima's largest working-class neighborhoods and raised in a family with very few economic means. Hence, the two men's possibilities to study and earn a living in Peru varied significantly before emigrating. Notwithstanding these differences, Goyo and Pedro have both suffered from racial and cultural discrimination because of their ethnic status in Peruvian society. Goyo descends from Chinese contract workers and Pedro's ancestors were enslaved Africans. The two men also share same migration trajectories. They both have emigrated to the United States, more specifically Los Angeles that has a huge Hispanic population of primarily Mexican origin. However, whereas Goyo left Peru because his family refused to recognize his marriage with a woman of non-Chinese descent economic necessity forced Pedro to emigrate. Although the specific circumstances that prompted them to emigrate differ both men state that they are content living in California, which has allowed them to eschew their ethnic status as Chinese and Afro-Peruvians and achieve recognition as both Peruvian and Hispanic. In other words, the migration experience has shaped both men's notion of home and idea of return migration in significant ways.

MESTIZO PERUVIANS

Silvio

Silvio, fifty-two, grew up in Huancayo, one of the major cities in Peru's highlands. His family belonged to the small group of mestizos who have traditionally played a dominant role in the city but who have seen their privileged position being challenged in the past two decades by the growing number of rural migrants of Andean origin. After Silvio graduated as a civil engineer, he married a local woman who was working as a schoolteacher and with whom he has had four children. A personal friend of the city's mayor, he was entrusted with being the leading contractor in the construction of a number of Huancayo's most notable public buildings (the Civic Hall, the University, etc.), and over the years he became not only one of Huancayo's wealthiest citizens, but also a prominent personality in the city's social and political life. In the late 1980s he invested money in a large lot of land on the outskirts of Huancayo, which he intended to parcel out and sell. However, his plans did not work out the way he had expected. A group of rural migrants invaded the lot and established one of Huancayo's largest shantytowns there, mostly inhabited by displaced people from other Andean areas affected by Peru's civil war in the late 1980s and early 1990s. Initially, Silvio responded by asking the police to clear the lot. However, as the invaders succeeded in drawing public attention to their struggle for land rights, the conflict became a delicate political issue for Silvio, who received death threats from the Shining Path and was eventually forced to flee.

Thus, Silvio and his family migrated to Miami in 1990, settling in Kendall, where Silvio invested the savings he had brought from Huancayo in real estate. As in Huancayo he bought a large lot of land in Kendall, which he parceled out and sold to other Peruvian migrants. Over the years these entrepreneurial activities have made him not only a wealthy but also a politically influential man within the Peruvian community. In 1998 he was elected president of the Miami chapter of AIPEUC (the national association of Peruvian institutions in the United States), and a year later his wife created a regional organization for Huancayo migrants in Miami and a local brotherhood in Kendall in honor of one of the Lord of the Miracles (see chapter 6). Today his four children are all studying in high school and at university, and he and his wife are considered important actors in the preservation of Peruvian folk culture and identity, in Miami as well as the rest of the United States.

When asked about his vision of home and desire to return, Silvio's wife says, "We're okay here. Our four children are studying, and two of them have entered university. When we came to Miami my husband and I had to confront the Peruvian establishment because we said we were proud of being Peruvian and because we wanted to demonstrate our Peruvian culture. But now they recognize our efforts. Of course, we must continue fighting. We would like to go back to Huancayo if the political situation changes in the future. Maybe we will return to Peru one day and recover the land we lost in Huancayo."

Ana

Ana, fifty-seven, was born in Lima, where she worked for twenty-four years as a schoolteacher. Her father also came from Lima, while her mother was born and raised in Callao, Lima's port. Ana's husband, who is sixty, is also from Lima and used to work in the city's transport company as a manager of the public bus system. Because Peru's economic and political crisis in the late 1980s made it increasingly difficult for Ana and her husband to maintain the family and pay for their three children's education, they started to explore the possibilities of emigrating. A friend of the family, who at that time was preparing to leave for the United States suggested that Ana's oldest daughter joined her on the trip planned to take them by land through Central America and Mexico to California. However, as the daughter was afraid of traveling illegally she decided to wait. Instead Ana and her daughter applied for a tourist visa at the American Embassy in Lima, which they were granted in 1989. The same year they two women flew to New York where the friend who had left a year earlier helped them to find a place to live. When the tourist visa expired three months later Ana returned to Peru. By contrast, her daughter decided to overstay her visa and become an unauthorized immigrant. Despite of her illegal status the daughter, who the studied electric engineering in Lima before emigrating, soon found work in a factory producing electronic devices. Later she married a Puerto Rican man, which gave her the right to American citizenship. She then moved to Kearney, New Jersey, the husband's hometown.

In 1993 Peru's economic crisis reached its peak, and Ana's husband was fired because the company had to cut down its activities. The couple then decided to leave together and later pull their two younger children and Ana's mother. The same year they both obtained tourist visas for the United States and left for Kearney, where their oldest daughter and her husband were waiting for them. After three months, however, Ana returned to Peru to take care of her two youngest children, leaving her husband in Kearney as an unauthorized immigrant. In 1993 she traveled to the United States for a third time, now through the family reunification program, having been invited by her daughter, who had become an American citizen. The daughter also applied for a green card for her father, which he obtained after a few months. Moreover, Ana, who is now an American citizen, has invited her mother to come to the United States through the family reunification program together with her two youngest children, who are studying in Lima.

Ana and her husband have both found work in Kearney and continue to send money back to Ana's mother and their children, who live off the allowances that her husband received after he was laid off from his former job in Lima. Their plan is to reunite the entire family in the United States. Although this plan seems close to being fulfilled, they are not content with their new life. Ana says, "My husband doesn't like living here. He works in a factory in Kearney and has no hope of finding other jobs. He was better off in Peru. I would like to go back to Peru too. We had a good life there. We still have our house there. But our children can have a better future here. We told them to study professions they can use in the United States."

From Mestizo Peruvian to Peruvian Hispanic

Although Silvio and Ana originate from different regional and cultural environments in Peru they both lived stable middle-class lives before emigrating. However, Peru's economic and political crisis in the late 1980s and early 1990s radically changed their lives; Silvio because he received death threats and Ana because her husband lost his job. In effect, they both decided to emigrate to the United States, Silvio to Miami and Ana to New Jersey. Both migrants first entered their new country of residence on a tourist visa but while Silvio later asked for and was granted political asylum Ana continued to travel back and forth to assist her relatives in their efforts to get to the United States. Eventually, she was granted legal residence through family reunification. The two migration trajectories show that migrants' class and economic status in Peru play an important role for their possibilities of traveling legally.

They also reveal that although Silvio and Ana managed to create new middle-class lives in the receiving society they both regret the loss of their former status as mestizos in Peru and deplore their new status as Hispanics in the United States. To them, home is inextricably associated with a stable middle-class life in Peru. Not surprisingly, both Silvio and Ana continue to dream of a future return.

EUROPEAN PERUVIANS

Roberto

Roberto, fifty, was brought up in Miraflores, an upper-class neighborhood in Lima. His family belongs to an exclusive group of upper-class Peruvians, who claim descent from European immigrants and invoke this to distinguish themselves from the rest of the population. He went to school at Leoncio Prado, a famous military school for boys. Although the school's main function is to provide new recruits for Peru's armed forces, it also serves as educational institution for the children of the country's middle and upper classes. After finishing school Roberto underwent training to become a pilot, hoping to make a career in one of Peru's airlines. However, because of the political changes that followed the military coup against the democratic government of Belaúnde in 1968, these plans never materialized. The new regime installed by the military introduced a reform policy that gave land and voice to Peru's marginal and powerless rural population at the cost of the dominant upper-class of European descent. As a result, Roberto and his family, who felt that the military regime threatened their privileged position in Peruvian society, decided to emigrate.

In 1968 Roberto traveled by air to Los Angeles on a tourist visa, which he later succeeded in converting into a student visa. He recalls, "I didn't have any close family in Los Angeles, only a couple of friends who offered me a place to stay. They also told me how I could get a job to make money to get started." In 1978 Roberto became an American citizen after marrying a Mexican woman, who had obtained U.S. citizenship. This allowed him to bring first his brothers and sisters and then his aging parents to Los Angeles, where they died a few years later. Today his entire family lives outside Peru. Roberto's first job in the United States was as a parking assistant, but after a few years he managed to obtain a license to fly and got work in a commercial air company. Roberto later started his own business, and now he owns a tourist and travel agency in Hollywood. Moreover, he has become a respected person in the Peruvian community in Los Angeles and is currently the president of the local chapter of the national association of Peruvian organizations in the United States.

Roberto says he has no plans of returning to Peru. Although he takes active part in the Peruvian community in Los Angeles and occupies a leading role in migrant associations in the United States he feels more at home outside than inside Peru. Today Roberto's closest relatives are scattered in both Europe and the United States. Furthermore, his status as *leonciopradino*, that is, a former student of the Leoncio Prado school in Lima, links him up to a global network of fellow migrants who have formed associations in various parts of the United States (see chapter 5). The aim of this network is to create ties based on solidarity and support among *leonciopradino* migrants wherever they live. Roberto says, "We're part of one family, and we always support each other to get jobs and get along, wherever we travel or migrate. I don't think I'll ever go back to Peru. I feel at home here in Los Angeles, but maybe I'll go to Europe one day. Who knows?"

Alma

Alma, forty-five, was born in one of Lima's upper-class neighborhoods of parents of European descent. Her mother was born in Peru but of immigrants from northern Europe. Her father, on the other hand, was born in Spain and spent most of his youth in England until he migrated to Peru as an adult. As a child Alma was taught that she was different from most of the rest of the Peruvian population and that her status as an upper-class Peruvian constitutes an important resource that she is expected to draw on whenever necessary. Similarly, she was raised with the idea that she belongs to a family network of ties that reach far beyond Peru and include relations in Europe as well as the United States. This notion of belonging to a world reserved for a small group of privileged families that descend directly from European immigrants was also prevalent in the elite school where Alma was educated. Here the teachers only taught in English, which was also the usual language of communication at Alma's home, except with the maids. She says, "My family comes from Europe, and in school many of my classmates were like me. They had non-Spanish European surnames and they were brought up with the idea that they were different from other Peruvians. In fact, I never felt Peruvian in the way that many others do." Although Alma grew up in Peru, then, she never fully identified as a Peruvian.

Political developments in Peru in the 1970s, which ended the control of the country's ruling families, reformed the land tenure system, and integrated the subordinated classes into the political system, changed the life world of Alma's family, and prompted her family to emigrate to the United States and

Europe. In the 1980s Alma left for Miami, where she married a Cuban and settled in Coral Gable, an exclusive neighborhood in the southern part of the city. She now studies at the University of Miami and participates in the local Hispanic community. However, she only has a few Peruvian friends in Miami, and rarely attends events organized by the local Peruvian community.

Alma says she has no wish to return to Peru. She asserts, "I have no future there. Today 50 percent of my former classmates live outside Peru, and we often communicate, mostly by e-mail. One lives in Japan, where he is directing an international project. Another lives in Thailand, one has gone back to France where his parents come from, and one is living in England. Another even lives here in Miami. But you couldn't tell that he is Peruvian. His surname is German, and he is the director of the office of one of Spain's major banks here in Miami." Hence, Alma is part of a global network of not merely family members but also former classmates, some of whom still live in Peru, though many have emigrated like herself. Ironically, she feels uncomfortable in the company of the local community of other upper-class Peruvians living in Miami's newly rich areas such as Key Biscayne. She says, "When I'm together with Peruvians here in Miami, they know that I'm from the upper class. So they think I'm not a real Peruvian. But when I go to one of those Peruvian restaurants where the really rich people come, they know from the way I dress and spend money that I'm not one of them. You see, I belong somewhere in the middle. I'm not like the rest, but neither am I part of the upper class."

From European Peruvian to Peruvian Cosmopolitan

Roberto's and Alma's migration histories share many commonalities. They both come from families that claim European ancestry and grew up in upper-class neighborhoods in Lima; likewise, they were both raised to believe that they are different from other Peruvians because of their descent and privileged economic position in Peruvian society. Furthermore, they both attended elite schools in Lima, which reinforced their class identity. However, the reforms introduced by Peru's military regime in the late 1960s and early 1970s undermined the economic and political privileges that Roberto's and Alma's families used to enjoy and prompted them to emigrate. In the United States they both married well off North Americans of Hispanic descent, obtained U.S. citizenship, and settled in exclusive neighborhoods in Los Angeles and Miami. Today Roberto and Alma have family members in Europe and the United States and form part of small networks of former students from Lima elite schools, which make them identify as cosmopolitan and Peruvian at one and the same time. In effect, both migrants feel at home in most cities of the modern world.

DESCENDANTS OF INDIGENOUS PERUVIANS

Lizet

Lizet, twenty-eight, comes from the city of Trujillo on Peru's northern coast, where she studied to be a teacher after graduating from school. However, she decided to emigrate before finishing her studies because of the economic situation in Peru. In fact, Lizet had received several offers from relatives of hers living in different countries. Her preferred destination was Japan, where one of her cousins was living and where she had been told that the salaries were higher than elsewhere. Moreover, Lizet felt convinced that "In Japan you live more quietly and better organized than in other parts of the world." Nevertheless, when she was told that another cousin of hers had been detained at the airport in Tokyo and deported while trying to enter Japan on a forged passport, she changed her mind and made contact with another relative who was living in Italy. Once again, however, Lizet was forced to change plans, this time because the costs of traveling illegally were too high. Eventually she decided to go to Argentina, where her mother had been working in Buenos Aires for a number of years and which was the least expensive of the options available to Lizet.

In 1994 she entered Argentina on a tourist visa, which later she overstayed. Now an unauthorized immigrant living she was hired by three Argentine women to take care of their mother, who is handicapped and needs attention twenty-four hours a day. Although at five hundred dollars her salary is higher than the average, Lizet does not feel content with the job. She says that the youngest of the three sisters blames her for the bad health of her ailing mother. She says, "It's like she thinks it's my fault that the mother doesn't get better. But how can that be? She feels guilty because she lets me take care of her mother. The truth is that I know more about her illness than she does. That's why she's jealous and that's why she reproaches me all the time. But what can I do? I prefer to take care of children, but in Argentina there are more old people than children, and people pay others to take care of them."

Two years ago Lizet pulled two of her brothers to Argentina. However, they have both had difficulties finding work and are forced to make a living washing cars in the streets of downtown Buenos Aires. Lizet declares, "I really can't complain, although I don't like my work. Look at my brothers? It's like in Peru. Washing cars in the street. The only difference is that they make a little more here than there. But only a little bit. That's how life is in Argentina. Here there's only work for women. The men should stay at home!" But Lizet's prospects of achieving social mobility in Argentina are not very promising. She says, "I do not want to stay but I don't want to go back to Peru neither. In Peru I had no future. Here I have work but it does not lead me any-

where. I would like to go to Spain or Italy but I have no one there to pull me."
Indeed, Lizet does not seem to feel at home anywhere and is always looking
for somewhere else to go.

Cecilia

Cecilia, who is twenty-three, was born in Trujillo in on Peru's northern coast.
Her parents come from Otuzco in the highlands not far from Trujillo and migrated to this city when they were young. The father works as a truck driver
whereas her mother sells food at a local market. Cecilia and her two older sisters and two younger brothers grew up and went to school in Esperanza, a
shantytown at the outskirts of Trujillo where the family owns a humble house.
After finishing school in 1988 Cecilia studied to become a nurse and was
lucky to find work as assistant at a laboratory in Trujillo. However, she found
the salary to be very low and after a couple of years she decided to emigrate.
Before leaving Peru she agreed with her older sisters that they would all emigrate for periods of three years to work and send money back to their
younger brothers so that they could study.

The first to emigrate in Cecilia's sibling group were Cecilia's two sisters
who traveled to Japan in 1992. Having entered the country on tourist visas
they took work in a factory where they made almost US$3,000 a month each.
After three months they two sisters overstayed their tourist visas and became
unauthorized immigrants. As they remitted most of their earnings to their parents in Trujillo the family's economic income increased substantially. However, the following year their stay in Japan was unexpectedly disrupted after
they were arrested and deported by the Japanese police. Yet instead of returning to Peru the sisters ended up in the United States. Cecilia relates, "My
sisters were put in a flight to Miami with connection to Lima. But as they
traveled during Christmas and the airport in Miami was very busy they managed to escape their officers that looked after them and enter the United
States." She goes on, "Then they went to Chicago where they have married
Mexican men and now live."

Cecilia, on the other hand, emigrated to Spain in 1994. She entered the
country on a tourist visa becoming an unauthorized immigrant after this expired. In Barcelona she found work taking care of a senior Catalan woman
who later helped her applying the Spanish authorities for a *cupo* (a time limited work permit). She then returned to Peru where she stayed until the Spanish Embassy in Lima called and asked her to collect her work permit. Once
again Cecilia traveled to Spain, which she entered this time as a legal immigrant, and in Barcelona she took up the job as care taker of the Catalan woman.
Because the work requires that Cecilia lives in the woman's apartment she

saves and remit most of her earnings to her family in Trujillo. She says, "I am very worried for my younger brothers in Peru. I hope that they can study and later find work. That's why I send almost all the money I make. My sisters in Chicago are married and have children so they cannot help much. And I don't think they'll ever return to Peru."

Although the Catalan woman treats and pays Cecilia well she does not feel at home in Spain. She says, "I miss my family. I don't feel well here." She rents a room together with another Peruvian woman where she spends her Sundays off. However, instead of going out she sits in the room writing letters to her relatives. Cecilia declares, "In Spain I work to forget myself," and adds "but I can't go back. I have no future in Peru." To her, home is neither in Spain nor Peru.

From Excluded Peruvian to Estranged Alien

Lizet and Cecilia come from families that have migrated from Peru's highlands to the shantytowns of the country's major cities with the aim to *progresar* and change social and ethnic status. The vernacular term for such rural-urban migrants as well as their descendants is *cholo*, a strongly charged word that incarnates their excluded status in Peruvian society. In the past fifteen years Peruvians belonging to this social strata have emigrated in large numbers to escape from cultural prejudices and economic poverty in Peru and seek social mobility in other parts of the world. Whereas Lizet decided to go to Argentina, which can be reached at a relatively low cost, and entered the country on a tourist visa, Cecilia went to Spain also on a tourist visa. After three months both women became unauthorized immigrants. Yet Lizet's and Cecilia's different choices of destination also point to important differences in the two women's room for maneuver. To Lizet emigrating to Argentina was the last and only option available to her. Cecilia, on the other hand, traveled to Spain where not only the salaries are higher than in Argentina but where the immigration policy and labor market offer her better possibilities of achieving social mobility. Thus in Spain Cecilia was fortunate to obtain a work permit and become a legal immigrant whereas Lizet continued to work illegally.[4] Yet despite these differences both women feel estranged in their new countries of residence. They also declare that they have no other places to go. To them, home is always somewhere else.

DISCUSSION

The twelve migrant trajectories demonstrate that Peru's economic crisis and political conflict constitute two major push factors in contemporary Peruvian emigration. They show, first, that the political reforms introduced by the military government in the late 1960s and 1970s prompted members of the country's ruling class to emigrate (Roberto and Alma), and second, that the economic crisis and the violent conflict that affected Peru in the late 1980s and early 1990s led Peruvians from the urban middle-class and the country's shantytowns to emigrate too (Silvio, Ana, Lizet, and Cecilia). This indicates that Peru's exodus resembles other Latin American migrations, such as the Cuban (Pérez 1992), which have also taken the form of waves of migrants from particular social classes emigrating in response to economic and political changes in their country of origin. However, the trajectories also suggest that structural causes alone cannot account for the recent emigration of more than two million Peruvians. They reveal that Peru's minorities in particular are inclined to emigrate because of their migration histories and the regional and ethnic status accorded to them as indigenous peasants or the descendants of former rural-urban migrants, slaves, or contract workers. More bluntly, the trajectories suggest that Peru's current exodus to a large extent is propelled by the inclusive exclusion and the relations of inequality and domination that shape Peruvian society.

Migration clearly constitutes a leitmotif in Inja's life course. Born in Japan he immigrated to Peru as a young man but returned to his country of origin as an old man; indeed, in his transpacific travels Inja has experienced being treated as an ethnic foreigner in both Peru and Japan. Arguably, the same experience is immanent in the migration history of Antonio's family, although he had no personal migration record before going to Japan. Silvia and Livio, on the other hand, who spent their childhood in the rural Andes and moved to the city before growing up, regard Miami as just another destination in their search for social mobility and struggle to change social and ethnic status. Moreover, although the migration history is not present as an active memory in the personal or family trajectories of Goyo or Pedro, the two men clearly consider emigration an important resource in escaping the ethnic discrimination they suffered in Peruvian society due to their ancestry and in seeking social mobility in the United States. Today both Goyo and Pedro insist that emigrating has made them identify as more Peruvian than they use to. For Livio, Silvia, Inja, Antonio, Goyo, and Pedro, who all belong to Peru's ethnic minorities, then, geographical mobility and social mobility are two sides of the same coin.

Unlike Peru's indigenous peasantry, Peruvians who descend from European immigrants and Peruvians who identify themselves as mestizos point out that they emigrate because of political instability and economic crisis rather than racial discrimination or ethnic prejudice. However, the migration trajectories discussed in this chapter also indicate that the two groups of Peruvians perceive emigration in very different ways. Thus, while middle-class mestizos, whether from provincial cities like Huancayo or from Lima, regard it as a temporary strategy to regain lost economic opportunities and social status in Peru, with the possibility of returning to what they consider their home country (Silvio and Ana), Peruvians of European descent tend to view it as a way of strengthening their economic and social positions, not merely in Peruvian society, but also within the existing diasporic networks of the country's economic and ethnic elite (Roberto and Alma). In other words, whereas middle-class mestizos emigrate because they feel that their economic and social position is being jeopardized, Peruvians of European descent regard migration as a strategy that confirms existing relations of control and power. Yet, as demonstrated by Alma's testimony, the question of who is accepted into the country's elite continues to be an issue of contestation, both within and outside Peru.

Peruvians who descend from Peru's indigenous population but live in the shantytowns of the country's major cities generally take great pains to distance themselves from their Andean past and to win recognition as Spanish-speaking, western-oriented mestizos. However, because they are notoriously classified as *cholos*, these recently urbanized Indians are constantly being reminded of their family's rural roots and migration activities. During the economic and political crises of the past two decades, the deteriorating prospects of escaping poverty and achieving social mobility have prompted large numbers of these rural-urban migrants to reconsider their family's migration and livelihood strategies and use this experience to emigrate and search for new ways of making a living outside Peru. Lizet and Cecilia initially entered their new countries of residence on tourist visas, but became unauthorized immigrants once these had expired. Arguably, the stigma that the two women suffer in their new countries of residence as ostracized immigrants reminds them both of their previous experiences as *cholos* in Peru. And although both migrants acknowledge that they have improved their living conditions compared to their situation before emigrating they still claim that they do not feel at home in their new countries of residence and that they would like to go somewhere else. Hence, like Peruvians belonging to Peru's indigenous population and minority groups, Lizet's and Cecilia's migration histories have clearly influenced the two women's decision to emigrate. However, unlike Livio, Silvia, Goyo, and Pedro, who claim to feel more Peruvian after emigrating, but like Inja and Antonio, Lizet and Cecilia have few hopes that their lives as immigrants will lead to any improvement in their social status, suggesting that the context of their reception in their new countries of residence is playing a critical role in migrants' own expectations.

CONCLUSION

Although most Peruvians living outside Peru feel united by a common idea of national origin, the notion of home varies, depending on migrants' previous migration experiences and their social statuses before emigrating. Mi-

grants from the country's urban middle class, who are predominantly mestizos, tend to associate home with their place of origin. For them emigration is
a strategy of escape from Peru's economic depression and political instability, which implies a temporary uprooting of their natural ties of belonging.
Upper-class Peruvians of European descent, on the other hand, often dissoci-
ate their place of origin with the notion of home, which they conceive as a diasporic network of social ties rather than any specific city or country. From
this perspective Peru is only one among many places to which they may feel
attached, and unlike many middle-class Peruvians, who subscribe to an ideology of nationalism that equates home with their country of origin, upper-
class Peruvians prefer to stress their class status rather than their national
identity. By contrast, migrants with an ethnic or a minority background tend
to associate home with the experience of being recognized as Peruvian on
equal terms with Peruvians of mestizo and European descent in their new
place of residence. Rather than attaching the idea of nationality to a particular territory or cultural history, they regard national identity as a relationship
of belonging that emerges from their new status as emigrant Peruvians. Finally, migrants of classified as *cholos* and subject to cultural prejudices in Peruvian society often emigrate to elude racial and social discrimination as
much as to achieve social and economic mobility. However, because they
rarely have access to support networks, they are forced to travel to destinations that are easy to get to and do not require work or residence visa. Not
only does this lack of support networks limit their possibilities of changing
economic and social status but it also means that they spend long periods of
time at the margins of the receiving society.

The twelve migration trajectories are evidence of the inclusive exclusion
that molds Peruvian society and prompts thousands of Peruvians to emigrate
to achieve upward mobility. They also demonstrate how economic, regional,
and ethnic difference in Peru continues to shape migrants' ideas of what it implies to be Peruvian as well as their dreams of home and return migration. As
discussed in chapters 5 and 6, such notions periodically cause conflicts and
divisions within migrant associations and institutions. In the following chapter I explore how the exclusive inclusion and in particular the illegalization of
Peruvians in the United States, Spain, Japan, and Argentina affect their possibilities of creating new lives in these countries.

NOTES

1. In Peru regionality is often used as a euphemism for ethnicity. Hence, the semantic difference between the two forms of classification is difficult to establish. Yet
when asked to identify themselves most Peruvians prefer to refer to their regional

rather than ethnic origin thus eluding the cultural prejudices and racial discrimination attached to the latter form of classification.

2. Mendoza argues that we should take ethnicity and race to be historically defined categories. She claims that when studying inequality in Peru "To use the concept of either ethnicity or race alone to analyze the category of 'mestizo,' as well as categories of 'Indian,' 'cholo' (intermediate category of 'Indian' and 'mestizo'), and white, would only limit such analysis" (2000: 10).

3. Today most of the country's African minority lives in Lima and the southern coastal towns of Cañete, Chincha, and Ica, and belong to Peru's impoverished urban working class.

4. Supposedly, Lizet has been granted legal residence by the amnesty dictated by the Argentinean government in 2004.

Chapter Eight

Tales from the Shadow

Migrants can be divided into two groups: those who possess proper ID and therefore travel, work, and take up residence without violating the immigration laws in their new countries of residence, and those who do it illegally because they cannot comply with the requirements to obtain legal status. In this chapter I focus on the latter group and explore how the "cat and mouse" game described in chapter 4 unfolds from the perspective of the undocumented or unauthorized immigrant. The chapter examines the many pathways, geographically as well as socially, that migrants traveling without ID pursue in order to avoid detention and deportation; likewise, it explores the implications of the struggle to obtain legal status and the required ID for the lives of undocumented or unauthorized immigrants. My aim is to scrutinize the meaning of "illegality" from the perspective of those classified as illegals and to investigate the consequences of illegal status for their ability to achieve the goals and ambitions that led them to emigrate in the first place.

My approach to illegality is to view it as a state of being, one may say a form of liminality in Turner's sense of the term, that the majority of Peruvians living outside Peru go through at some point during their lives as migrants (Chávez 1992: 4–6). Whereas many enter this state as soon as they leave Peru (i.e., as undocumented immigrants), others become illegals after first entering their new countries of residence on a legal entry visa, which they later overstayed (i.e., as unauthorized immigrants). Yet others continue to change status as documented and unauthorized immigrants. Thus many migrants who enter the United States illegally manage to obtain temporary residence permits as students or political refugees. However, when these expire they become unauthorized immigrants again. As Ngai states, "The line between legal and illegal status can be crossed in both directions. An illegal alien, can, under certain conditions, adjust his or her status and become legal and hence eligible for citizenship. And legal aliens who violate certain laws can become illegal and hence expelled and, in some cases, forever barred from reentry and the possibility of citizenship" (2004: 6). Rather than constituting a separate sphere in the lives of Peruvians, then, illegality is a condition that they continuously enter and leave and therefore constantly have to respond to and act upon.

Many Peruvians who travel illegally originate from Peru's Andean highlands and the shantytowns of Lima or other major cities and belong to the country's excluded population. Although the economic and social circumstances that trigger their emigration often are the same, the avenues they use in emigrating vary considerably. Some eschew illegality all together and enter their new country of residence as legal immigrants because they possess professional skills that are considered valuable by the receiving society (e.g., as agricultural workers or artists), belong to a particular ethnic group that is granted special rights by the immigration law (e.g., as *nikkeijin*), or are related by ties of kinship to a national citizen or an immigrant with a permanent residence permit who is entitled to family reunification. Yet others travel illegally because they are denied an entry visa to their new countries of residence but manage to convert their illegal status into a legal one subsequently. However, migrants from Peru's peasantry and urban working class are not the only Peruvians who struggle to obtain legal papers in the new countries of residence. Indeed, many middle- and even upper-class Peruvians, who have professional titles as dentists, medical doctors, engineers, teachers, or architects, pass long periods working as unskilled workers such as cleaning assistants, restaurant workers, and gardeners, because these are the only jobs they can find as undocumented immigrants. While some succeed in legalizing their stay in the receiving society and establishing their professional title within a short time of their arrival, many continue to struggle to get established for several years often experiencing downward mobility and loss of social status compared to their position in Peruvian before emigrating.

My scrutiny of illegality comprises three aspects of the life of undocumented and unauthorized immigrants. First, I explore the many detours and problems that Peruvians who travel illegally are faced with when crossing international borders, entering the countries of the First World, and looking for work and somewhere to live in their new countries of residence. Second, I discuss how illegality and the lack of ID shape the life worlds of individual migrants and influence their relationships with family, friends, and fellow migrants and the surrounding society. Third, I examine how migrants navigate through the labyrinths of illegality once they have arrived and settled in their new countries of residence and, more specifically, how they negotiate and contest the relations of dependence and dominance to which they submit themselves when embarking on illegal traveling.

THE PATHWAYS OF ILLEGALITY

Illegal traveling is an important aspect of modern, globalized life that is of great concern to all social actors involved in migration processes (Düvell and Jordan 2003; Kyle and Kolowski 2001). From the perspective of the First World, undocumented migrants are aliens who cross international borders without proper ID such as passports and take up residence in foreign countries without complying with the requirement to obtain legal status (Andreas 2001). Moreover, because undocumented immigrants are denied many of the rights that legal immigrants and natural citizens are granted, their presence challenges the moral and democratic values that dictate the identity politics of many First World countries. Similarly, they reveal the dilemma of placing people in juridical and political categories such as legal and illegal, and account for the administrative inconsistency that the term's conceptual ambiguity creates in bureaucratic practice. As such they represent an enormous challenge to social order and are addressed by politicians and the public media in very different and often contradictory ways depending on their political stance (Friman 2001). While some portray undocumented and unauthorized immigrants as uncontrolled, invading aliens, others regard them as the helpless victims of economic poverty and social injustice (de Genova 2005: 56–94).

From the point of view of the undocumented or unauthorized immigrant, on the other hand, illegality implies living at the edge of society and in the twilight between law and criminality. Traveling and living without documentation implies the risk of not only being detained and deported to your country of origin but also abused by the local police, cheated or blackmailed by travel agents, and in the last resort, assaulted, raped, or perhaps even murdered by people-smugglers or others who are trying to exploit the vulnerable situation of migrants as individuals without ID and therefore a status as "lawless" (Kyle and Dale 2001). Hence, migrants' travel narratives are often dramatic descriptions of how, either by astuteness or plain luck, they managed to overcome the many dangers of their journey and the obstacles they encountered in reaching their final destination (Spener 2001). Once in their new country of residence, undocumented and unauthorized immigrants are forced to take jobs that documented immigrants and native citizens refuse to take, and to accept salaries and working conditions that are often at variance with the statutory minimum wage and labor market regulations in the country.

Moreover, because undocumented and unauthorized immigrants lack ID, they may be denied access to a number of services that other people enjoy, such as renting a flat or house, taking out a bank loan, or applying for a driving license; similarly, they cannot claim protection from the police against threats or crimes, and are often exploited by their employers, who benefit from their lack legal rights. Indeed, in some countries such as Argentina, undocumented and unauthorized immigrants avoid the police not merely out of fear of being deported, but also of being robbed or raped. In other countries such as Japan, illegality is regarded as a criminal act and can therefore be punished by not merely deportation but also imprisonment.

The following eight migration trajectories describe the many dangers and difficulties that migrants in the United States, Spain, Japan, and Argentina experience when traveling illegally. They also illustrate how migrants design strategies and navigate their ways in and out of illegality in their efforts to create new lives in their new countries of residence. Thus while some of the migrants have entered their new country of residence legally only to become unauthorized because they remain in the country after their tourist visa expires or they loose their refugee status others arrive without any form of documentation but succeed to convert their illegal status to a legal status at a later point of time. Yet others continue to zigzag in and out of illegality and legality without ever obtaining permanent legal residence. Finally, the eight trajectories demonstrate not merely the particular forms and meanings that illegality takes in the United States, Spain, Japan, and Argentina but also the consequences these forms and meanings of illegality have for migrants' individual lives and their capacity to make future plans in their new countries of residence and for instance go back to Peru and visit their families.

Andrea

In chapter 7 I described my first encounter with Silvia in 1990. Indeed, Silvia's situation resembled that of Andrea, her elder sister, who arrived in Florida in 1989. Before emigrating she signed a contract with a travel agency in Lima, which charged her US$7,000 to arrange the journey, planned to end in San Diego. An aunt (*tía*) living in Miami lent her the money to finance the journey, which took three and a half months and first brought her to Panama by air. Here she took another flight to El Salvador, from where she continued the journey by land together with a group of other undocumented migrants, including five Peruvians. A local agent instructed Andrea and her traveling companions how to bribe the border police when entering Guatemala. Andrea relates that once across the border she returned her Peruvian passport to Peru by mail and continued the journey without any form of personal documentation. She states, "My passport could only cause trouble. If the American police catch you and see your passport they return you to Peru, but if you don't have any papers they only return you to Mexico."

After the group had spent a month in a hotel in Guatemala another agent, who guided them to a lake that separates Guatemala from Mexico, contacted them. The group then tried to enter Mexico by crossing the lake on a car tire in the middle of the night. However, they were all caught by the Mexican Federal Police (*los federales*) and returned to Guatemala the same day. Andrea exclaims, "*Los federales* treat the illegals very badly. That was the worst part of the trip." But she adds, "Actually I was lucky. One of the girls in the group was raped by a contact person who helped us cross the border." Later the group made a second attempt to cross the border, this time without getting caught. Although they all managed to enter Mexico in good health, two Peruvian male companions disappeared before they reached Tijuana several weeks later. The rest of the group crossed the U.S.-Mexican border at night without major problems and continued to San Diego, where it split up. Here Andrea bought an air ticket to Miami, where she was received by *la tía*, who helped her to find somewhere to live.

Andrea's trip over land from Peru to the United States shows the obstacles and dangers that thousands of Peruvians go through when traveling illegally. It emphasizes how migrants are transformed into illegal subjects, not merely because they fail to meet the requirements for obtaining legal status in the receiving country, but also because they lack the documentation to verify who they are. It also sheds light on how undocumented immigrants reproduce the logic of identification embodied in identity papers through their own actions and discourses. From the point of view of the undocumented immigrant, travel papers are synonymous with identification and thus trouble, whereas anonymity allows them to alter their identities according to circumstance.

Sonia

Sonia, twenty, who has six brothers and sisters, describes herself as the most adventurous of all her siblings. Her parents originate from a small village in the province of Huarochirí in the department of Lima, but moved to Lima, where Sonia and her siblings were born. After finishing school Sonia found work in a factory in Lima, but she had to leave the job because her fiancé disapproved of her taking salaried work. However, in 1992 she broke off her engagement and decided to emigrate to the United States to find work and start a new life. Sonia says, "My mother always told me to be independent even after marrying. So I decided to leave the country and try my luck elsewhere." Although no one in her own nuclear family had migrated outside Peru, more than a hundred villagers from her parents' native community were already living in Houston and Dallas, Texas. In fact, the first villager to leave Peru was one of Sonia's *tíos* (uncles), an engineer, who had been brought to Texas by the American company he was working for in the 1960s. She borrowed money from a friend to pay a travel agency in Lima to arrange the trip to the United States and flew to Panama, entering on a tourist visa. After waiting for three months, she traveled illegally by land to Mexico in a group that included Cubans, Colombians, and Ecuadorians as well as Peruvians. According to Sonia the hardest part of the trip was passing through Nicaragua. She says, "We had to sit in a truck for two days without eating." Later they continued to the border to Honduras and El Salvador. Sonia recalls, "We crossed the border to Honduras walking in a minefield, and in El Salvador we drove in dirt roads to avoid the police and got dust in out eyes and ears." In Mexico they crossed the border to the United States without major difficulty.

After a short break in Los Angeles Sonia continued the trip to Houston, where she spent two weeks with her *tío*. However, rather than accept the offer to stay in Texas and draw on his support as well as that of the migrant community of her parents' native community in Peru, she decided to go to Miami, where a friend of hers offered her a place to stay. In Miami she found a job as a live-in domestic servant for an American family, for whom she works six days a week. Her Sundays she spends in a room she rents in the house of a Peruvian family. Whereas the job allows her to send monthly remittances to her family in Peru, it does not allow her to find a place of her own to live, to obtain an education or otherwise to achieve social mobility in Miami. Moreover, Sonia's status as an undocumented immigrant cripples her geographical mobility and prevents her from leaving the country and traveling to Peru to visit her family. When I met Sonia in 1998 she told me that she was exploring the possibilities of entering a marriage in order to obtain a green card. She said, "My father is very ill. Last year I sent all the money I had saved so that he could have an operation, and now my family depends on the money I send them every month. So I have to continue working in the United States. But I'm afraid that he will die before I can go back and see him. If I get a green card I can visit Peru and return to the United States without problems. That's why I'm thinking of marrying someone who has citizenship."

Sonia is truly trapped in the labyrinths of illegality. On the one hand, she cannot travel to Peru because it would jeopardize her stay in the United States and thus her plans to support her family economically, in particular the hospital bill for her ailing father. On the other hand, she is becoming increasingly worried that her father will die before she can acquire legal status in the United States and can thus go back to see him. To make things worse, Sonia's job as domestic servant restricts her social network to the family she is working for, as well as the time she has to visit other Peruvians and fellow migrants to express her concerns, exchange experiences, and explore the possibilities of legalizing her status in the United States, a situation I became aware of when interviewing her in 1998. Indeed, during our conversation Sonia began to cry while recounting the sufferings she was going through. She later excused herself and told me that the interview had taken her by surprise, as it was the first opportunity she had had to share her concerns with anyone else since leaving Peru. She said, "I work all week and only have Sunday off. It's very rare that I can talk with anyone else about these things."

Avelino

Before emigrating, Avelino, who comes from the department of San Martín in the Peruvian jungle, lived in Lima with his wife and seventeen-year-old daughter. Whereas his wife made a living as a hairdresser in the neighborhood where they lived, Avelino served as a Sinchi, that is, a soldier in the Peruvian army's elite corps trained to combat the country's terrorist groups. One day in 1987 Avelino got into trouble during his service and was forced to abandon his duties and emigrate. He states, "I cannot tell you what happened, but I just had to leave the country that very day. I had no choice. I didn't even have time to say good-bye to my wife and daughter. In those days I always carried my passport on me, so I went straight to the airport." As one of his brothers was living in Barcelona, Avelino decided to take the first flight to Spain, which he entered on a tourist visa. After three months he overstayed the visa and became an unauthorized immigrant. Later he applied to the Spanish authorities for political asylum, which he was granted after a few months. Avelino says, "I couldn't tell them that I had been a Sinchi, so I said that I had been persecuted by the police. In those days it was easy to get asylum." His new status allowed him to take work, and after some months a Spanish construction and demolition company took him on. He says, "The company hired me because I had been trained to work with explosives as a Sinchi in Peru." Later he married a Peruvian woman living in Barcelona, with whom he has two children. Because the woman was already a legal resident in Spain at the time of the marriage, this enabled Avelino to apply for a permanent residence permit in Spain and later for citizenship, which he has now obtained.

Avelino's migration history resembles that of many other Peruvians who emigrated to Spain during the 1990s. Because this country recognized the victims of Peru's civil war as political refugees in this period, large numbers of Peruvians were granted political asylum in Spain. Ironically, as Avelino's trajectory indicates, this group included not merely civilians who had been persecuted, but also members of the armed forces and the country's rebel groups. Indeed, along with hundreds of other law-enforcement agents, Avelino twisted his testimony to make him appear as the persecuted instead of the persecutor. His trajectory also sheds light on the concerns that guide the strategies that immigrants pursue when navigating through the muddy terrain of illegality and searching for pathways to obtain a legal status. Thus, during his more than fifteen years in Spain, Avelino's legal status has changed from tourist to political refugee to unauthorized immigrant and, finally, Spanish citizen.

Aurora

Aurora, fifty-six, has spent most of her life in Peru. She grew up and spent most of her youth together with her seven siblings in the department of Cajamarca. At the age of seventeen she got a job as teacher in the local school, a profession that became her livelihood after she moved to Lima ten years later. The first in the family to leave Cajamarca was one of Aurora's younger sisters, who went to Chiclayo to finish her *secundario*, the last five years of elementary school. Then the sister moved to Lima where she worked for a while as an educator before emigrating to Spain in 1976. Shortly after Aurora's three brothers also migrated to Lima to study. Whereas one of them stayed in Peru the two latter went to Canada and the United States where they both live with their Peruvian wives and children. In the late 1970s two of Aurora's sisters moved to Lima too whereupon they emigrated. One left for Spain in 1984 and settled in Barcelona whereas the other went to the United States with her Peruvian husband and their two children. When Aurora's father retired, her parents also moved to Lima together with Aurora and her younger sister. In Lima the sister found work as schoolteacher but in the late 1980s she emigrated to Spain. Today she lives in Barcelona.

Unlike her nine siblings, Aurora never married. Moreover, instead of emigrating she continued working in Lima as a schoolteacher, which allowed her to stay with and take care of her parents in the family's house in Lima until they passed away in the early 1990s. In 1995, however, she decided to visit her siblings living in Barcelona. She first flew to Germany on a tourist visa. A remote relative living there then arranged the trip by land to Spain that she entered as an undocumented immigrant. Aurora had never thought of staying in Spain for a longer period of time nor had she planned to take work. However, when a Catalan woman asked her to work for her as a domestic servant Aurora accepted the offer, which allowed her to spend more time with her siblings in Barcelona. In effect, her employer applied for a *cupo* that would give her the right to hire Aurora as domestic. Once the paper work had been done Amelia returned to Peru and waited until the Spanish Embassy in Lima informed her that she had been granted the work permit. Two months later she traveled to Spain for a second time now as a legal immigrant with the permission to stay and work as long as her employer offered her employment.

Although Aurora was hired to clean and cook, the employer became so fond of her that she asked Aurora to work as her personal waitress and promised to hire another female Peruvian immigrant to do the domestic work. Aurora decided to accept the offer and over the next two years she worked as the woman's waitress accompanying her in her daily doings and regular traveling between the two houses she owns in Spain. However, after two years Aurora decided to quit the job and return to Peru. She says, "I got tired of working for the woman. I spent all my time with her and never got time to see my siblings in Barcelona. I also missed Peru. I never wanted to stay in Spain." To Aurora, one cannot buy human love with money. She thinks that the woman is very lonely despite her wealth. Aurora asks, "Why should I continue to work for the lady? She needed me more than I needed her. She keeps writing asking me to come back. She considers me her personal friend but that's not the way to make friendships. Even after she remarried and moved together with her new husband she wanted me to stay with her. But I have my pension as a schoolteacher in Peru and I can always go back to Barcelona and get another job." Aurora adds, "I visited her once after quitting the job. She became so happy. I told her that I would look for another Peruvian woman to replace me. But I never found someone who wanted the job. I'm sure the woman would put me in her will if I came back. But I won't."

Unlike many of her fellow female migrants, Aurora is not undocumented but has obtained one of the desired *cupos*, which gives her the right to stay and take work in Spain, as long her employer requires her labor as a domestic servant. However, for Aurora and many other Peruvian women working on a *cupo* in Spain, legality is a fragile status that she may lose at any moment. If her employer refuses to renew her work contract, Aurora can be forced to leave the country or become an unauthorized immigrant again unless she finds a new employer within a very short time. Paradoxically, this dependence on her employer's good will urges Aurora to treat the woman with extra care and makes the "fortunes" of the two women intimately intertwined. On the one hand, the employer's health is in the hands of Aurora; on the other hand, Aurora's *cupo* can only be renewed as long as her employer stays alive and she approves of Aurora's work. The bonds of interdependence between the national employer and the foreign employee, then, are shaped by power relations that not merely favor the former, but may also be of use to the latter. Although Aurora ceased working for her Catalan employer and returned to Peru, the woman still writes asking her to come back. The mutual dependence between this wealthy but lonely Catalan woman and Aurora, who eventually opted to spend more time with her own family at the cost of ending a work contract that not only assured her of a *cupo* but also the possibility of inheriting from the employer when she dies, illustrates the many layers of meaning embedded in the domestic care industry that Peruvians and other Third World immigrant workers engage in (Hondagneu-Sotelo 2001: 114–210; Salazar Parreñas 2001: 150–96; Zimmerman, Litt, and Bose 2006).

Roberto

In 1990 Roberto, forty-six, decided to emigrate after he had been laid off from his work as a truck driver in Lima. He traveled to Japan on a tourist visa, which he overstayed when it expired three months later, thus becoming an unauthorized immigrant. Because he is not of Japanese descent, Roberto is not entitled to a work permit or permanent residence in Japan. Moreover, his illegal status makes it difficult to find factory work, as most other immigrants in Japan do, or to obtain ID papers such as driver's license. Despite these obstacles, however, Roberto has little trouble finding work. He contends, "It is always possible to find *contratistas* who are willing to hire illegal workers" and continues, "They pay you less and you are always in danger of being caught by the police, but it is still worth it." Currently, he makes a living by assisting a Japanese truck driver who delivers goods to shops in Isesaki. His employer pays him between US\$7 and 8 an hour, which is much less than legal immigrants doing factory work make (between US\$12 and 13). At the weekends, Roberto supplements his income by doing occasional work for a Peruvian businessman.

Roberto claims that the most troubling part of his life as an unauthorized immigrant is that he has not seen his wife and two daughters for eight years. They traveled to Italy in 1999, where they obtained legal residence after entering marriages with three Italian men. In return for this service, the men charged the women a considerable amount of money and made them promise to go through a divorce once they obtain residence permits. Roberto says that he plans to follow his wife and two daughters in the near future and find an Italian marriage partner like they did in order to acquire legal residence. Although he knows little about Italy or about Europe in general, he says that he is looking forward to being united with his family. He says, "In Italy we can all get work as domestic servants taking care of old people. I hope I'll have a better life there than here."

Unlike Andrea, but like Avelino, Roberto initiated his trajectory as a migrant by entering Japan legally as a tourist. However, in contrast to Avelino, who is now a Spanish citizen, Roberto has no way of legalizing his presence in Japan, which only allows *nikkeijin* to take work. Hence he has spent more than a decade as an unauthorized immigrant in the country. Roberto's history is especially compelling because it illustrates the constraints and restrictions implied by illegality for undocumented and unauthorized immigrants. Constantly hiding, he must shun contact with the authorities and with Japanese society in general; moreover, his illegal status prevents him from traveling outside Japan to visit his family in Peru. Indeed, the only options he faces in the current situation are either to marry a *nikkeijin* who already has legal residence in Japan and thus obtain the right to a temporary residence permit, or else leave the country at the risk of being detained as an undocumented immigrant at the airport. Finally, Roberto's history documents how Peruvians design migration strategies that allow them to navigate in and out of the world of legality and illegality, not only in the country where they are living, but also in other First World countries.[1]

Linda

In 1991 Linda, who was born in Callao of non-Japanese Peruvians and is twenty-eight years of age, married a Peruvian *sansei*. The same year the couple traveled together to Japan. As the wife of a *nikkeijin*, she was granted a three-year residence permit, which can be renewed indefinitely. After a few years Linda learned to speak a little Japanese and was hired by a Peruvian shopkeeper to help in his business. Linda sends most of her earnings back to Peru to support her family. Over the past ten years these remittances have not only provided her parents with a monthly income, but also allowed them to pay back a loan that they took out to support one of Linda's younger sisters, who went to the United States to study for two months in 1995. Although Linda feels happy that her sister had an opportunity to study abroad, she believes that it was a bad investment. She says, "After the two months my sister returned to Peru but couldn't find work." Moreover, the commitment to send remittances and pay off the loan has prevented Linda from saving money from her earnings for herself and returning to Peru to visit her family. When I interviewed her in 1999, she said, "I haven't been back since I came to Japan. All the money I have saved so far I have used to support my family. But next year my parents will have paid back the loan, and then I'll be free to save the money I earn and go back to Peru."

A year after she left Peru, Linda, who at that time was the only member of her family to emigrate, "pulled" one of her younger brothers to Japan, who entered the country on a tourist visa and found work at a factory through a Japanese contractor. Three months later he overstayed his visa and became an unauthorized immigrant. However, the following year he married a Peruvian *nikkeijin*, which gave him the right to apply for a residence and work permit.

Linda, meanwhile, separated from her *sansei* husband a few years after she
came to Japan, though as long as the husband refrains from asking her for a
divorce, she can continue renewing her temporary residence permit in the
country. Linda says, "That's how life is. I was legal when I got to Japan, and
now I may turn illegal if my husband asks for a divorce. My brother was first
illegal, but then turned legal because he married a *nikkei*."

When I visited Japan again in 2001, I was told that Linda had returned to
Peru. In fact, during my first stay in Japan she had told me that she was tired
of living there and wanted to go to the United States, where she has relatives
in Paterson and Los Angeles. However, in order to apply for a tourist visa for
the United States, she first needed to go back to Peru. Whether Linda ever
made it to the United States is not known to me. Yet what her migration story
does suggest, like Roberto's, is that many Peruvians regard illegality as a state
of being that is inextricably bound up with emigration and that may affect
their lives at any point of time and in many different ways. However, it is also
evident from both Roberto's and Linda's testimonies that, although their understanding of immigration policies in the First World and the bureaucratic
rationale that places immigrants in such categories as legal and illegal is often very limited, they are highly capable of exploiting the loopholes that
emerge from the inconsistencies that are inherent in this distinction. Not only
have they both lived in Japan as unauthorized immigrants for many years,
they have also designed new strategies with the aim of taking them to alternative destinations.

Marta

Marta, forty-eight, was born in Lima. Before emigrating she lived in La Perla,
a lower middle-class neighborhood, together with her twenty-year-old daughter, who helped her run a business sewing and selling women's clothes. Marta
claims that she raised her daughter alone without the support of her husband,
who abandoned her many years ago. She claims, "He is not of any use to me."
In 2000 she decided to emigrate to Argentina, where her two sisters-in-law
were working as the live-in caretakers of elderly Argentineans. She sold the
cloth she had stocked in her workshop in La Perla and used the money to finance the trip, which took her first to Bolivia and Brazil, and finally to Argentina, which she entered on a tourist visa after bribing the border police.
While searching for a job as a live-in domestic servant in Buenos Aires, Marta
lived in the flat of the employer of one of her sisters-in-law. When I met
Marta in late 2000 she was still looking for work and, to make things worse,
she had become an unauthorized immigrant by overstaying her tourist visa,
which restricted her ability to negotiate her salary and working conditions, as
well as exposing her to the abuses of the Argentinean police. Marta says,

"When the police discover that we're illegal, they force us to bribe them." Another of Marta's many concerns was finding somewhere to live. She says, "I really don't know what to do. My sister-in-law says that she is afraid that the old woman she is taking care of will discover that I am staying there. She may lose her job, she says." Marta is considering returning to Peru or going to the United States, where some of her distant relatives live. So far she has not made up her mind. She says, "I believe I have better opportunities to find work in the United States. But how can I get there? After all, it's easier going to Argentina as an illegal than to the United States."

Most migrants regard Argentina, together with Chile, as the easiest destination to have access to in Peru's contemporary emigration flows. Geographically, the country is much closer to Peru than the United States, southern Europe, or Japan, which makes it easy to reach by bus without the assistance of people-smugglers or other agents. Furthermore, Peruvians can enter the country on a tourist visa without major difficulties and obtain work and residence permits if they find work, their employer agrees to inform the authorities of the work contract, and the immigrant agrees to pay several hundred dollars for the paperwork. However, as Marta's migration history demonstrates, because many immigrants fail to find work they remain unauthorized for long periods of time. Furthermore, even when they do get a job many immigrants are reluctant to spend their hard-earned money in legalizing their status, which may cost up to US$400. Rather, they prefer to remain illegal and await an opportunity to re-migrate to another destination. From the perspective of the immigrants, therefore, illegality is an inevitable but temporary condition that permits them to pursue long-term migration strategies in the direction of other horizons.

Graciela

Graciela, twenty-two, was born in Morobe, a small town close to the city of Chiclayo on Peru's northern coast, where she went to school. After finishing *primaria*, the first five years of elementary school, she moved to Chiclayo, where she found work as a domestic servant, a job she kept until marrying at the age of twenty. In 1997 she and her husband decided to emigrate because of economic problems. Graciela first attempted to emigrate to Japan, where one of her cousins had been living since 1994. However, because the agent whom she had paid to provide a forged *koseki* (the Japanese national ID document) and apply for a work visa at the Japanese Embassy in Lima as a *nikkeijin* took so long, she decided to go to Argentina, where another cousin of hers was working as domestic servant for an Argentinean family. The cousin had told Graciela that the employer needed an extra domestic servant and that he was ready to lend Graciela the money to finance the trip from Peru to Buenos

Aires. So Graciela traveled to Argentina, which she entered on a tourist visa. Upon her arrival she immediately started to work as a live-in domestic servant for her cousin's employer, and after three months she overstayed her tourist visa and became an unauthorized immigrant. In order to make Graciela pay back the debt, her employer withheld her monthly salary through the following year, also keeping her passport to prevent her from running away. To her surprise, her employer continued to withhold her salary even after she had finally paid back the loan. Graciela says, "The man took advantage of my situation as an illegal." Thus, she decided to quit her job. She bitterly remarks, "I never received any money for my work, and he never returned my passport."

Today Graciela works as a live-out nanny and cleaning assistant and is paid by the hour. In 1998 her husband traveled to Argentina on a tourist visa, which he overstayed, becoming an unauthorized immigrant after three months. Shortly afterwards he was hired by a transport agency for occasional jobs. Within a year of his arrival Graciela gave birth to their first child, which automatically gave both parents the right to legal residency. Tragically, the baby suffered an accident and perished in the day nursery that was taking care of it while Graciela and her husband were working. Graciela says, "Imagine, first I lost my baby and because of that I didn't get my residence and work permit. So I'm still illegal. I want to go to Italy when I've saved money for the trip."

Graciela's migration story provides evidence not merely of the precarious job situation of Peruvian women working as domestic servants in the developed world and the relations of exploitation and abuse to which they are subject as live-in servants, but also the predicaments they face as unauthorized immigrants. In contrast to Marta, Graciela was lucky to receive help to finance her travel expenses and to find work immediately upon her arrival. However, her employer exploited her illegal status and refused to pay her a salary, also withholding her passport, hoping that this would force her to continue working for free. Eventually, Graciela decided to quit and look for other job opportunities. However, her misfortunes did not end. The tragic death of her child occurred at a moment when both Graciela and her husband expected to be granted work and residence permits in Argentina. In light of the country's deteriorating economic situation, however, none of them have much hope of finding steady work or of legalizing their presence in Argentina; likewise, their prospects of re-migrating to Italy or any other country (except Chile) look gloomy.

THE INCONSISTENCY OF ILLEGALITY

In many countries illegality is a highly inconsistent concept that is difficult to define in juridical terms (Coutin 2000: 27–47). While granting undocumented or unauthorized immigrants certain rights in, for instance, the labor market and thus implicitly accepting their presence in some spheres of society, their lack of legal residence status implies that they risk deportation if they are required to verify themselves. This is evident in the immigration policies of many First World countries, which indirectly recognize and, in some cases, even encourage the importation of undocumented immigrants to meet the need for cheap labor in the nation's industries while publicly prohibiting it, thus exposing a latent contradiction between modern universal human rights and the civil and legal rights that individuals obtain through national citizenship (Apap 1997; Casaravilla 1999; 141–51; Martin 1992; Shimada 1994: 3–11; Vasta 1993: 94–95). As De Genova suggests, "The category 'illegal alien' is a profoundly useful and profitable one that effectively serves to create and sustain a legally vulnerable—and hence, relatively tractable and thus 'cheap'—reserve of labor" (2002: 440).

The policy of benign neglect in simultaneously accepting and prohibiting illegality pursued by many governments in the developed world can be practiced in various ways. In Japan illegal migration is perceived as a potentially criminal act that is often punished severely (Matsumoto and Gashu 1998: 46–71; Watkins 1999: 73), a policy that, according to Roberto, has thwarted his plans to give up his illegal life in Japan and travel to Italy to initiate a new life there as a migrant together with his wife and daughter. Conversely, in the United States, and to some extent also Spain and Italy, illegal immigration is regarded as a simple breach of the law that in theory leads to the deportation of the migrant but in practice is often tolerated by the authorities and permitted by law (Coutin 2000: 79–104). Indeed, such policies have from time to time led different governments in the United States, Spain, Italy, Argentina, and other countries in the developed world to carry out so-called amnesties granting undocumented immigrants legal status (De Genova 2002: 419–20), which both Vanesa (in chapter 3) and Tito (see below) have benefited from.

The inconsistencies in the immigration policies of governments in the developed world not only affect migrants who travel without documents, but also those who travel with them. In fact, for many migrants living in the United States, Europe, or Japan on temporary work visas, the distinction between what is legal and what is illegal is far from clear, as the following case illustrates.

Victor

I have already presented Victor in chapter 5. This man who is forty-five was brought up in Pachacayo, a cattle ranch in the central highlands of Peru that belonged to the American-owned Cerro de Pasco Mining Corporation before the land reform. His father was an employee of the company and worked with the Peruvian engineer in charge of recruiting new herders in Lima. This connection has had a critical impact on the life course of Victor's family. Today Victor and his three brothers all live in the United States, his father and sister being the only members of the family who have remained in Peru. Victor's experience of migration began when he moved to Lima as a young man to be apprenticed to a tailor. Later he set up his own tailor's workshop, married, and had several children. However, the economic crisis of the late 1980s had a disastrous effect on Victor's business and forced him to seek help from among his relatives. At that time two of his brothers were already working in the United States.

The first to leave in the family was a cousin of Victor's, who had formerly worked as a veterinarian in the SAIS Túpac Amaru cooperative. He left on his first contract in 1979, then returned on a second in 1982, and finally ran away and became an unauthorized immigrant before the contract expired. Four years later he was granted U.S. residence. Today he works as a gardener in New Mexico, where he lives with his daughter, who came to the United States through the family reunification program. The cousin later recommended Victor's oldest brother, Hugo, to his employer, who made the arrangements for him to come. The brother migrated in 1988 after the factory he was working in Lima closed down, leaving his wife and three children in a newly built house in the shantytown of Huaycán. Hugo is currently working on his fourth contract for a ranch owner in Wyoming. Another brother, Máximo, left in 1989, and in 1991 Victor also traveled to work on a three-year work contract as a shepherd in Bakersfield, California.

When Victor completed his work contract in 1994, he decided to overstay his H-2A visa and settled in Bakersfield, where he met a group of Peruvian migrants who, like him, had gone into illegality instead of returning to Peru. In fact, by the mid 1990s the city had become a center for the growing number of Peruvian shepherds in California who had overstayed their visas and settled in the United States as unauthorized immigrants. They now make up a community of more than a hundred Peruvians, who come together every Sunday to play soccer and drink beer. Some of them, including Victor, have married local women of Hispanic origin and thus become legal residents. Others have applied for political asylum or spent years as unauthorized immigrants looking for work in the service sector or the manufacturing industry.

Victor's migration history demonstrates that the borderline between illegality and legality is blurred, and reminds us of the political economy that shapes the immigration policy of the United States. Essentially, the H-2A visa serves the interests of American farmers and ranchers by providing them with a cheap, unorganized rural labor force, while at the same time permitting Peruvians to take work legally as shepherds for many years. However, a growing number of these rural workers have discovered that their legal status submits them to semi-feudal relations of exploitation, a situation they can only escape by running away and becoming unauthorized immigrants. Although many of these ex-rural workers have spent long periods in the world of illegality, a growing number have managed to legalize their presence in the United States either by applying for political asylum or by marrying Hispanic or Chicana women who already have citizenship. Ironically, illegality is regarded an avenue to obtaining civil rights and becoming a legal immigrant.

MIRROR, MIRROR ON THE WALL: WHO'S THE PERSON IN MY GREEN CARD?

Most citizens in First World countries think of ID papers as indispensable in carrying out their daily chores. Such documents prove people's names, ages, addresses, occupations, and marital statuses, as well as their physical appearance, thus allowing the appropriate authorities to verify whether the person who claims to be the owner of the papers really is the person identified in them, that is, that the people actually are who they give themselves out to be (Lund 2001: 4).[2] Historically, European states have used written records to document the movements of its subjects since the early medieval transition from oral to written procedures.[3] Torpey contends that, "In order to monopolize the legitimate means of movement, states and the state system have been compelled to define who belongs and who does not, who may come and go and who not, and to make these distinctions intelligible and enforceable. Documents such as passports and identity cards have been critical to achieving these objectives" (2000: 13). In essence, these documents verify people's legal status in the country where they live (Caplan and Torpey 2001: 2). Such a status may provide the right to live in the country, but may also include the right to work, study, buy property, receive social benefits, engage in financial activities, and take out insurance, that is, the legal rights that are normally included in national citizenship. In short, ID papers document people's identities and provide evidence of the fact that they have legal status.

Although undocumented and unauthorized immigrants lack proper ID and therefore live on the margins of society, many conduct what appear to be normal, legal lives. As Coutin suggests, "Though they are not legally present, the undocumented get jobs, rent apartments, buy property, go to school, get married, have children, join churches, found organizations, and develop friendships. The undocumented thus move in and out of existence" (2000: 40). She adds, "The borders between existence and nonexistence remain blurred and permeable" (Coutin 2000: 40). In other words, illegality is a muddy space in which immigrants alternate between the official world of normality and in the invisible world of lawlessness. This sense of existing in incommensurable life domains is reflected in the ambivalent, often contradictory sentiments many undocumented and unauthorized immigrants have toward ID. On the one hand, personal identification provides immigrants as well as other people with a magic power to satisfy basic needs such as getting a job, finding a place to live, and obtaining the right to public welfare; on the other hand, immigrants who fail to present the required ID papers or, perhaps even worse, are caught with false ID papers run the risk of deportation.

Most newly arrived, undocumented immigrants shun any form of self-identification that may disclose their "true" identity and reveal their status as illegal immigrants. They spend their first months or years as illegal subjects without engaging with the host society and confined to exclusive networks of fellow migrants. This strategy confines immigrants to a self-producing "culture of illegality" and prevents them from pursuing the goals that could later lead them to become documented immigrants. As time goes by, however, many migrants learn to deal with the bureaucracy and the judicial system in their new countries of residence, thus discovering the "tricks" involved in acquiring the necessary ID papers to get on with their daily activities. Moreover, some First World countries recognize the possibility of converting an illegal into a legal status, given that migrants have already acquired some kind of identification, such as a driving license or health insurance cards. This makes ID papers a Janus-faced device that is an issue of concern as well as desire for many undocumented immigrants. Tito's struggle to obtain his green card is evidence of this. He emigrated to the United States as a "wetback" in 1986. The same year the U.S. government issued an amnesty for all undocumented and unauthorized immigrants who could prove that they had been living in the country since 1982. Tito therefore paid an American cattle rancher in California US$250 to make a contract stating that he had worked for him between 1982 and 1986. The same year Tito received his green card.

Among the most wanted ID papers are residence and work permits, birth and marriage certificates, driving licenses and social security card. Often these papers can be obtained by a simple request to the local authorities, who in many places take people's identity for granted and therefore neglect to investigate their legal status in the country. Another way is to acquire fake ID papers (e.g., green cards and social security cards), which in most major cities in the United States can be purchased on the streets at prices varying between US$20 to 100 (Mahler 1995: 167; Margolies 1994: 117–20). Insofar as these documents allow immigrants to acclaim that they are legal residents or citizens, they provide the means of conducting a semi-legal life, as well as insurance against the danger of arbitrary detention and deportation (Coutin 2000: 55–63). The next step toward legalization involves converting their illegal status into a legal status. In order to achieve this, it is vital that the immigrant presents his or her "situation" to the immigration authorities to convince them that they are actually entitled to a legal residence and work permit. This involves them in accounting for all their actions and movements after entering the country and explaining the intentions and rationale behind these in such a way that the immigrant does not place him- or herself in conflict with the law, despite having an illegal status. Or, as Coutin phrases it, "individuals" immigration status is determined by their legal histories" (Coutin 2000: 52). Unfortunately, this often leads to a misconception among immigrants of what legality actually means. Thus Coutin suggests that, "because documents are required to demonstrate eligibility for rights and services, and because those who demonstrate eligibility are materially situated in particular positions (as citizens, legal permanent residents, and so on), enforcing immigration law makes it appear that *status inheres in paper, not persons*" (Coutin 2000: 55). In other words, immigrants tend to ignore the fact that for the authorities, ID papers are only the means by which a resident or citizen documents his or her personal status and identity.

Of course, the predicaments inherent in the legitimization of people's personal status and the documentation of their private identity are in no way peculiar to the situation of undocumented or unauthorized immigrants. The tension between a person's self and the identity imposed on her or him, and the question of who has the right to define an individual's identity, are compelling issues for any anthropological study (Coutin 2000: 178). But as Anthony Cohen points out, while the intricacy of how individuals address the latent conflict between external identification and the identity of the self is a topic often exploited in the literature of fiction, it has not resonated among anthropologists. However, Cohen asserts, the difference between the two forms of identity "is a matter of consciousness, of *self* consciousness, not of official license and recognition" (1994: 179). Rather than treating the people they study as performing selves, then, anthropologists should regard them as self-conscious agents who create their sense of being individuals in response to their experience of external identification; that is, in the interface between the self and the persona that this self is made into.

Such a perspective is particularly relevant when studying undocumented and unauthorized immigrants and other individuals whose identity is called to being question by the legal authorities of the nation-state or whose physical presence within its territory is classified as "illegal," and who therefore find themselves caught in a predicament of identification because their personal status does not entitle them to the civic and legal rights that citizens enjoy. It is important to emphasize that by using the phrase "predicament of identification," I am not implying that immigrants suffer from an "identity" crisis, nor am I arguing that immigrants do not know who they are themselves because they have to conceal their own identity or identify themselves as someone else. Quite the contrary, illegality and marginalization often prompt immigrants to cling to their identity as an ethnic and migrant minority and to strengthen their ties with their relatives in their countries of origin and settlement. Rather, I argue that the lack of a legal status seriously restricts immigrants' agency and hampers their ability to plan and control their own lives, as Silvia's migration story, described below, illustrates.

Illegality affects the lives of immigrants in very different ways, depending on the circumstances of their presence in the country in which they are residing. As Andrea's and Sonia's migration stories suggest, many Peruvians initiate their new lives as immigrants as undocumented immigrants because they enter the United States, Spain, Japan, and Argentina without the required documentation. Some, however, manage to convert their illegal status into a legal one by, for instance, enrolling themselves in a student program, applying for political asylum (as did Avelino in this chapter and Silvio in chapter 7, or finding employment (as did Goyo in chapter 7). Others enter their new countries of residence as legal aliens, for instance as tourists, but become unauthorized immigrants because they remain in the country after their visa has expired (so-called visa overstayers) (as did Maritza in this chapter and Lizet and Cecilia in chapter 7). Moreover, it is not unusual for Peruvians to take on the identity of another person in order to obtain a work or residence permit and thus live in the name of somebody else,[4] as Adela's migration experience illustrates.

In 1985 Adela married an American, applied for a green card at the American Embassy in Lima, and emigrated to California, where she settled together with her husband. In 1996 her sister Myrtha traveled to Tijuana in Mexico and crossed the U.S.-Mexican border illegally by hiding in the car of Adela and her husband, who had come to pick her up. In Los Angeles Myrtha bought a forged green card and security card for US$30 each. The ID documents were issued in Adela's name, but had a photo of Myrtha. She says, "The papers are OK as long as you don't look carefully." She now works at the Grand Canyon at a restaurant for tourists. In 1998 Myrtha's daughter Ursula also made it to Tijuana. Just like her mother two years before, she was met by Adela and her husband on the Mexican side of the border and brought to Los Angeles. And just like Myrtha, Ursula bought a forged green card shortly after her arrival. However, unlike her mother's ID papers, which were duplicates of her sister's papers, a legal resident in the United States, Ursula had her green card issued in her own name, that is, as an individual without legal status in the country. Effectively, Ursula now figures as the daughter of Adela in the forged ID papers that Myrtha uses, which has complicated Adela's life. She says, "It now appears as if Ursula is my daughter and not my niece. This can create trouble for me." The confusion caused by Myrtha's and Ursula's use of phony ID papers has been further complicated by the fact that Myrtha became pregnant shortly after she arrived in the United States and that the ID documents issued in the name of the child to be born will make it appear as the offspring of Adela and not Myrtha.

Other undocumented and unauthorized immigrants buy forged papers that provide them with a fake identity, that is, their ID papers are issued in the name of a nonexistent person. Such a strategy may cause severe existential problems that sometimes lead immigrants to give up and return to Peru. One Peruvian woman in Kakegawa in Japan told me that she had decided to leave the country because she became pregnant. The woman, a non-*nikkeijin* Peruvian who had lived in Japan using a fake *koseki* with a Japanese name and forged ID papers for several years, said she was concerned that her child would be born with a Japanese first name and a surname that was different from the mother's Peruvian surname. She said, "I know my real name and who I am and where I come from. But what about my child? That's why I have decided to return to Peru."

Illegality forces immigrants to spend long periods of time in isolation from close relatives at home. Marco left Peru in 1996 and traveled illegally to the United States, which he entered as "wetback." A year later his wife Maria followed him and they settled together in Los Angeles. When I interviewed the couple in 1998, Marco was working as a parking assistant in a mall, and Maria still was looking for a job. Maria says, "We have a lot of land in Lima where we want to build a house. My mother lives just next to the lot. She takes care of our children. I only left because Marco wanted me to come. And he left because he lost his job. We both want to make some money and then go home again." However, she now regrets that they left Peru because she misses the children. She says, "We can't go home. If we do, we'll have to make it all the way to the United States again as illegals." In other words, illegality seriously restricts the mobility of Marco and Maria, who also feel that they are constantly having to hide because they lack ID papers in the United States. Marco says, "I have a car and drive to work every day. That's the only way to get around in Los Angeles. But I don't have a driving license. If the police stop me one day, they may deport me."

Two of the most popular ways of obtaining legal residence and, eventually, citizenship in the host society are through family reunification and by marrying immigrants who already have permanent residence permits or citizenship or marrying native citizens. In chapter 4 I dealt extensively with Peruvians' use

of the first strategy as a means of creating networks and of "pulling" relatives
and fellow villagers. The following case demonstrates how migrants seek to
legalize their stay in the United States by using the second strategy, which to
many represents the most direct avenue toward obtaining legal status in the
country in which they were living. However, as Silvia's story suggests, this
strategy may involve dramatic changes in the lives of the immigrants.

Silvia

When I met Andrea and Silvia for a second time in Miami in 1998, the two
sisters had become legal residents in the United States. Andrea had obtained
a permanent green card in 1994 after marrying Amador, a man of Cuban descent who was a legal immigrant at the time of the marriage, while Silvia had
married Danny, an American from Illinois, in 1996, an arrangement that initially provided her with a temporary green card and, after waiting another
year, gave her the right to apply for a permanent residence permit. Although
both women arrived as "wetbacks" and share many experiences as undocumented immigrants in the United States, and although they both married men
who are legal immigrants or American citizens and thus chose the same path-
way out of illegality, their lives have taken very different directions. Whereas
Andrea married Amador primarily out of affection, Silvia's interest in Danny
was more pragmatic: to get out of illegality.

   Before marrying Danny, Silvia worked as a waitress in a coffee bar in
Ventura Mall. As an undocumented immigrant, the employer paid her less
than the minimum wage, but because Silvia only spoke a few words of English, she was not acquainted with her employment rights in the United States.
She therefore engaged an American lawyer to help her obtain legal residence. The man encouraged her to apply for political asylum but said that
she would have to provide evidence supporting such a petition. Silvia therefore invented a narrative that represented her as a political refugee who had
had to escape from Sarayka, her native village, and leave Peru after the Peruvian army and the Shining Path had both threatened to kill her. Silvia says,
"The story was true, except that I told my father's story, not my own. He was
a leader of an Evangelical group in Sarayka and was persecuted by the Army
as well as the terrorists." However, the immigration authorities turned the
petition down. According to Silvia, the lawyer failed to satisfy the immigration authorities because he had reduced her story to a brief version that did
not contain sufficient evidence of persecution. She says, "I paid him US$700
and wasted all the money. He didn't even speak Spanish." Later she con-
sulted another lawyer, who told her that the only way to obtain a green card

was to marry an American citizen. Consequently, Silvia started to search for a husband.

In 1996 one of Silvia's Hispanic workmates introduced her to Danny, who was working in the valet parking service of Ventura Mall. Shortly afterwards the couple decided to marry and live together for two years until Silvia could apply for a permanent residence visa. In return for this service, she agreed to pay Danny US$3,500. They immediately moved into a three-room apartment in the northeast part of the city, which made them look like a conventional married couple. Although sharing the living room and the kitchen, however, they slept in separate bedrooms. During their first few months together the couple had difficulties in communicating. Danny, who comes from the Midwest, did not know a single word of Spanish, and Silvia's proficiency in English was still rudimentary at that time. However, when I met Silvia again in 1998, she told me that their communication skills had improved and that they had come to know each a lot better, so well, in fact, that she was becoming concerned that Danny had fallen in love with her and would therefore refuse to divorce her when she obtains her green card, as originally agreed. Her concern has been confirmed by the fact that Danny's mother moved into the couple's apartment soon after they married and is now sharing a bedroom with her son. Silvia says, "Danny's mother moved in from one day to the next, just like that. I don't understand Danny. I could never fall in love with a man like him. He doesn't want to make progress in life. He doesn't want to study and is content with the job he has at the Mall. He spends all day together with his mother in the bedroom watching television and playing computer games. How will I ever get a life of my own?"

Silvia's statement indicates that the marriage, which was originally a merely formal arrangement, has evolved into a complicated and committed relationship, which Silvia and Danny both have difficulties explaining not merely to each other, but also to the surrounding world. In fact, Danny's mother is not the only person to show concern for the future of their marriage. Silvia says, "Andrea and Amador didn't approve of my marrying Danny. And now they keep on saying that I should make up my mind and decide whether I'm going to stay with him." Moreover, unlike her sister, who sent pictures of Amador to her family in Peru after they had married, Silvia has been reluctant to introduce Danny to her parents and siblings. She exclaims, "I cannot let my parents know who Danny is. What will they think? That I have married someone that I'm going to divorce after two years?" Although she traveled to Peru to visit her family in 1996 after she married Danny and obtained a temporary green card, she refrained from telling them about him. She states, "When I was illegal I couldn't go to Peru because I wouldn't be let back into the United States. Now I can go but I can't show my family pictures of the man I have married."

THE SPIDER'S WEB OF ILLEGALITY

In her study of Salvadorans in California, Menjívar says that Salvadoran migrants' networks tend to be fragile (2000). In contrast to Menjívar's findings, my data suggest that Peruvian networks are often very powerful. They also reveal that networks can play a highly ambiguous role in migrants' lives. On the one hand, for many migrants networks are the primary and sometimes only resource available to them in traveling and looking for work and somewhere to live. On the other hand, once migrants become established and start creating new lives for themselves, their networks often constrain their agency as much as they empower it. This is particularly true when migrants travel illegally and are forced to ask for help from relatives to take out loans in order to finance their migration and the first months in their new country of residence. Indeed, many discover that the same relations that helped them emigrate and thus lead them into the world of illegality may later prevent them from obtaining legal status and integrating in the receiving society. As Mahler, who studied Hispanic immigrants on Long Island, points out, "When the innocence of neophyte immigrants is exploited by more experienced co-ethnics, the newcomers are introduced to the opportunity structure they will face and learn to use to their own ends." In such a situation, the newcomers "learn the hard way that one of the best avenues available is utilizing resources within their own community to their advantage" (Mahler 1995: 104).

In the following I examine two cases showing how migrants renegotiate their relationships with other migrants and establish new relationships in the attempt to legalize their status in their country of residence.

Andrea and *la tía*

I have already introduced Silvia and Andrea and their struggle to make the journey to the United States as undocumented migrants. I have also described how Andrea's trip was financed by a loan from an aunt (*tía*) living in Miami. Before emigrating *la tía* worked as a seamstress in Lima making a modest income, but because she wanted to offer her children a better future she decided to travel to the United States on her own. According to Andrea, the journey as an undocumented migrant was far from easy. She says, "*La tía* suffered a lot. She was fifty-six when she left Peru and fat. Imagine traveling all the way to the United States by land alone at that age and with that weight." After a couple of years living in Miami, she saved enough money to pull her five children one by one. Once her family was reunited in Miami she decided to pull some of her nieces too,[5] and in 1989 *la tía* offered Andrea a loan of US$ 7,000 to finance her journey to the United States.

In Miami Andrea learned that *la tía* expected her to return the loan and the support she had been offered at high rates of interest, both economically and morally. A few days after her arrival, *la tía* asked Andrea to take over her duties as a domestic servant for a Cuban woman in Miami, who had lent her money to pay for the journey to the United States. In other words, *la tía* used Andrea to pay off her own debt and to escape from the working relationship she had been forced into when she arrived in Miami.[6] Moreover, although *la tía* and the Cuban woman had both told Andrea that they would help her legalize her undocumented status in the United States they never kept their promise, and it was only when the *la tía* died that Andrea's debt was redeemed. In effect, she was released from her moral obligations to the woman and freed to find work elsewhere. *La tía*'s sudden death also allowed Andrea to alter position in the *jalar* chain and become a puller by offering Silvia a loan, who thus assumed the role of newcomer.

Elena and *la tía*

Elena, twenty-six, was born in the department of Apurímac in the Peruvian highlands, but migrated to Lima with her parents when she was a child. Later her family moved to Callao, Lima's port, and after finishing school she started to work in one of the city's hospitals. However, after a short while she received an offer from one of her aunts to emigrate. *La tía* had been acting as a "puller" of not only her own children but also her brothers and sisters and nieces and nephews since she left for the United States in late 1960s.[7] In fact, over the years she had managed to convert the "pulling" mechanism into an organized business by paying Puerto Ricans, who in the United States are legal residents or U.S. citizens, first to contract a marriage with her relatives in Peru, and then to invite them to the United States through the family reunification program.

In 1989 she paid a Puerto Rican woman to go to Lima to marry one of Elena's brothers. Upon her return the newly married woman applied for family reunification, and within a couple of months the brother emigrated to the United States and settled in Paterson as a legal immigrant. Once he had obtained his green card, he divorced the Puerto Rican woman and started to pay back his debt to *la tía*. In 1991 the aunt paid another Puerto Rican, this time a man, to travel to Lima to marry one of Elena's nieces. However, as the niece changed her mind at the last minute and decided to stay in Lima, the aunt sent a letter to Elena's family and told them to find someone to replace her. Thus, Elena was given the chance to marry the man and emigrate. She recalls, "My family said to me, 'Go, don't stay in Peru. Here things can only get worse with the Fujimori government.' So I married the man and left for the United States, although I had never thought of leaving the country before." Like her brother, Elena divorced the Puerto Rican once she had obtained her green card. In the following years a number of Elena's close relatives benefited from the same arrangement, including three of Elena's brothers.

Although the aunt's "pulling" business represented a unique possibility for Elena and her family to emigrate and obtain legal residence in the United States, it also has its dark side. Elena says, "One of my uncles was offered the chance to marry a Puerto Rican too and come to the United States. But he said no, because his wife got jealous. Later he did the trip alone by land as an illegal." On another occasion her father declined a similar offer because her mother opposed the arrangement. In Elena's view, however, this could have been of great use to the family because her father could have acted as the "puller" of Elena's remaining sisters still living in Peru. She claims, "My father could have applied for family reunification for my sisters, and that wouldn't have cost anything. Now we have to pay *la tía* a huge amount of money to make the arrangement." In fact, *la tía*'s "pulling" business has caused much tension in Elena's family, who increasingly regard the woman as a cynical moneymaker rather than their altruistic savoir. Elena says, "I once asked *la tía*, 'Why do you treat my family this way? How come you have become so cruel?' And she said, 'Well, that was the way I was treated. Now I have become so too.'"

CONCLUSION

The data presented in this chapter suggest that the judicial distinction between immigrants who qualify for temporary or permanent residence visas and are therefore allowed to conduct legal lives in their new countries of residence, and those who are forced to travel illegally and live as undocumented or unauthorized immigrants and thus unwanted subjects, constitutes a critical divide within immigrant communities, not only along ethnic and class lines, but also between the individual members of families and households. The above testimonies also show that the classification of migrants into legal and illegal subjects is a source of conflict and tension because the newly arrived migrants are forced to make use of the "pulling" mechanism and thus submit themselves to relations of inequality and ties of dependency in order to finance their travel and solve the daily problems that illegality involves. As Andrea's and Elena's stories demonstrate, these networks generate a generalized system of exchange that urges migrants to "pull" newcomers and obliges them to send remittances to relatives and friends who remain in Peru. As a result, migrants become dependent not only on moneylenders, travel agents, people-smugglers, employers, lawyers, and bureaucrats, but also on their own relatives, friends, and fellow countrymen, who help them pay their travel expenses, obtain visas, provide them with new ID papers, and find work. In other words, the ties and bonds that initially help the "mouse" to escape the "cat" when it crosses the border and enters the First World are transformed into a "cat" that holds the "mouse" prisoner and prevents it from moving on and creating its own life as a legal immigrant.

Ironically, then, the immigration policies and economic demands in the developed countries and the relations of exclusive inclusion that these policies and demands give rise to prompt migrants to reproduce the same relations of inclusive exclusion that they are trying to escape by emigrating. As pointed out in the previous chapter, Peruvian associations and institutions are often the battlefield of conflicts and strife between migrants from different social classes and regional and ethnic groups in Peru. The data discussed in this chapter indicate that these tensions are reinforced by the fact the bulk of Peruvians who decide to emigrate are forced to pass long periods of time as undocumented or unauthorized immigrants and that "illegality" hereby enhances social inequality among Peruvians.

NOTES

1. Roberto no longer lives in Japan. When I visited the country in 2005 I was told that the Japanese truck driver and Roberto had had a traffic accident. Subsequently, the police interrogated the two men and when they discovered that Roberto was an unauthorized immigrant they first detained and later deported him.

2. Lund, who studies ID paper, citizenship practices, and bureaucratic spaces in Peru, states, "Explicitly, the quest for documents is about acquiring a written identity comprised of a hierarchy of affidavits that construct the legal person. The individual elements or entries on each document and the relationship of one document to another in a dossier represent an objective written reality about the applicant" (Lund 2001: 4).

3. Caplan and Torpey state that this "need to identify and track those who had wandered or traveled beyond the circle in which they were personally known was an original and continuing stimulus to the development of the portable identify document in its modern form" (2001: 2).

4. In fact, awareness of being an illegal is so widespread among Peruvians in Japan, where the government pursues a very strict immigration policy and considers illegality a potential crime punishable not merely by deportation but also by a jail sentence,

that some migrants employ the term to identify themselves. Thus at a soccer tournament in Mooka in which immigrant groups from not only Latin America but also Asia participated, I noticed that one of the Peruvian teams called itself *los ilegales* (the illegals). Naturally, the designation also indicated a certain irony and a certain distance from the official use of the term.

5. In 1989 I had the opportunity to meet *la tía* in Lima just before Andrea left for the United States. The woman had informed Andrea's and Silvia's family that she expected to arrive from Miami on a certain date. However, she did not give them the number of the flight or the time of its arrival. Thus, Andrea and Silvia both spent the entire day waiting at Lima airport. Eventually, it turned out that *la tía* had changed her flight and arrived on a later day. A couple of days later the woman invited the entire family to a reception to be held in the house of one of Andrea's and Silvia's relatives. At this event, all her nieces and nephews who were considering taking advantage of *la tía*'s offer to help pull them to the United States were present, trying to gain the woman's attention and her possible support in emigrating.

6. In fact *la tía* is not a biological relative of Andrea and Silvia, but their father's brother's wife. She had been pulled by one of her goddaughters living in Miami, who lent her money to travel illegally to the United States. Andrea states, "*La tía* was very brave. She traveled all the way on land, although she was fifty-six and fat."

7. In fact, *la tía* acted as "puller" even before emigrating. While living in Lima, this woman, who originates from Apurímac in the Andean highlands and left her native village as a young girl, had helped several of her close relatives migrate to the capital.

Chapter Nine

Conclusion

Between Hope and Despair

In this study, I have defined transnationality and diaspora as two analytical categories that are applicable to all migrant populations (Brubaker 2005; Butler 2001). These categories allow me to identify those aspects of Peruvian emigration that may be called transnational or diasporic, and to distinguish them from other dimensions, such as labor migration, temporary migration, return migration, or immigration. By the transnational dimension I understand the ties that migrants establish to social or political institutions or their relatives in Peru and enable them to engage in a continuous relationship of exchange with their place of origin. By the diasporic dimension, on the other hand, I refer to the networks that Peruvians form with their fellow countrymen in other countries and cities, which they use to achieve social mobility in their new countries of residence and to distinguish themselves as a national or ethnic group from other minorities in the receiving society.

TRANSNATIONAL TIES

My study shows that although contemporary Peruvian emigration contains aspects of both transnationality and diaspora, the two dimensions are only developed in a rudimentary manner. As to the former, my study points to five important transnational aspects. First, for several decades Peruvians from the Andean highlands have established transnational ties between their new countries of residence and their places of origin in Peru. As demonstrated in chapters 2 and 4, these ties are based on a livelihood strategy and migration practice that brought thousands of not merely Peruvians of indigenous origin but also Chinese and Japanese contract workers to the Peruvian coast to work

229

in the sugar and cotton plantations in the late nineteenth and early twentieth centuries. Between the 1950s and the 1980s, Andean women who had been working as domestics for Peruvian and American upper-class families in Lima and were then brought to Miami and other North American cities by their employers began to pull first female and later male migrants from their native villages to the United States by extending already existing rural-urban ties based on kinship, vicinity, and relations of reciprocity. In effect, in contrast to other Andean migrations (Bratton 2005: 33–36; Grimson 1999; Grimson and Paz Soldán 2000; Herrera, Carillo, and Torres 2005: 21–22) women spearheaded Peruvian emigration to the United States (and other countries) and created a series of long-lasting transnational networks linking migrants to their villages of origin economically, socially, and culturally.

Second, Peruvians of Japanese descent working in Japan have formed transnational organizations such as Kyodai by reactivating networks the created by their parents and grandparents before World War II. The aim of these institutions is to strengthen migrants' ties with Peru by helping them to remit their savings to relatives in their home cities. They also prompt migrants to engage in transnational economic activities between Japan and Peru and to create ethnic businesses such as the importation of video recordings by Marco and his two brothers discussed in chapter 5.

Third, a number of migrant institutions in the United States habitually organize collections to help their countrymen in Peru, such as the victims of the el Niño disaster and the country's violent conflict with Ecuador. Although these activities often deepen existing relations of mistrust between the Peruvian state and emigrant populations, they enhance national sentiments among migrants and strengthen their sense of belonging to Peru. Other migrants create unions to not only defend their labor rights, but also draw the attention of the Peruvian migrant community and public opinion in their country of origin to their problems, as happened when the conditions of Peruvian shepherds in the United States became an issue of conflict in both countries. Migrants' formation of political movement in Buenos Aires and Paterson in support of former president Toledo during his presidential campaign in 2000 is another example of Peruvian transnational political engagement. Among its many activities, the movement promoted a migrant residing in Argentina as a candidate in the Peruvian parliamentary elections the same year.

Fourth, migrants in the United States, Spain, Argentina, and Japan form transnational agencies and companies specializing in the export and import of Peruvian articles, particularly food and beverages. In the course of this trade, hundreds of shops and restaurants selling Peruvian products have appeared in New York, Miami, Los Angeles, Madrid, Barcelona, Rome, Buenos Aires, Santiago, Tokyo, and other cities that allow Peruvians in different parts of the world to consume produce from their regions of origin and create an illusion of "living in Peru." Other migrants establish agencies specializing in remitting money and making travel arrangements to Peru.

Fifth, migrants engage in transnational activities on an individual basis. Thus, as demonstrated in chapter 5, over the past decade Nicario, a reputed folk artist, and his family have created workshops in Lima as well as in Florida, in which he exhibits and sells his works. This transnational engagement has triggered a shift in Nicario's notion of what it means to be an artist and induced him to promote his works in the United States as art rather than as folklore. Moreover, it has urged him to contest conventional notions of ethnic identity in Peru and has provoked heated debates within the migrant community in Miami about what it implies to be Peruvian.

DIASPORIC BONDS

Unlike the transnational engagement of Peruvians, which encompasses a broad variety of activities and involves a relatively large number of migrants from different social strata and ethnic groups, their diasporic networking is rudimentary and limited to an exclusive segment of migrants. These networks are of three kinds.

First, Peruvian male medical doctors in the United States, Spain, and Argentina have formed organizations to promote their professional interest as a national group in their new countries of residence. Their activities include frequent meetings of Peruvian doctors in the three countries and the collection of aid to countrymen in need. Whereas most Peruvian medical doctors in Spain and Argentina have studied outside Peru, later contracting marriages with local women and establishing families in their new countries of residence, the majority of Peruvians practicing medicine in the United States received their training in Peru before emigrating. The difference between the migration histories of the two groups is reflected in their feelings of belonging and their degree of transnational involvement. In contrast to the former group, who are mainly concerned about their new lives as Spanish or Argentinean citizens or residents, the economic and political development of Peru constitutes an important point of reference for the latter.

Second, groups of male migrants from Peru's middle and upper classes, who attended the same schools and academies before emigrating, form exclusive networks with the aim of supporting newcomers in their search for jobs and a place to live. Although most of these networks are based in New York, Miami, Los Angeles, and other cities with major concentrations of Peruvians, they show little interest in social and cultural events arranged by other migrant institutions, and rarely engage in transnational activities or make much effort to maintain contact with Peru.

Third, migrants in the United States, Spain, Italy, Argentina, Chile, Japan, and other countries form religious brotherhoods honoring Catholic saints from their home cities and regions. These institutions organize annual processions that take their icons into the streets of the cities where they live and arrange different kinds of social activities. Although faith in these saints represents a symbol of national identity to most Peruvians, conflicts over the meaning of their social and religious practices cause splits in many brotherhoods. Moreover, few of them maintain contact with their mother institutions in Peru or with other brotherhoods outside the country.

PERSISTENCE AND TRANSFORMATION

These observations suggest that Peruvians' transnational and diasporic involvement is many-stranded and includes economic, social, and political as well as religious activities. Among these the most salient are the economic networks established by producers and traders of Peruvian food and beverages, the remittance agencies that service migrants in their major cities of settlement, the religious brotherhoods that migrants have created in more than fifty cities, and the umbrella institution that migrants in the United States and Canada have formed, with the aim of bringing together the many local migrant associations in the two countries. However, it also follows that the scale and intensity of these activities are relatively low. In other words, Peruvian emigration has not resulted in strong transnational or diasporic relations (Portes, Guarnizo, and Landolt 1999).

This becomes particularly clear when comparing my study with the growing body of literature by North American scholars on Caribbean, Mexican, and Central American migrations to the United States. In contrast to the research presented in this book, these studies demonstrate that Dominican, Cuban, Haitian, and Mexican migrants engage in intense relations of exchange, economically, socially, and politically, with their countries of origin, and that emigration itself is an important issue in the domestic politics of all the sending countries (Glick Schiller and Fouron 1999; Kearney 1996; Levitt 2000; Tweed 1997). Similar studies of migrant groups in other parts of the world show that migration processes triggered by political and religious persecution may lead to the emergence of a diasporic identity and a claim to national sovereignty (Axel 2001). Yet although the patterns of migration of Peruvians and other Latin Americans resemble one another with regard to the economic, social, and political determinants that trigger them, as well as to the contexts of reception in the countries where the migrants settle, the transnational and diasporic involvement of the former is far less developed than that of the latter.

The fact that Peruvian emigration has not developed strong transnational relations and diasporic identities can be attributed to several factors. First of all, Peruvians tend to disperse in many countries and cities, which undermines their ability to establish organized migrant communities in the receiving countries and to create firm economic, social, and political ties with their country of origin or between different migrant settlements. A second factor is that, with the exception of the United States, which has been the destination of Peruvian migrants since the mid 1950s, Peru's exodus has only recently gained momentum. In addition, Peru's emigrant population is extremely heterogeneous and includes migrants of both sexes, as well as from almost all social strata and ethnic and regional groups. Moreover, unlike some governments in the Caribbean, Mexico, and parts of Central America, which have put migration on the top of their political agenda, the Peruvian state shows little concern for its emigrant population, which only rarely makes it into the headlines of Peru's public media. In fact, the flow of information between the country and its emigrant population is surprisingly thin, and except for recurrent estimates of migrants' remittances and their impact on the country's development, the only news that appears in the Peruvian media are occasional reports about migrants who have been caught by the police or immigration authorities because of they have broken the law or traveled illegally. By contrast, the fact that Peruvian food today is served in hundreds of restaurants owned and run by migrants and thus constitutes an important ethnic cuisine in some of the major cities in the world, or that Peruvian religious icons are brought into the main streets of such metropolises as New York, Miami, Milan, Barcelona, and Buenos Aires by more than fifty Catholic brotherhoods, only makes it into the newspapers in Peru in their Sunday editions[1] and seems to attract very little attention from businessmen, politicians, reporters, researchers or ecclesiastical leaders in Peru. In other words, Peru's growing emigration has not yet given rise to long-distance nationalism (Glick Schiller and Fouron 1999); nor has it triggered a diasporic awareness (Schnapper 1999).

Under these circumstances, it is pertinent to ask whether the emergence of a transnational community or diasporic consciousness among Peruvians is imminent at all. A brief consideration of the migration history of the modern world suggests that it is not. Although millions of Europeans, Japanese, and Chinese emigrated to the New World in the late nineteenth and early twentieth centuries, these migrations did not become an issue of importance for previous governments or the dominating political parties in Europe, Japan, and

China at that time. Of course, a major difference between population movements and other globalization processes at the threshold to the twentieth century and today is the development of new technologies of transportation and communication (R. Smith 2000). By generating a growing sense of the compression of time and space and a feeling of simultaneity among migrants and their fellow countrymen in their places of origin, modern technologies have facilitated the creation of transnational ties and the formation of a diasporic awareness in societies that are the objects of extensive migration movements. By the same token, as several studies have pointed out, the growing marginalization and discrimination that many migrants from the Third World living in the First World experience is leading the latter to strengthen their ties with their countries of origin rather than seek integration in their new countries of settlement (Glick Schiller and Fouron 1999). Yet I argue that, rather than clinging to their countries of origin or their national identities and developing patterns of transnational engagement or diasporic identities like Caribbean, Mexican, and Central American migrants, the majority of Peruvians in the United States, Spain, and Italy will seek to adapt to their new countries of residence and assume new identities. Whether a similar process of adaptation will take place in Argentina, Chile, and Japan is far less clear.

As already mentioned, Peruvians tend to emigrate to the same countries that produced the immigrants that Peru received in the nineteenth and twentieth centuries. This is particularly evident when contemporary Peruvian emigration is compared with previous immigration flows in Peru originating from Japan, Spain, and, to a certain extent, Italy suggesting that there is a strong element of persistence in Peruvian migration history and that Peruvians' choice of destination when emigrating is greatly influenced by national origin and ethnic status. Two more indicators of this continuity are of interest to this study: the correlation between the current influx of Peruvians in southern Europe and the flow of young male Peruvians from the country's middle and upper classes who left for Spain (and Argentina) in the 1950s and 1960s to study and later married local women and established families in their new countries of residence; and the correlation between previous internal migration processes in Peru and contemporary emigration flows spearheaded by women. Thus, Peruvians from the country's Andean peasantry and urban working class, who began to emigrate to the United States in the 1950s and to Spain, Italy, Argentina, and Chile in the 1990s, have drawn extensively on the same networks and livelihood strategies that Peru's rural-urban migrants used throughout the second half of the twentieth century in their quest to change social status and create new lives in the country's major cities. In sum, the migration practices and livelihood strategies that Peruvians from the country's rural and urban working class, as well as the middle and upper classes and ethnic minorities, engage in and pursue have a long history in Peru.

GLOBAL INCLUSION AND EXCLUSION

Throughout this book I have applied the terms inclusion and exclusion to explore the relations of power and control that, on the one hand, propel Peruvians to emigrate and, on the other hand, shape their adaptation to the receiving societies. I have defined the mechanism of exclusion that grants Peruvians who belong to Peru's urban and rural working classes or the country's ethnic minorities formal citizenship but in real life prevents them from exercising this as an inclusive exclusion. By contrast I have called the mechanism of exclusion that denies Peruvians the legal rights that the majority population in the receiving societies are entitled to but in practice tolerates their continuous presence in these countries as an exclusive inclusion. My aim has been to examine how not only these two forms of exclusion mold Peruvian emigration but also how Peruvians negotiate and transform them and, eventually, how the migration process alters their own ideas of economic inequality and social difference. The findings of this exploration are that migrants tend to reproduce the relations of power that divide them in Peru as much as they contest them. This is specially evident from the tensions and strives that recurrently occur within the networks and institutions Peruvians create in the United States, Spain, Japan, and Argentina. Such conflicts are not merely the outcome of traditional divisions in Peruvian society but also a response to the policies of immigration and labor markets that contain Peruvians' mobility and exclude migrants in the four countries. As the receiving contexts in the United States, Spain, Japan, and Argentina offer Peruvians very different possibilities of finding work and achieving social mobility the scale and significance of the tensions that cause conflicts within the migrant communities in these countries vary considerably.

In recent years Peruvians in the United States find themselves increasingly divided into those who have ID papers and those who do not. This split has been caused by the tightening of immigration control and the "illegalization" of Latin American immigrant but takes different forms in the cities where Peruvians settle. In Miami, which is strongly influenced by Cuban and other Hispanic immigrants and which primarily has received migrants from both Peru's urban upper and middle classes and the Andean highlands, Peruvians have engaged in during conflicts over the interpretation of national symbols and what it implies of being Peruvian. By contrast, in Paterson, which is a traditional industrial city and which mostly has received Peruvians from Lima's working-class neighborhoods, strife and divisions are often political and tend to follow the divides of Peru's political parties. On the other hand, in Los Angeles where migrants live scattered over the city and where the Peruvian community is more fragmented than in Miami and Paterson tensions rarely occur. Overall, a growing number of Peruvians in the United States experience what North American scholars have denoted fragmented assimilation. In other words, rather than integrating into the majority population they adopt a multicultural identity as Hispanics.

For the last fifteen years the Peruvian community in Spain has been divided into a small group of predominantly male migrants who traveled to the country to study in the 1950s and 1960s and a group of both male and female migrants who arrived in large numbers in the early 1990s to take work as domestic servants, many of them as undocumented or unauthorized immigrants. This rift in the Peruvian community has been deepened by the job quota policy pursued by shifting Spanish governments, which offers an annual number of *cupos* to Peruvians to take work in the domestic servant industry. However, given that the same governments not merely have granted periodical amnesties to the country's undocumented and unauthorized immigrant population but also allowed Latin Americans to apply for citizenship within a period of two years after they have obtained legal residence the vast majority of Peruvians in Spain are today legal immigrants.[2] This policy has urged many to find work outside the domestic servant industry and apply for family reunification with their spouses, children, and parents in Peru. In effect, Peruvians are increasingly achieving social mobility and integrating in Spanish society.

In Japan Peruvians are of two kinds: those who descend from Japanese emigrants or are married to descendants of Japanese emigrants and therefore are allowed to stay and work in the country and those who are not of Japanese descent and therefore are undocumented or unauthorized immigrants. Although the marginalization and exclusion that most immigrants experience in Japan have prompted many Peruvians of Japanese descent to revise their ideas of Japaneseness the ethnic boundaries generated by Japanese immigration policy continues to cause divides within the Peruvian community in this country. This split has been deepened by the Japanese governments' growing persecution of the country's undocumented and unauthorized immigrant population.[3] So far there are few signs that Peruvians in Japan will succeed to overcome the internal tensions that separate them in ethnic groups and legal status and, eventually, achieve social mobility. Rather, a growing number of migrants are considering the possibility of re-emigrating to the United States and other countries.

Much like migrants in Spain Peruvians in Argentina are divided into a group of male migrants who arrived more than thirty years ago to study at the country's universities and who later have married local Argentinean women and established families and a group of mainly female migrants who have traveled to Argentina in the second half of the 1990s to work as domestics. Moreover, just like in Spain recurrent amnesties granted by shifting Argentinean governments have reduced the conflicts generated by this split. However, unlike in migrants Spain but similar to migrants in Japan Peruvians in Argentina, which has been haunted by economic and political crisis in the recent five years, find that the prospects of achieving social mobility are bleak. In effect, many regard Argentina as less attractive than other migration destinations and refrain from applying for legal residency when the Argentinean governments grant amnesties. Rather they think of their stay in Argentina as temporary and use the country as a hub to emigrate to other places such as Spain and Italy.

CONCLUSION

The analytical implication of my study is that Peruvians from almost all social classes and ethnic groups regard geographical mobility as an important means of achieving social mobility and are therefore inclined to adapt to the receiving societies rather than maintain existing ties with their country of origin. However, my data also lead us to be cautious in drawing definitive conclusions concerning the opportunities of migrants to achieve social mobility. First of all, Peruvians have only recently started to emigrate in large numbers, and the country's emigrant population still consists almost exclusively of first-generation migrants. Moreover, there are many indications that Peruvians, like other Latin Americans, will continue to suffer from marginalization and discrimination in their new countries of residence for many years to come, and that their attempts to achieve upward mobility may therefore last several generations.

Although Peru has experienced considerable economic growth and although its political situation has stabilized in the last couple of years, unemployment and poverty is still widespread in both urban and rural areas. As a consequence, Peruvians continue to emigrate in large numbers, driven by a desire to improve their living conditions and create a better future for their children.[4] So far there are few signs that this development will change, that the current emigration will start to decline significantly or that the country's emigrant population will begin returning to Peru on a major scale. Thus, it seems appropriate to end this book by asking what the future of Peruvians as immigrants, residents, or citizens in the receiving countries looks like. The prospects vary significantly, depending on not only migrants' individual skills and social backgrounds in Peru, but also the strategies they pursue in emigrating, as well as the context of their reception in the countries where they settle. By and large, migrants can be divided into two groups according to their success or failure to make *progreso*. In the United States, Spain, and Italy, a growing number of Peruvians, are experiencing upward mobility, inducing them to seek assimilation into the receiving society. From the point of view of this group of migrants, the United States in particular is an attractive destination because of its cultural diversity and the economic opportunities that it offers its immigrant population. However, rather than improving their lives, many Peruvians in the United States end up living on the margins of society, with few possibilities ever to climb the social ladder. A large group of Peruvians in Japan and Argentina (and also Chile), who feel that they are either the victims of exclusion and discrimination or that they have become marginalized because they cannot find work, may well suffer the same fate. Hence, from their perspective social mobility is something to be achieved somewhere else; indeed, for them it is difficult to tell the difference between hope and despair.

NOTES

1. *El Comercio* Aug. 8, 2004, b4 Economía.

2. According to INE (Spain's National Institute of Statistics), in 2006 the total number of undocumented immigrants in Spain was one million. Of these, only 4,367 were Peruvians (*El País* July 26, p 17, 2006).

3. *El Comercio* April 23, 2006, a 31.

4. According to INEI (Peru's National Institute of Statistics and Information), 263,441 Peruvians emigrated between January and September 2004. The average number of Peruvians leaving the country during this period is 29,271 (*El Comercio* Nov. 3, 2004). On the other hand, Altamirano claims that 450,000 Peruvians left Peru in 2005 (2006: 119).

References

Adepoju, Aderanti. 1995. Emigration Dynamics in Sub-Saharan Africa. *International Migration. Quaterly Review* 18 (3/4): 315–90.

Agamben, Giorgio. 1998. *Homo Sacer. Sovereign Power and Bare Life*. Stanford: Stanford University Press.

Aguirre, Carlos. 2005. *Breve historia de la esclavitud en el Perú: Una herida que deja de sangrar*. Lima: Fondo Editorial del Congreso del Perú.

Alberti, Giorgio, and Fernando Fuenzalida. 1969. Pluralismo, dominación y personalidad. In *Dominación y cambios en el Perú rural*, ed. J. M. Mar, W. Whyte, J. Cotler, L. Williams, J. O. Alers, F. Fuenzalida, G. Alberti, 285–325. Lima: Instituto de estudios peruanos.

Alicea, Marixsa. 1997. "A Chambered Nautilus": The Contradictory Nature of Puerto Rican Women's Role in the Social Construction of a Transnational Community. *Gender & Society* 11 (5): 597–626.

Allen, Catherine. 1988. *The Hold Life Has: Coca and Cultural Identity in an Andean Community*. Washington, D.C.: Smithsonian Institution Press.

Allen, James and Eugene Turner. 1997. *The Ethnic Quilt. Population Diversity in Southern California*. Northridge: The Center for Geographical Studies, California State University.

Altamirano, Rua, Teófilo. 1990. *Los que se fueron: Peruanos en Estados Unidos*. Lima: Pontificia Universidad Católica del Perú.

———. 1992. *Exodo: Peruanos en el exterior*. Lima: Pontificia Universidad Católica del Perú.

———. 1996. *Migración, el fenómeno del siglo: Peruanos en Europa, Japón y Australia*. Lima: Pontificia Universidad Católica del Perú.

———. 2000. *Liderazgo y organización de peruanos en el exterior: Culturas transnacionales e imaginarios sobre el desarrollo*. Vol. 1. Lima: Pontificia Universidad Católica del Perú.

———. 2006. *Remesas y nueva "fuga de cerebros": Impactos transnacionales*. Lima: Pontificia Universidad Católica del Perú.

Andreas, Peter. 2001. The Transformation of Migrant Smuggling across the U.S.-Mexican Border. In *Global Human Smuggling: Comparative Perspectives*, ed. D. Kyle and R. Koslowski, 107–25. Baltimore: The Johns Hospkins University Press.

Anthias, Floya. 2000. Metaphors of Home: Gendering New Migrations to Southern Europe. In *Gender and Migration in Southern Europe: Women on the Move*, ed. F. Anthias and G. Lazaridis, 15–48. Oxford: Berg.

Apap, Joanna. 1997. Citizenships Rights and Migration Policies: The Case of Maghrebi Migrants in Italy and Spain. In *Southern Europe and the New Immigrants*, ed. R. King and R. Black, 138–57. Sussex: Sussex Academic Press.

Appadurai, Arjun. 1998. *Modernity at Large. Cultural Dimensions of Globalization*. Minneapolis and London: University of Minnesota Press.

Arango, Joaquín. 2000. Becoming a Country of Immigration at the End of the Twentieth Century: The Case of Spain. In *Eldorado or Fortress? Migration in Southern Europe*, ed. R. King, G. Lazaridis, and C. Tsardanidis, 253–76. London: MacMillan Press.

Arguedas, José María. 1980. *Todas las sangres*. Vol. 1–2. Lima: Editorial Milla Batres.

Avila Molero, Javier. 2003. Lo que el viento (de los Andes) se llevó: Diásporas campesinas en Lima y los Estados Unidos. In *Comunidades locales y transnacionales, Cinco estudios de caso en el Perú*, ed. C. I. Degregori, 167–261. Lima: IEP.

———. 2005. Worshipping the Señor de Qoyllur Riti in New York: A Transnational Andean Ethnography. *Latin American Perspectives* 32 (1): 174–92.

Axel, Brian. 2001. *The Nations' Tortured Body. Violence, Representation and the Formation of a "Sihk" Diaspora*. Durham, N.C.: Duke University Press.

Bakewell, Peter. 1997. *A History of Latin America: Empires and Sequels 1450–1930*. Oxford: Blackwell Publishers.

Balán, Jorge. 1988. International Migration in Latin America: Trends and Consequences. In *International Migration Today: Vol. 1. Trends and Prospects*, ed. R. Appleyard, 210–63. Unesco: University of Western Australia.

———. 1992. The Role of Migration Policies and Social Networks in the Development of a Migration System in the Southern Cone. In *International Migration Systems. A Global Approach*, ed. M. Kritz, L. Lim, and H. Zlotnik, 115–30. Oxford: Clarendon Press.

Ballard, Roger. 1987. The Political Economy of Migration. Pakistan, Britain, and the Middle East. In *Migrants, Workers, and the Social Order*, ed. J. Eades, 17–41. ASA Monographs 26. London: Tavistock Publications.

Banchero, Raúl Castellano. 1972. *Lima y el mural de pachacamilla*. Lima: Aldo Raúl Arias Montesinos.

Banerjee, Biswajit. 1983. Social Networks in the Migration Process: Empirical Evidence on Chain Migration in India. *The Journal of Developing Areas* 17 (1): 185–96.

Barnes, J. A. 1969. Networks and Political Processes. In *Social Networks in Urban Situations: Analyses of Personal Relationships in Central African Towns*, ed. J. C. Mitchell, 51–76. Manchester: Manchester University Press.

Basch, Linda, Nina Glick Schiller, and Cristina Blanc-Szanton. 1994. *Nations Unbound: Transnational Projects, Postcolonial Predicaments and Deterritorialized Nation-States*. Langhorne: Gordon and Breach.

Bebout, John, and Ronald Grele. 1964. *Where Cities Meet: The Urbanization of New Jersey*. Princeton: D. Van Nostrand Company.

Benencia, Roberto. 1999. El fenómeno de la migración limítrofe en la Argentina: interrogantes y propuestas para seguir avanzando. *Estudios migratorios latinoamericanos* (Buenos Aires) 13/14: 40–41, 419, 448.

Benencia, Roberto, and Grabriela Karasik. 1995. *Inmigración limítrofe: Los bolivianos en Buenos Aires*. Buenos Aires: Centro Editor de América Latina.

Berg, Ulla. 2005. ¿Enmarcando la "peruanidad"? La poética y la pragmática de un espectáculo público entre los migrantes peruanos en Nueva Jersey. In *El Quinto Suyo. Transnacionalidad y formaciones diaspóricas en la migración peruana*, ed. U. Berg and K. Paerregaard, 37–68. Lima: Instituto de Estudios Peruanos.

Bernard, William. 1998. Immigration: History of U.S. Policy. In *The Immigration Reader. America in a Multidisciplinary Perspective*, ed. D. Jacobsen, 48–71. Malden, Mass.: Blackwell.

Bernasconi, Alicia. 1999. Peruanos en Mendoza: Apuntes para un ¿nuevo? modelo migratorio. *Estudios migratorios latinoamericanos* 13/14 (40–41): 639–58.

Bodega, Isabel, Juan Cebrian, T. Franchini, G. Lora-Tamayo, and A. MartínLou. 1995. Recent Migrations from Morocco to Spain. *International Migration Review* 14 (3): 800–819.

Brochmann, Grete. 1999a. The Mechanisms of Control. In *Mechanisms of Immigration Control*, ed. G. Brochmann and T. Hammar, 1–28. Oxford: Berg.

———. 1999b. Controlling Immigration in Europe. In *Mechanisms of Immigration Control*, ed. G. Brochmann and T. Hammar, 297–334. Oxford: Berg.

Brodwin, Paul. 2003. Pentecostalism in Translation: Religion and the Production of Community in the Haitian Diaspora. *American Ethnologist* 30 (1): 85–101.

Brubaker, Rogers. 2005. The "Diaspora" Diaspora. *Ethnic and Racial Studies* 28 (1): 1–19.

Burawoy, Michael. 2000. Introduction. In *Global Ethnography. Forces, Connections, and Imaginations in a Postmodern World*. Burawoy, et. al., 1–40. Berkeley: University of Califormia Press.

Burrell, Jennifer. 2005. Migration and the Transnationalization of Fiesta Customs in Todos Santos Cuchumatán, Guatemala. *Latin American Perspectives* 32 (5): 12–32.

Butler, Kim. 2001. Defining Diaspora, Refining a Discourse. *Diaspora* 10 (2): 189–220.

Calavita, Kitty. 1992. U.S. Immigration and Policy Responses: The Limits of Legislation. In *Controlling Immigration: A Global Perspective*, ed. W. Cornelius, P. Martin, and J. Hollifield, 55–82. Stanford: Stanford University Press.

Campani, Guivanna. 2000. Immigrant Women in Southern Europe: Social Exclusion, Domestic Work and Prostitution in Italy. In *Eldorado or Fortress? Migration in Southern Europe*, ed. R. King, G. Lazaridis, and C. Tsardanidis, 145–69. London: MacMillan.

Cánepa Koch, Gisela. 1998. *Máscara: Transformación e identidad en los Andes*. Lima: Pontificia Universidad Católica del Perú.

Caplan, Jane, and John Torpey. 2001. Introduction. In *Documenting Individual Identity: The Development of State Practices in the Modern World*, ed. J. Caplan and J. Torpey, 1–12. Princeton: University of Princeton Press.

Carrón, Juan. 1979. Shifting Patterns in Migration from Bordering Countries to Argentina: 1914–1970. *International Migration Review* 13 (3): 475–87.

Casanova, José. 1997. Globalizing Catholicism and the Return to a "Universal" Church. In *Transnational Religion and Fading States*, ed. Susanne H. Rudolph and James Piscatori, 121–43. Boulder: Westview Press.

Casaravilla, Diego. 1999. *Los laberintos de la exclusión. Relatos de inmigrantes ilegales en Argentina*. Buenos Aires: Lumen-humanitas.

Castillo, Manuel Angel. 1994. A preliminary Analysis of Emigration Determinants in Mexico, Central America, Northern South America, and the Caribbean. *International Migration: Quarterly Review* 17 (2): 269–306.

Chaney, Elsa. 1985. Agripina. In *Sellers & Servants: Working Women in Lima, Peru*. X. Buntser and E. Chaney, 11–80. New York: Praeger.

Chaney, Elsa, and Mary Garcia Castro, eds. 1989. *Muchachas No More. Household Workers in Latin America and the Caribbean*. Philadelphia: Temple University Press.

Chapin, Wesley. 1996. The Turkish Diaspora in Germany. *Diaspora* 5 (2): 275–301.

Chávez, Leo. 1992. *Shadowed Lives: Undocumented Immigrants in American Society*. Ft. Worth: Harcourt, Brace & Jovanovitch.

Ciccarelli, Orazio. 1988. Fascist Propaganda and the Italian Community in Peru during the Benavides Regime, 1933–1939. *Journal of Latin American Studies* 20 (2): 361–88.

Clifford, James. 1994. Diaspora. *Cultural Anthropology* 9 (3): 302–38.

———. 1997. *Routes: Travel and Translation in the Late Twentieth Century*. Cambridge: Harvard University Press.

Cohen, Anthony. 1994. *Self Consciousness: An Alternative Anthropology of Identity*. London: Routledge.

Cohen, Robin. 1997. *Global Diasporas: An Introduction*. Seattle: University of Washington.

Cook, David Noble. 1981. *Demographic Collapse. Indian Peru, 1520–1620*. Cambridge: Cambridge University Press.

Cornelius, Wayne. 1992. Spain: The Uneasy Transition from Labor Exporter to Labor Importer. In *Controlling Immigration: A Global Perspective*, ed. W. Cornelius, P. Martin, and J. Hollifield, 331–69. Stanford: Stanford University Press.

Coutin, Susan Bibler. 2000. *Legalizing Moves: Salvadorean Immigrants' Struggle for U.S. Residency*. Ann Arbor: The Universtiy of Michigan Press.

Das Veena and Deborah Poole. 2004. State and Its Margins: Comparative Ethnographies. In *Anthropology in the Margins of the State*, ed. V. Das and D. Poole, 3–34. Santa Fe: School of American Research Press and James Curry.

Davies, Thomas. 1974. *Indian Integration in Peru: A Half Century of Experience, 1900–1948*. Lincoln: University of Nebraska Press.

De Certeau, Michel. 1988. *The Practice of Everyday Life*. Berkeley: University of California Press.

De Genova, Nicholas P. 2002. Migrant "Illegality" and Deportability in Everyday Life. *Annual Review of Anthropology* 31: 419–47.

——. 2005. *Race, Space, and "Illegality" in Mexican Chicago*. Durham, N.C.: Duke University Press.

de la Cadena, Marisol. 2000. *Indigenous Mestizos. The Politics of Race and Culture in Cuszo, Peru, 1919–1991*. Durham, N.C.: Duke University Press.

Dirección General de Ordenación de las Migraciones. 1996. *Anuario de Migraciones*. Madrid: Ministerio de Trabajo y Asuntos Sociales.

——. 2002. *Anuario de Migraciones*. Madrid: Ministerio de Trabajo y Asuntos Sociales.

Dobyns, Henry. 1966. Estimating Aboriginal American Population. An Appraisal of Techniques with a New Hemisphere Estimate. *Current Anthropology* 7: 395–449.

Dobyns, Henry, and Paul Doughty. 1976. *Peru: A Cultural History*. New York: Oxford University Press.

Douglass, Mike. 2000. The Singularities of International Migration of Women to Japan: Past, Present and Future. In *Japan and Global Migration: Foreign Workers and the Advent of a Multicultural Society*, ed. M. Douglass and G. Roberts, 91–119. London: Routledge.

Douglass, Mike, and Glenda Roberts. 2000. Japan in a Global Age of Migration. In *Japan and Global Migration: Foreign Workers and the Advent of a Multicultural Society*, ed. M. Douglass and G. Roberts, 3–37. London: Routledge.

Driessen, Henk. 1998. The "New Immigration" and the Transformation of the European-African Border. In *Border Identities: Nation and States at International Frontiers*, ed. T. Wilson and H. Donnan, 96–116. Cambridge: Cambridge University Press.

Duany, Jorge. 2002. *The Puerto Rican Nation on the Move: Idenetities on the Island and in the United States*. Chapel Hill: The University of North Carolina Press.

Dunn, Marvin, and Alex Stepick. 1992. Blacks in Miami. In *Miami Now! Immigration, Ethnicity, and Social Change*, ed. G. Grenier and A. Stepick III, 41–56. Gainesville: University Press of Florida.

Düvell, Franck, and Bill Jordan. 2003. *Irregular Migration: The Dilemmas of Transnational Mobility*. Cheltenham: Edward Elgar.

Eades, Jeremy. 1987. Anthropologists and Migrants: Changing Models and Realities. In *Migrants, Workers, and the Social Order*, ed. J. Eades, 1–18. ASA Monographs 26. London: Tavistock.

Epstein, A. L. 1969. The Network and Urban Social Organization. In *Social Networks in Urban Situations. Analyses of Personal Relationships in Central African Towns*, ed. J. C. Mitchell, 77–116. Manchester: Manchester University Press.

Escrivá, Angeles. 1997. Control, Composition, and Character of New Migration to Southwest Europe: The Case of Peruvian Women in Barcelona. *New Community* 23 (1): 43–57.

——. 1999. *Mujeres peruanas del servicio doméstico en Barcelona: Trayectorias socio-laborales*. Tesis doctoral. Departamento de Sociología. Facultad de Ciencias politicas y Sociología. Universidad Autónoma de Barcelona.

——. 2000. The Position and Status of Migrant Women in Spain. In *Gender and Migration in Southern Europe: Women on the Move*, ed. F. Anthias and G. Lazaridis, 199–226. Oxford: Berg.

———. 2003. Conquistando el espacio laboral extradoméstico. Peruanas en España. *Revista Internacional de Sociología* (RIS). Tercera Epoca, No 36, Septiembre–Diciembre: 7–31.

———. 2004. Formas y motives de la acción transnacional. Vinculaciones de los peruanos con el país de origin. In *Migración y desarrollo*. Estudios sobre remesas y otras practices transnacionales en España. Angeles Escrivá y Natalia Ribas (eds). Pp. 149–81. Córdoba: Consejo Superior de Investigaciones científicas/Instituto de Estudios Sociales de Andalucía.

———. 2005. Peruanos en España: ¿de migrantes a ciudadanos? In *El Quinto Suyo: Transnacionalidad y formaciones diaspóricas en la migración peruana*, ed. U. Berg and K. Paerregaard, 133–72. Lima: Instituto de Estudios Peruanos.

Flores, Juan, John Attinasi, and Pedro Pedraza. 1987. Puerto Rican Language and Culture in New York City. In *Caribbean Life in New York City: Sociocultural Dimension*, ed. C. Sutton and E. Chaney, 207–19. New York: Center for Migration Studies of New York, Inc.

Foner, Nancy. 1978. *Jamaica Farewell: Jamaican Migrants in London*. Berkeley: University of California Press.

Foreign Press Center of Japan. 1999. *Facts and Figures of Japan, 1999 Edition*. Tokyo: Foreign Press Center/Japan.

Friman, Richard. 2001. Immigrants, Smuggling, and Treats to Social Order in Japan. In *Global Human Smuggling: Comparative Perspectives*, ed. D. Kyle and Koslowski, 294–317. Baltimore: The Johns Hospkins University Press.

Fukumoto, Mary. 1997. *Hacia un nuevo sol: Japoneses y sus descendientes en el Perú*. Lima: Asociación Peruano Japonesa del Perú.

Gardiner, Harvey. 1981. *Pawns in a Triangle of Hate: The Peruvian Japanese and the United States*. Seattle: University of Washington Press.

Gardner, Katy. 1995. *Global Migrants, Local Lives. Travel and Transformation in Rural Bangladesh*. Oxford: Clarendon Press.

Geertz, Clifford. 1973. *The Interpretation of Cultures*. New York: Basic Books.

Gelles, Paul. 2005. Transformaciones en una comunidad andina transnacional. In *El Quinto Suyo: Transnacionalidad y formaciones diaspóricas en la migración peruana*, ed. U. Berg and K. Paerregaard, 69–96. Lima: Instituto de Estudios Peruanos.

Gille, Zsuzsa, and Seán Ó Riain. 2002. Global Ethnography. *Annual Review of Sociology* 28: 271–96.

Gillin, John. 1960. Some Signposts for Policy. In *Social Change in Latin America Today: Its Implications for United States Policy*, ed. R. Adams, O. Lewis, J. Gillin, R. Patch, A. Holmberg, and C. Wagley, 14–62. New York: Vintage Books.

Glick Schiller, Nina, and Georges Fouron. 1999. Terrains of Blood and Nation: Hatian Transnational Social Fields. *Ethnic and Racial Studies* 22 (2): 340–67.

Gratton, Brian. 2005. Ecuador en la historia de la migración internacional ¿Modelo o aberración? In *La migración ecuatoriana: Transnacionalismo, redes e identidades*, ed. G. Herrera, M. Carillo, and A. Torres, 31–56. Quito: FLACSO.

Grenier, Guillermo, and Alex Stepick. 1992. Introduction. In *Miami Now! Immigration, Ethnicity, and Social Change*, ed. G. Grenier and A. Stepick, 1–17. Gainesville: University Press of Florida.

Grimson, Alejandro. 1999. *Relatos de la diferencia y la igualadad: Los bolivianos en Buenos Aires*. Buenos Aires: Felafacs & Eudeba.

Grimson, Alejandro, and Edmundo Paz Soldán. 2000. *Migrantes bolivianos en la Argentina y los Estados Unidos*. Cuaderno de Futuro 7. La Paz: Programa de la Naciones Unidas para el Desarrollo (PNUD).

Guarnizo, Luis E., and P. Michael Smith. 1998. The Locations of Transnationalism. In *Transnationalism from Below: Comparative Urban & Community Research*. Vol. 6, ed. M. Smith and Guarnizo, 64–102. New Brunswick: Transaction Publishers.

Gudeman, Steven. 1976. Saints, Symbols, and Ceremonies. *American Ethnologist* 3 (4): 709–30.

Gupta, Akhil, and James Ferguson. 1997. Discipline and Practice: "The Field" as Site, Method, and Location in Anthropology. In *Anthropological Locations: Boundaries and Grounds of a Field Science*, ed. A. Gupta and J. Ferguson, 1–46. Berkeley: University of California Press.

Gurak, Douglas, and Fe Caces. 1992. Migration Networks and the Shaping of Migration Systems. In *International Migration Systems: A Global Approach*, ed. M. Kritz, L. Lim, and H. Zlotnik, 150–76. Oxford: Clarendon Press.

Hagan, Jacqueline, and Helen Ebaugh. 2003. Calling Upon the Sacred: Migrants' Use of Religion in the Migration Process. *International Migration Review* 37 (4): 1145–62.

Hannerz, Ulf. 1996. *Transnational Connections. Culture, People, Places*. London: Routledge.

Herbert, Wolfgang. 1996. *Foreign Workers and Law Enforcement in Japan*. London: Kegan Paul International.

Herrera, Gioconda, María Cristina Carillo, and Alicia Torres. 2005. Introducción. In *La migración ecuatoriana: Transnacionalismo, redes e identidades*, ed. G. Herrera, M. Carillo, and A. Torres, 13–27. Quito: FLACSO.

Heyman, Josiah. 1998. *Finding a Moral Heart for U.S. Immigration Policy: An Anthropological Perspective*. American Ethnological Society Monograph Series, Number 7. Arlington: American Anthropological Association.

Hirabashi, Lane. 1993. *Cultural Capital. Mountain Zapotec Migrant Associations in Mexico City*. Tucson: The University of Arizona Press.

Hirabayashi, Jane. 1986. The Migrant Village Association in Latin America. *Latin American Research Review* 21 (3):7–29.

Hollifield, James. 1999. Ideas, Institutions, and Civil Society: On the Limits of Immigration Control in France. In *Mechanisms of Immigration Control: A Comparative Analysis of European Regulation Policies*, ed. G. Brochmann and T. Hammar, 59–96. Oxford: Berg.

Hondagneu-Sotelo, Pierrette. 2001. *Immigrant Workers Cleaning and Caring in the Shadows of Affluence*. Berkeley: California University Press.

Hondagneu-Sotelo, Pierette, and Ernestine Avila. 1997. "I'm Here, But I'm There": The Meaning of Latina Transnational Motherhood. *Gender & Society* 11 (5): 548–71.

INEI (Instituto nacional de estadística e información). 2005. Censo nacional X de población y V de vivienda. Lima: INEI.

Isbell, Billie Jean. 1985. *To Defend Ourselves: Ecology and Ritual in an Andean Village*. Prospect Heights: Waveland Press.

Itzigsohn, José, Carlos D. Cabral, Esther H. Medina, and Obed Vásquez. 1999. Mapping Dominican Transnationalism: Narrow and Broad Transnational Practices. *Ethnic and Racial Studies* 22 (2): 316–39.

Izquierdo, Antonio. 1996. *La inmigración inesperada: La población extranjera en España (1991–1995)*. Madrid: Editorial Trotta.

Jokisch, Brad, and David Kyle. 2005. Las transformaciones de la migración transnacional del Ecuador, 1993–2003. In *La migración ecuatoriana: Transnacionalismo, redes e identidades*, ed. G. Herrera, M. Carillo, and A. Torres, 57–70. Quito: FLACSO.

Julca, Alex. 2001. Pervuvian Networks for Migration in New York City's Labor Market, 1970–1996. In *Migration, Transnationalization, and Race in a Changing New York*, ed. H. Cordero-Guzmán, R. Smith, and R. Grosfoguel, 239–57. Philadelphia: Temple University Press.

Kasinitz, Philip, and Judith Freidenberg-Herbstein. 1992. The Puerto Rican Parade and West Indian Carnival: Public Celebrations in New York City. In *Caribbean Life in New York City. Sociocultural Dimensions*, ed. Constance Sutton and Elsa Chaney, 305–25. New York: Center for Migration Studies.

Kearney, Michael. 1986. From the Invisible Hand to Visible Feet: Anthropological Studies of Migration and Development. *Annual Review of Anthropology* 15: 331–61.

——. 1996. *Reconceptualizing the Peasantry: Anthropology in Global Perspective*. Boulder: Westview Press.

Kerri, James. 1976. Studying Voluntary Associations as Adaptive Mechanisms: A Review of Anthropological Perspectives. *Current Anthropology* 17: 23–47.

Kilroy, Paul. 1993. *The Black Atlantic: Double Consciousness and Modernity*. Cambridge, Mass: Harvard University Press.

King, Russell. 2000. Southern Europe in the Changing Global Map of Migration. In *Eldorado or Fortress? Migration in Southern Europe*, ed. R. King, G. Lazaridis, and C. Tsardanidis, 1–26. London: MacMillan Press.

King, Russell, and Isabel Rodríguez-Melguizo. 1999. Recent Immigration to Spain: The Case of Moroccans in Catalonia. In *Into the Margins: Migration and Exclusion in Southern Europe*, ed. F. Anthias and G. Lazaridis, 55–82. Aldershot: Ashgate.

King, Russell, and Richard Black, eds. 1997. *Southern Europe and the New Immigrations*. Brighten: Sussex Academic Press.

Klaren, Peter F. 1970. *Formación de las haciendas azucareras y orígenes del APRA*. Perú Problema 5. Lima: Instituto de Estudios Peruanos.

Kosinski, Leszek, and Mansell Prothero. 1975. Introduction: The Study of Migration. In *People on the Move: Studies in Internal Migration*, ed. L. Kosinski and M. Prothero, 1–17. London: Methuen & Co.

Kritz, Mary and Dougles Gurak. 1979. International Migration Trends in Latin America: Research and Data Survey. *International Migration Review* XIII (3):407–27.

Kritz, Mary, and Hania Zlotnik. 1992. Global Interactions: Migration Systems, Processes, and Policies. In *International Migration Systems: A Global Approach*, ed. M. Kritz, Mary L. Lim, and H. Zlotnik, 1–16. Oxford: Clarendon Press.

Kyle, David Jané. 2000. *Transnational Peasants: Migrations, Networks, and Ethnicity in Andean Ecuador*. Baltimore: Johns Hopkins University.

Kyle, David, and Rey Koslowski. 2001. Introduction. In *Global Human Smuggling: Comparative Perspectives*, ed. D. Kyle and R. Koslowski, 1–25. Baltimore: The Johns Hospkins University Press.

Kyle, David and John Dale. 2001. Smuggling the State Back. In *Agents of Human Smuggling Reconsidered. In Global Human Smuggling. Comparative Perspectives*, eds. D. Kyle and R. Kolowski: 29–57. Baltimore: The Johns Hopkins University Press, 1996.

Landolt, Patricia. 1999. From Hermano Lejano to Hermano Mayor: The Dialectics of Salvadorean Transnationalism. *Ethnic and Racial Studies* 22 (2): 290–316.

León, Pericles. 2001. Peruvian Sheepherders in the Western United States. *Nevada Historical Society Quaterly* 44 (2): 147–65.

Levitt, Peggy. 2001. *The Transnational Villagers*. Berkeley: University of California Press.

———. 2003. "You Know. Abraham Was Really the First Immigrant": Religion and Transnational Migration. *The International Migration Review* 37 (3): 847–73.

Levitt, Peggy, and Nina Glick Schiller. 2004. Conceptualizing Simultaneity: A Transnational Social Field Perspective on Society. *The International Migration Review* 38 (3): 1002–39.

Lie, John. 2000. The Discourse of Japaneseness. In *Japan and Global Migration: Foreign Workers and the Advent of a Multicultural Society*, ed. M. Douglass and G. Roberts, 70–90. London: Routledge.

Lim, Lin L. 1992. International Labour Movements: A Perspective on Economic Exchanges and Flows. In *International Migration Systems*, ed. M. Kritz, Mary L. Lim, and H. Zlotnik, 133–49. Oxford: Clarendon Press.

Linde, Charlotte. 1993. *Life Stories: The Creation of Coherence*. Oxford: Oxford University Press.

Linger, Daniel. 2001. *No One Home: Brazilian Selves Remade in Japan*. Stanford: Stanford University Press.

Lockhart, James. 1968. *Spanish Peru: 1532–1560: A Colonial Society*. Madison: University of Wisconsin Press.

Lomnitz, Larissa. 1977. *Networks and Marginality: Life in a Mexican Shantytown*. New York: Academic Press.

Lopez, David, Eric Popkin, and Edward Telles. Central Americas. At the Bottom, Struggling to Get Ahead. In *Ethnic Los Angeles*, eds. R. Waldinger and M. Bozorgmehr, 278–304. New York: Russell Sage Foundation.

Lund, Sarah. 1994. *Lives Together, Worlds Apart: Quechua Colonisation in Jungle and City*. Oslo: Scandinavian University Press.

———. 2001. Bequeathing and Quest. Processing Personal Identification Papers in Bureaucratic Spaces (Cuzco, Peru). *Social Anthropology* 9 (1): 3–24.

Mahler, Sarah. 1995. *American Dreaming. Immigrant Life on the Margins*. Princeton, N.J.: Princeton University Press.

———. 1998. Theoretical and Empirical Contributions toward a Research Agenda for Transnationalism. In *Transnationalism from Below: Comparative Urban and Community Research*, ed. Michael P. Smith and Luis E. Guarnizo, 64–100. New Brunswick: Transaction Publishers.

Mahler, Sarah, and Katrin Hansing. 2005. Toward a Transnationalism of the Middle: How Transnational Religious Practices Help Bridge the Divides between Cuba and Miami. *Latin American Perspectives* 32 (1): 121–46.

Maingot, Anthony. 1992. Immigration from the Caribbean Basin. In *Miami Now! Immigration, Ethnicity, and Social Change*, ed. G. Grenier and A. Stepick III, 18–40. Gainesville: University Press of Florida.

Mallki, Liisa. 1992. National Geographic: The Rooting of Peoples and the Territorialization of National Identity among Scholars and Refugees. *Cultural Anthropology* 6 (4): 466–503.

Mallon, Florencia. 1983. *The Defense of the Community in Peru's Central Highlands. Peasant Struggle and Capitalist Transition, 1860–1940*. Princeton, N.J.: Princeton University Press.

Marcus, George. 1995. Ethnography in/of the World System: The Emergence of Multi-sited Ethnography. *Annual Review of Anthropology* 24: 95–117.

Margolies, Maxine L. 1994. *Little Brazil. An Ethnography of Brazilian Immigrants in New York City*. Princeton: Princeton University Press.

Marshall, Adriana. 1979. Immigrant Workers in the Buenos Aires Labor Market. *International Migration Review* 13 (3): 488–501.

———. 1981. Structural Trends in the International Labor Migration: The Southern Cone of Latin America. In *Global Trends in Migration. Theory and Research on International Movements*, ed. M. Kritz, C. Keely, and S. Tomasi, 234–58. New York: Center for Migration Studies.

Martin, Philip. 1992. The United States: Benign Neglect toward Immigration. In *Controlling Immigration: A Global Perspective*, ed. W. Cornelius, P. Martin, and J. Hollifield, 83–99. Stanford: Stanford University Press.

Martínez, Ubaldo Veiga. 1997. *La integración social de los inmigrantes extranjeros en España*. Madrid: Editorial Trotta/Fundación 1° de mayo.

Marzal, Manuel. 1988. *Los caminos religiosos de los inmigrantes en la gran Lima: El caso de El Augostino*. Lima: Pontificia Universidad Católica del Perú.

Massey, Douglas, Rafael Alarcón, Jorge Durand, and Humberto González. 1987. *Return to Aztlán: The Social Process of International Migration from Western Mexico*. Berkeley: University of California Press.

Massey, Douglas, Joaquin Arango, Graeme Hugo, Ali Kouaouci, Adela Pellegrino, and J. Edward Taylor. 1998. *Worlds in Motion: Understanding International Migration at the End of the Millennium*. Oxford: Clarendon Press.

Matsumoto, Juan Alberto, and Irene Gashu. 1998. *Residencia permanente y naturalización—todo lo referente a los visados y sobre la adopción de la nacionalidad japonesa*. Yokohama: Idea Books.

McAlister, Elisabeth. 1998. The Madonna of 115th Street Revisited: Vodou and Haitian Catholicism in the Age of Transnationalism. In *Gatherings in the Diaspora: Re-*

ligious Communities and the New Immigration, ed. S. Warner and J. Wittner, 123–60. Philadelphia: Temple University Press.

McKeown, Adam. 2001. *Chinese Migrant Networks and Cultural Change: Peru, Chicago, Hawaii, 1900–1936.* Chicago: University of Chicago Press.

Meisch, Lynn A. 2002. *Andean Entrepreneurs: Otavalo Merchants & Musicians in the Global Arena.* Austin: University Press of Texas.

Mendoza, Zoila. 2000. *Shaping Society through Dance. Mestizo Ritual Performance in the Peruvian Andes.* Chicago: Chicago University Press.

Menjívar, Cecilia. 1999. Religious Institutions and Transnationalism: A Case Study of Catholic and Evangelical Salvadoran Immigrants. *International Journal of Politics, Culture and Society* 12 (4): 589–612.

———. 2000. *Fragmented Ties: Salvadoran Immigrant Networks in America.* Berkeley: University of California Press.

Mera, Carolina. 1998. *La inmigración coreana en Buenos Aires: Multiculturalismo en el espacio urbano.* Buenos Aires: Eudeba.

Merino, Hernando, and María Asunción. 2002. *Historia de los inmigrantes peruanos en España: Dinámicas de exclusión e inclusión en una Europa globalizada.* Madrid: Consejo superior de investigaciones científicas/Centro de estudios históricos.

———. 2004. Politics of Identity and Identity Policies in Europe: The Case of Peruvian Immigrants in Spain. *Identities: Global Studies in Culture and Power* 11: 241–64.

Mitchell, J. Clyde. 1969. The Concept and Use of Social Network. In *Social Networks in Urban Situations. Analyses of Personal Relationships in Central African Towns*, ed. J. C. Mitchell, 1–50. Manchester: Manchester University Press.

———. 1974. Social Networks. *Annual Review of Anthropology* 3: 279–300.

———. 1984. Case studies. In *Ethnographic Research: A Guide to General Conduct*, ed. R. F. Ellen, 237–41. London: Academic Press.

Molinié, Antoinette. 1999. Dos celebraciones "salvajes" del Cuerpo de Dios (los Andes y la Mancha). In *Celebrando el Cuerpo de Dios*, ed. A. Molinié, 245–79. Lima: Pontificia Universidad Católica del Perú.

Monaghan, Ray. 1973. *Chile, Peru, and the California Gold Rush of 1849.* Berkeley: California University Press.

Mori, Hiromi. 1997. *Immigration Policy and Foreign Workers in Japan.* London: MacMillan Press.

Morimoto, Amelia. 1999. *Los japoneses y sus descendientes en el Perú.* Lima: Fondo Editorial del Congreso del Perú.

Naciones Unidas. 1998. *Perú: Un examen de la magración internacional de la comunidad andina usando datos censales.* Proyector sistema de información sobre migración internacional en los países de la comunida andina (SIMICA). Santiago de Chile: CEPAL, CELADE, OIM.

Ngai, Mae. 2004. *Impossible Subjects: Illegal Aliens and the Making of Modern America.* Princeton, N.J.: Princeton University Press.

Noble, Mary. 1973. Social Network: Its Use as a Conceptual Framework in Family Analysis. In *Network Analysis: Studies in Human Interaction*, ed. J. Boissevain and C. Mitchell, 3–14. The Hague: Mouton.

Nuñez, Lorena. 2002. Peruvian Migrants in Chile. In *Transnational Identities: A Concept Explored: The Andes and Beyond*. Part II, ed. T. Salman and A. Zoomers, 61–72. Antropologische Bijdragen 16. Amsterdam: CEDLA.

Nuñez, Lorena, and Dany Holper. 2005. "En el Peú, nadie se muero de hambre": pérdida de peso y prácticas de alimentación entre trabajadoras domésticas peruanas en Chile. In *El Quinto Suyo. Transnacionalidad y formaciones diaspóricas en la migración peruana*, ed. U. Berg and K. Paerregaard, 291–314. Lima: Instituto de Estudios Peruanos.

Oboler, Suzanne. 1995. *Ethnic Labels, Latino Lives: Identity and the Politics and (Re)Presentation in the United States*. Minneapolis: University of Minnesota Press.

Ochs, Elinor, and Lisa Copps. 1996. Narrating the Self. *Annual Review of Anthropology* 25: 19–43.

Ortiz, Vilma. 1996. The Mexican-Origin Population: Permanent Working Class or Emerging Middle Class? In *Ethnic Los Angeles*, ed. R. Waldinger and M. Bozorgmehr, 247–78. New York: Russel Sage Foundation.

Oteiza, Enrique, Susana Novick, and Roberto Aruj. 1996. *Política inmigratoria, inmigración real y derechos humanos en la Argentina*. Documento de trabajo. Buenos Aires No. 5. Instituto de Investigación Gino Germano.

Pacecca, María Inés. 1998. *Los inmigrantes peruanos en el area metropolitana*. Buenos Aires: Informe de investigación para Secretaría de Cultura de la Nación, 1–47.

———. 1999. *Working and Living in Buenos Aires: Peruvian Migrants in the Metropolitian Area*. Paper presented at the International Sociological Association (ISA)'s meeting in Buenos Aires, Nov. 2000.

Paerregaard, Karsten. 1987. *Nuevas Organizaciones en comunidades campesinas: El case de Usibamba y Chaquicocha*. Lima: Pontificia Universidad Católica del Perú.

———. 1997a. *Linking Separate Worlds: Urban Migrants and Rural Lives in Peru*. Oxford: Berg.

———. 1997b. Imagining a Place in the Andes: In the Borderland of Analyzed, Invented, and Lived Culture. In *Siting Culture: The Shifting Anthropological Object*, ed. K. Hastrup and K. Olwig, 39–59. Oxford: Routledge.

———. 1998. The Dark Side of the Moon: Conceptual and Methodological Problems of Studying Urban Migrants and Their NativeVillage. *American Anthropologist* 100 (2): 397–408.

———. 2002. Business as Usual: Livelihood Strategies and Migration Practice in the Peruvian Diaspora. In *Work and Migration: Life and Livelihoods in a Globalizing World*, ed. K. Olwig and N. Soeresen, 126–44. London: Routledge.

———. 2003. Migrant Networks and Immigration Policy: Shifting Gender and Migration Patterns in the Peruvian Diaspora. *JCAS Symposium Series* 19: 1–18. Osaka: The Japan Center for Area Studies/National Museum of Ethnology.

———. 2005a. Inside the Hispanic Melting Pot: Negotiating National and Multicultural Identities among Peruvians in the United States. *Latino Studies* 3 (1): 76–96.

———. 2005b. Contra viento y marea: redes y conflictos entre ovejeros peruanos en Estados Unidos. In *El Quinto Suyo: Transnacionalidad y formaciones diaspóricas en la migración peruana*, ed. U. Berg and K. Paerregaard, 97–129. Lima: Instituto de Estudios Peruanos.

———. 2005c. Callejón sin salida: estrategias e instituciones de los peruanos en Argentina. In *El Quinto Suyo: Transnacionalidad y formaciones diaspóricas en la migración peruana*, ed. U. Berg and K. Paerregaard, 231–60. Lima: Instituto de Estudios Peruanos.

———. in review. The Show Must Go On: The Role of Fiesta in Andean Transnational Migration. *Latin American Perspectives*.

Peacock, James, and Dorothy Holland. 1993. The Narrated Self: Life Stories in Process. *Ethos* 21 (4): 367–83.

Perera, Pintado, and Ana Cecilia. 2005. Religion and Cuban Identity in a Transnational Context. *Latin American Perspectives* 32 (1): 147–73.

Pereyra, Brenda. 1999. Más allá de la ciudadanía formal. La inmigración chilena en Buenos Aires. *Cuadernos para en debate* No. 4. Programa de investigaciones Socioculturales en el Mercosur. Buenos Aires: Instituto de Desarrollo Económico y Social.

Pérez, Lisandro. 1992. Cuban Miami. In *Miami Now! Immigration, Ethnicity, and Social Change*, ed. G. Grenier and A. Stepick III, 83–108. Gainesville: University Press of Florida.

Plataforma sudamericana de derechos humanos, democracia y desarrollo. 2000. *Los derechos humanos de los migrantes: Situación de los derechos económicos, sociales y culturales de los migrantes peruanos y bolivianos en Argentina y Chile*. La Paz: CEDLA-Comisión chilena de derechos humanos-CEDAL-CELS.

Popkin, Eric. 1999. Guatemalan Mayan Migration to Los Angeles: Constructing Transnational Linkages in the Context of the Settlement Process. *Ethnic and Racial Studies* 22 (2): 267–89.

Portes, Alejandro. 2001. Introduction: The Debates and Significance of Immigrant Transnationalism. *Global Networks* 1 (3): 181–93.

Portes, Alejandro, Luis Guarnizo, and Patricia Landolt. 1999. Introduction: Pitfalls and Promise of an Emergent Research Field. In Special Issue of *Transnational Communities. Ethnic and Racial Studies* 22 (2): 217–37.

Portes, Alejandro, and Rubén Rumblatt. 1996. *Immigrant America: A Portrait*. Berkeley: University of California Press.

Portes, Alejandro, and Alex Stepick. 1993. *City on the Edge: The Transformation of Miami*. Berkeley: University of California Press.

Pribilsky, Jason. 2004. "*Aprendemos a convivir*": Conjugal Relations, Co-parenting, and Family Life among Ecuadorian Transnational Migrants in New York City. *Global Networks* 4 (3): 313–34.

Pries, Ludger. 1999. New Migration in Transnational Spaces. In *Migration and Transnational Social Spaces*, ed. L. Pries, 1–35. Aldershot: Ashgate Publishing.

Pulis, John W. 1999. *Religion, Diaspora, and Cultural Identity: A Reader in the Anglophone Caribbean*. Amsterdam: Gordon and Breach Publishers.

Ramella, Franco. 1998. Redes sociales and mercado de trabajo en un caso de emigración. Los obreros italianos y los otros en Paterson, New Jersey. *Estudios migratorios latinoamericanos* (Buenos Aires) 39, Agosto: 331–72.

Reimers, David. 1992. New York City and Its People: An Historical Perspective up to World War II. In *Caribbean Life in New York City: Sociocultural Dimensions*, ed. C. Sutton and E. Chaney, 30–50. New York: Center for Migration Studies.

Ribas-Mateos, Natalia. 2000. Female Birds of Passage: Leaving and Settling in Spain. In *Gender and Migration in Southern Europe. Women on the Move*, eds. F. Anthias and G. Lazardis. 199–226. Oxford: Berg.

Rodríguez Pastor, Humberto. 2000. *Historia de la comunidad china en el Perú*. Lima: Fondo Editorial del Congreso del Perú.

Rogers, Alisdair, and Steven Vertovec. 1995. Introduction. *The Urban Context: Ethnicity, Social Networks, and Situational Analysis*, ed. Alisdair Rogers and Steven Vertovec, 1–33. Oxford: Berg.

Rollins, Judith. 1985. *Between Women: Domestics and Their Employers*. Philadelphia: Temple University Press.

Ross, Marc Howard, and Thomas Weisner. 1977. The Rural-Urban Migrant Network in Kenya: Some General Implications. *American Ethnologist* 4 (2): 359–76.

Rostworowski, María de Diez Canseco. 1992. *Pachacamac y el Señor de los Milagros: Una trayectoria milenaria*. Lima: Instituto de Estudios Peruanos.

Rouse, Roger. 1991. Mexican Migration and the Social Space of Postmodernism. *Diaspora* 1 (1): 24.

———. 1995. Questions of Identity: Personhood and Collectivity in Transnational Migration to the United States. *Critique of Anthropology* 15 (4): 351–80.

Rowe, John. 1963. Inca Culture at the Time of the Spanish Conquest. In *Handbook of South American Indians*. Vol. 2, ed. J. Steward, 183–330. Bureau of American Ethnology Bulletin 143. Washington, D.C.

Rudolph, Susanne Hoeber. 1997. Introduction: Religion, States, and Transnational Civil Society. In *Transnational Religion and Fading States*, ed. S. H. Rudolph and J. Piscatori, 1–24. Boulder: Westview Press.

Ruíz Bahúa, Larissa. 1999. Rethinking Transnationalism: Reconstructing National Identities Among Peruvian Catholics in New Jersey. Special Issue Religion in America. *Journal of Interamerican Studies and World Affairs* 41 (4): 93–109.

Sabogal, Elena. Viviendo en la Sombra. The Immigration of Peruvian Professionals in Southern Florida. *Latino Studies* 3 (1): 113–31.

Safan, William. 1991. Diasporas in Modern Societies: Myths of Homeland and Return. *Diaspora* 1 (1).

Saignes, Thierry. 1985. *Caciques, Tribute, and Migration in the Southern Andes: Indian Society and the 17th Century Colonial Order (Audencia de Charcas)*. Paper published by the Institute of Latin American Studies, No. 15. London: University of London.

Sakuda, Alejandro. 1999. *El futuro era el Perú: Cien años o más de inmigración japonesa*. Lima: ESICOS (Empresa de Servicios Integrados en Comunicación Social).

Salazar Parreñas, Rhacel. 2001. *Servants of Globalization: Women, Migration, and Domestic Work*. Stanford: Stanford University Press.

Sallnow, Michael. 1987. *Pilgrims of the Andes. Regional Cults in Cusco*. Washington, D.C.: Smithsonian Institute Press.

Sarramone, Alberto. 1999. *Los abuelos inmigrantes: Historia y sociología de la inmigración argentina*. Buenos Aires: Editorial Azul.

Schnapper, Dominique. 1999. From the Nation-State to the Transnational World: On the Meaning and Usefulness of Diaspora as a Concept. *Diaspora* 8 (3): 225–54.

Sciortino, Guiseppe. 1999. Planning in the Dark: The Evolution of Italian Immigration Control. In *Mechanisms of Immigration Control*, ed. G. Brochmann and T. Hammar, 233–60. Oxford: Berg.

Sellek, Yoko. 1997. *Nikkeijin*: The Phenomenon of Return Migration. In *Japan's Minorities: The Illusion of Homogeneity*, ed. M. Weiner, 178–210. London: Routledge.

———. 2001. *Migrant Labour in Japan*. Basingstoke: Palgrave.

Shah, Nasra. 1995. Emigration Dynamics from and within South Asia. *International Migration: Quarterly Review* 18 (3/4): 559–626.

Shimada, Haruo. 1994. *Japan's "Guest Workers": Issues and Public Policies*. Tokyo: University of Tokyo Press.

Singhanetra-Renard, Anchalee. 1992. The Mobilization of Labour Migrants in Thailand: Personal Links and Facilitating Networks. In *International Migration Systems: A Global Approach*. M. Kritz, L. Lim, and H. Zlotnik, 190–204. Oxford. Clarendon Press.

Smith, Clifford Thorpe. 1970. Depopulation of the Central Andes in the 16th Century. Current Anthropology 11 (4–5):453–60.

Smith, Gavin. 1989. *Livelihood and Resistance: Peasants and the Politics of Land in Peru*. Berkeley: University of California Press.

Smith, James P., and Barry Edmonston, eds. 1997. *The New Americans. Economic, Demographic, and Fiscal Effects of Immigration*. Washington, D.C.: National Academy Press.

Smith, Margo. 1973. Domestic Service as a Channel of Upward Mobility for the Lower-Class Women: The Lima Case. In *Female and Male in Latin America: Essays*, ed. A. Pescatello, 191–208. Pittsburgh: University of Pittsburgh Press.

Smith, Michael, and Luis Guarnizo, eds. 1998. *Transnationalism from Below*. New Brunswick: Transaction Publishers.

Smith, Robert C. 2000. How Durable and New is Transnational Life? Historical Retrieval through Local Comparison. *Diaspora* 9 (2): 203–34.

Spener, David. 2001. Smuggling Migrants through South Texas: Challenges Posed by Operation Rio Grande. In *Global Human Smuggling. Comparative Perspectives*, ed. D. Kyle and R. Koslowski, 129–65. Baltimore: The Johns Hospkins University Press.

Stefoni, Carolina. 2002. *Inmigración peruana en Chile: Una oportunidad a la integración*. Santiago: FLACSO-Chile/Editorial Universitaria.

———. 2005. Inmigrantes transnacionales: la formación de comunidades y la transformación en ciudadanos. In *El Quinto Suyo. Transnacionalidad y formaciones diaspóricas en la migración peruana*, ed. U. Berg and K. Paerregaard, 261–90. Lima: Instituto de Estudios Peruanos.

Stepick, Alex. 1992. The Refuges Nobody Wants: Haitians in Miami. In *Miami Now! Immigration, Ethnicity, and Social Change*, ed. G. Grenier and A. Stepick III, 57–82. Gainesville: University Press of Florida.

Stratton, Jon. 1997. (Dis)placing the Jews: Historicizing the Idea of Diaspora. *Diaspora* 6 (3): 301–30.

Sugimoto, Yoshio. 1997. *Japanese Society: An Introduction*. Cambridge: Cambridge University Press.

Takenaka, Ayumi. 1999. Transnational Community and Its Ethnic Consequences: The Return Migration and the Transformation of Ethnicity of Japanese Peruvians. *The American Behavioral Scientist* 42 (9): 1459–74.

——. 2003. The Mechanisms of Ethnic Retention: Later-Generation Japanese Immigrants in Lima, Peru. *Journal of Ethnic and Migration Studies* 29 (3): 467–83.

——. 2004. The Japanese in Peru: History of Immigration, Settlement, and Racialization. *Latin American Perspectives* 32 (3): 77–98.

——. 2005. Nikkeis y peruanos en Japón. In *El Quinto Suyo: Transnacionalidad y formaciones diaspóricas en la migración peruana*, ed. U. Berg and K. Paerregaard, 37–68. Lima: Instituto de Estudios Peruanos.

Tamagno, Carla. 2002a. "You Must Win Their Affection . . . ": Migrants' Social and Cultural Practice between Peru and Italy. In *Work and Migration: Life and Livelihoods in a Globalizing World*, ed. N. N. Soerensen and K. F. Olwig, 106–25. London: Routledge.

——. 2002b. La Plaza del Duomo: Políticas de identidad y producción de localidad, el caso de los peruanos en Milán. In *Transnational Identities: A Concept Explores: The Andes and Beyond*. Part II, ed. T. Salman and A. Zoomers, 9–60. Antropologische Bijdragen 16. Amsterdam: CEDLA.

——. 2003a. *Entre Acá y allá. Vidas transnacionales y desarrollo: Peruanos entre Italia y Perú*. Ph.D. thesis. Dpt. of Sociology of Development. Wageningen University, Holland.

——. 2003b. Los peruanos en Milán. In *Comunidades Locales y Transnacionales: Cinco Estudios de caso en el Perú*, ed. C. I. Degregori, 319–98. Lima: Instituto de Estudios Peruanos.

——. 2005. Entre "celulinos" y "cholulares": prácticas comunicativas y la construcción de vidas transnacionales entre Perú y Italia. In *El Quinto Suyo: Transnacionalidad y formaciones diaspóricas en la migración peruana*, ed. U. Berg and K. Paerregaard, 173–204. Lima: Instituto de Estudios Peruanos.

Tilly, Charles. 1990. Transplanted Networks. In *Immigration Reconsidered: History, Sociology, and Politics*, ed. V. Yans-MacLaughlin, 79–95. New York: Oxford University Press.

——. 1998. *Durable Inequality*. Berkeley: University of California Press.

——. 1996. Rethinking Diaspora(s): Stateless Power in the Transnational Moment. *Diaspora* 5 (1):3–36.

——. 1996. Rethinking Diaspora(s): Stateless Power in the Transnational Moment. *Diaspora* 5 (1): 3–36.

Torales, Ponciano. 1993. *Diasnóstico sobre la inmigración receinte de peruanos en la Argentina*. Buenos Aires: Organización internacional para las migraciones (O.I.M.)

Tornos, A., et al. 1997. *Los peruanos que vienen: Quiénes son y como entienden típicamente la inmigración los inmigrantes peruanos*. Madrid: UPCO.

Torpey, John. 2000. *The Invention of the Passport: Surveillance, Citizenship, and the State*. Cambridge: University of Cambridge Press.

Trazegnies, Fernando. 1995a. *En el país de las Colinas de arena. Reflexiones sobre la inmigración china en el Perú del S. XIX desde la perspective del Derecho*. Vol. 1. Lima: Pontifica Universidad Católica del Perú.

———. 1995b *En el país de las Colinas de arena. Reflexiones sobra la inmigración china en el Perú del S. XIX desde la perspective del Derecho*. Vol. 2. Lima: Pontifica Universidad Católica del Perú.

Tsuda, Takeyuki. 1999. Transnational Migration and the Nationalization of Ethnic Identity among Japanese Brazilian Return Migrants. *Ethos* 27 (2): 145–79.

Tullis, La Mond F. 1970. *Lord and Peasant in Peru: A Paradigm of Political and Social Change*. Cambridge, Mass: Harvard University Press.

Tweed, Thomas. 1997. *Our Lady of the Exile: Diasporic Religion at a Cuban Catholic Shrine in Miami*. Oxford: Oxford University Press.

Ueda, Reed. 1998. The Changing Face of Post-1965 Immigration. In *The Immigration Reader: America in a Multidisciplinary Perspective*, ed. D. Jacobsen, 72–91. Malden, Mass.: Blackwell.

Urbano, Jesús Rojas, and Pablo Macera. 1992. *Santero y Caminante: Santoruraj—ñampurej*. Lima: Editorial Apoyo.

Vásquez, Mario C. 1970. Immigration and the Mestizaje in Nineteenth Century Peru. In *Race and Class in Latin America*, ed. M. Morner. New York: Columbia University Press.

Vasta, Ellie. 1993. Rights and Racism in a New Country of Immigration: The Italian Case. In *Racism and Migration in Western Europe*, ed. J. Wrench and J. Solomons, 83–98. Oxford: Berg Publishers.

Vázques, Manuel. 1999. Toward a New Agenda for the Study of Religion in the Americas. *Journal of Interamerican Studies and World Affairs* 41 (4): 1–20.

Vertovec, Steven. 1997. Three Meanings of "Diaspora" Exemplified among South Asian Religions. *Diaspora* 7 (2): 277–300.

———. 2000. *The Hindu Diaspora: Comparative Patterns*. London: Routledge.

Wachtel, Nathan. 1977. *The Vision of the Vanquished: The Spanish Conquest of Peru through the Indian Eyes*. Sussex: Harvester Press.

Wadia, Khursheed. 1999. France: From Unwilling Host to Bellicose Gatekeeper. In *The European Union and Migrant Labour*, ed. G. Dale and M. Cole, 171–202. Oxford: Berg.

Waldinger, Roger, and Mehdi Bozorgmehr. 1996. The Making of a Multicultural Metropolis. In *Ethnic Los Angeles*, ed. R. Waldinger and M. Bozorgmehr, 3–37. New York: Russel Sage Foundation.

Waldinger, Roger and David Fitzgerald. 2004. Transnationalism in Question. *The American Journal of Sociology* 109 (4):1177–95.

Waldinger, Roger and Michael Lichter. 1996. Anglos: Beyond Ethnicity? In *Ethnic Los Angeles*, eds. R. Waldinger and M. Bozorgmehr. 413–41. New York: Russell Sage Foundation.

Walker, Charles. 1988. Los peruanos en EE.UU. *QueHacer* (Lima) May–June: 76–92.

Warner, R. Stephen, and Judith Wittner, eds. 1998. *Gatherings in the Diaspora: Religious Communities and the New Immigration*. Philadelphia: Temple University Press.

Watkins, Montse. 1996. *Passageiros de um sonho: A experiencia recente dos brasileiros no Japao*. Kamakura: Luna Books (Tokyo).

———. 1999. *¿El fin del sueño? Latinoamericanos en Japón*. Kamakura: Luna Books.

Weiner, Michael. 2000. Japan in the Age of Migration. In *Japan and Global Migration. Foreign Workers and the Advent of a Multicultural Society*, eds. M. Douglass and G. Roberts. 52–69. London: Routledge.

Werbner, Pnina. 2002a. *Imagined Diasporas among Manchester Muslims: The Public Performance of Pakistani Transnational Identity Politics*. Oxford: James Currey.

———. 2002b. The Place Which Is Diaspora: Citizenship, Religion, and Gender in the Making of Chaordic Transnationalism. *Journal of Ethnic and Migration Studies* 28 (1): 119–33.

Weston, Marcela Olivas. 1999. *Peregrinaciones en el Perú: Antiguas rutas devocionales*. Lima: Universidad de San Martín de Porres.

Wightman, Ann. 1990. *Indigenous Migration and Social Change: The Forasteros of Cuzco, 1570–1720*. Durham, N.C.: Duke University Press.

Williams, William Carlos. 1992. *Paterson*. New York: New Directions Book.

Wilpert, Czarina. 1992. The Use of Social Networks in Turkish Migration to Germany. In *International Migration Systems: A Global Approach*, ed. M. Kritz, L. Lim, and H. Zlotnik, 177–89. Oxford. Clarendon Press.

Wolf, Eric. 1966. *Peasants*. Englewood Cliffs, N.J.: Printice Hall, Inc.

Wolf, Eric, and Edward Hansen. 1972. *Human Condition in Latin America*. New York: Oxford University Press.

Yamanaka, Keiko. 1996. Return Migration of Japanese-Brazilians to Japan: The *Nikkeijin* as Ethnic Minority and Political Construct. *Diaspora* 5 (1): 65–98.

Yamawaki, Chikako. 2002. *Estrategias de vida de los inmigrantes asiáticos en el Perú*. Lima: IEP and JCAS.

Zimmerman, Mary, Jacquelyn Litt, and Christine Bose. 2006. Globalization and Multiple Crisis of Care. In *Global Dimensions of Gender and Carework*, ed. M. Zimmerman, J. Litt, and C. Bose, 9–29. Stanford: Stanford University Press.

NEWSPAPERS

Actualidad (Los Angeles) 6 (82), April 1998.

Caretas (Lima) June 20, No. 1419, 1996.

Chasqui (Paterson) 3 (98), Feb. 1998.

El Comercio (Lima) Aug. 8, b4 Economía. 2004.

El Comercio (Lima) Aug. 8, b4 Economía, 2004.

El Comercio (Lima) Nov. 3, 2004.

El Comercio (Lima) April 23, a31, 2006.

El Heraldo del Perú (Buenos Aires) 3, Oct. 2000.

El País (Madrid) June 2000.

El País (Madrid) "Ecuatorianos de ida y vuelta." *El País* Semanal, Número 1.398. Domingo 13 de julio. Pp. 48–57. 2003.

El País (Madrid) July 28, 2005.

El País (Madrid) July19, Pp. 22, 2006.

El País (Madrid) July 26, p 17, 2006.

El Panamericano 5 (Los Angeles) (72), April 1998.

El Peruano News (Miami) Año 1, N. 8, Noviembre de 1996.

Gaceta del Perú (Buenos Aires) 217, Oct. 2000.

International Press (Tokyo) Aug., 1999.

La Primera de la Semana. Revista Semanal de Actualidad (Buenos Aires).

"La Invasión silenciosa," 4 de abril, Año 1, No. 3, 2000.

La Crónica (Miami) 5 (42), Jan. 1998.

La República (Lima) Aug. 16, Local, 1996.

La República (Lima) June 5, 2005, p. 4.

La República (Lima) May 3, 2006, p. 5.

L.A. Peruvian Times (Los Angeles) 7 (13), March 1998.

Los Angeles Times (Los Angeles) "Advocates Seek to Guard Shepherds From Exploitation" by Julie Tamaki. August 17: A 3 + A 23, 2000.

Newsweek (New York) "Mexico: Coyote Inc." by Alan Zarembo, August 30, 1999.

Oregon & The West (Oregon) "California Shepherds Endure Hardships in Quest for Work" by Evelyn Nieves. July 15: A21 + A24, 2001.

Perú al Día (Santiago) 15, Sept. 2002.

Perú de los 90 (Los Angeles) 9 (2), Feb. 1998, Dec. 1995.

Peru News (Miami) 2, Feb. and March 1998.

Peruvian Times (Los Angeles) 7 (13), March 1998.

The New York Sun (New York) Nov. 2004.

Ultima Hora (Los Angeles) 1 (5), April 1998.

Index

ADPEBA. *See* Asociación Deportiva
Peruana en Buenos Aires
Africans, 15, 18, 29; as domestic
servants, 39, 64; Lord of the
Miracles and, 148, 150, 158, 164;
migration links of, 2; in mining
industry/plantations, 39, 64;
population movements of, 74, 84;
as slaves, 38–40, 47, 147, 177,
188
Afro-Peruvians, 29, 38, 147, 186–87
agriculture, 54, 56, 64, 70, 71, 108, 128,
131, 135, 202
AIPEUC, 124, 139, 189; el Niño victim
assistance by, 122–23
Alien Registration Law, of Japan, 68
all the bloods *(todas las sangres),* 37, 40
amnesty: by Argentina, 72, 200n4, 215;
by Italy, 75n9, 104, 215; by Spain,
50n17, 65, 74, 99, 215; by United
States, 91, 215, 218
Andean migrants, 9, 17–18, 24, 29,
33n8, 90, 106, 126, 134, 151, 188;
as domestic servants, 45, 55, 60,
107, 110, 230; female, 55–56, 58,
81–82, 90, 107, 110, 230, 234;
illegality and, 202; music/folklore
of, 21, 32n32, 34n14, 125, 127;
retablos folk art and, 135–38,

142–43, 231; rural/urban networks
of, 82, 100
Argentina, 3, 13, 14, 27, 31, 43,
70–73, 103–4, 116, 160, 194, 234,
236–37; amnesty by, 72, 200n4,
215; deportation for illegality in,
204; depression in, 71; domestic
servants in, 9, 47, 73, 106, 212,
237; European immigration and, 54,
70–71; geographical access to, 213;
immigrant reception in, 48;
immigrants recruited by, 70;
immigration into, 17, 45, 48, 71–73,
109; immigration into, for
medicine/law, 45, 72, 128;
immigration policies in, 82; labor
agreement with Bolivia/Peru,
71–72; Lord of the Miracles
processions in, 157–58; map of, *17*;
migrant association in, 123; migrant
communities in, 13, 124; migrant
network in, 81–82; open door
policy of, 71; population/labor
market policies in, 47, 54; religious
brotherhoods, 152, 162–63; tourist
visa and, 49, 104, 212–14;
uncontrolled immigration into,
70–71; work permits in, 104, 106,
213. *See also* Buenos Aires

259

About the Author

Karsten Paerregaard is associate professor at the Department of Anthropology, University of Copenhagen. His publications encompass books and articles in English, Spanish, and Danish. They include *Linking Separate Worlds: Urban Migrants and Rural Lives in Peru* (Oxford: Berg, 1997), *El Quinto Suyo. Transnacionalidad y formaciones diaspóricas en la migración peruana* (edited with Ulla Berg) (Lima: IEP, 2005), and "Inside the Hispanic Melting Pot: Negotiating National and Multicultural Identities among Peruvians in the United States," *Journal of Latino Studies* 3 (2) (2005). His current research is focused on the impact that transnational migration has on Peru's development.